HISTORY AND LITERATURE

D1347065

The Triumph of
English 1350-1400

The Triumph of English 1350-1400

BASIL COTTLE, *M.A. (Wales), Ph.D. (Bristol).*
Senior Lecturer in English at the
University of Bristol

Blandford Press · London

First published 1969

© 1969 Blandford Press Ltd
167 High Holborn
London WC1

Library edition   SBN 7137 3603 8
Paperback   SBN 7137 3622 X

Text set in 11 on 13 pt Monotype Times
Printed and bound in Great Britain by
C. Tinling & Co. Ltd
Liverpool, London and Prescot
Blocks engraved by The Half-Tone Engraving Co. Ltd, London

Contents

ACKNOWLEDGEMENTS

Acknowledgement is due to the following for their kind permission to reproduce illustrations:

Robin Anderson and L. A. Hatch, No. 11
British Museum, Nos. 1, 4, 6, 8
Richard Burn, No. 5
Master and Fellows of Corpus Christi College, Cambridge, No. 22
Keith Durn, No. 2
National Gallery, No. 9
National Monuments Record, Nos. 3, 7, 12, 18
Radio Times Hulton Picture Library, No. 19
Society of Antiquaries, No. 14
University College, Oxford, No. 10
Nos. 15, 16, 17, 20 from drawings by the author
No. 21 from a photograph by the author

List of Illustrations

To
Cecile Mary Cottle
My Mother
Who taught me my first English
and History

Preface

THE aim of this book is to let the England of 1350–1400 speak for itself of those events and movements which appeared to it significant; we must not give way to our own hindsight in this, but admit the mingled perceptiveness and negligence with which writers treated the occasions and issues of their time. If we feel a disappointment at the silence over some big matters—for instance, the developments in trade, and on the other hand the effect of the war on wool-selling—we may excuse it either by acknowledging the blurred vision of too great nearness to the event, or by claiming that such subjects are not the stuff of poetry. The interests of the late fourteenth century were not always such as would now detain us, and we grow restive over the description of a Smithfield tournament when vital matters are left unrecorded; Chaucer now appears to many to have wasted the time he spent writing the prose *Astrolabie* and (if the ascription to him be correct) the prose *Equatorie of the Planetis*, but it is more reasonable to rejoice in the wide range of enthusiasm that dipped him in ink.

Fortunately we can for this period call on great minds to express themselves: Chaucer, his friend Gower, the poet of *Piers Plowman* tentatively called Langland, the utterly unnamed poet of *Sir Gawain and the Green Knight*, and Wyclif. This book could be inspiringly made up of their utterances; but it has been considered right, and it is often very entertaining, to include a host of lesser writers, usually anonymous, who could be as observant and impressed as the masters. The half-century is bounded for our purpose by two very handy dates—the ebbing of the Black Death in 1349, and the death of Chaucer in 1400; there were two monarchs only—the strong old king grown lustful and extravagant, and his imprudent grandson. How far this period can be seen through franker eyes than can its predecessors, may be judged by realizing that Chaucer is our first great layman poet, a man with an identity and a name, the founder of a 'school' (vitally, in London) and thus of a critique. That the writers sought to observe at all, and to record and annotate the things around them, belongs to an altogether new critical spirit; and for the first time there is an impression of national consciousness. It would be wrong to stress any new nationalism; but France was the clear enemy, and the expression of England as no longer merely a part of feudal society is beginning to be vocal.

It was a period rich in emphatic happenings, appalling in disasters, subtle in social and spiritual change, splendid in pageantry. Looked at in one way, it offered the glazing of windows, the topping of towers, the blare of trumpets, the Garter, Poitiers, a boy king bravely facing rebels, the great return of the English language; from another point of view, Chaucer—no pessimist—brusquely catalogued it thus:

> . . . in our dayes nis but covetyse
> And doublenesse, and tresoun and envye,
>   Poysoun, manslauhtre, and mordre in sondry wyse.

[. . . in these days there is nothing but covetousness and duplicity, and treason and envy, poison, manslaughter, and various kinds of murder. *The Former Age*, ll. 62–64]

Yet the reason why this period is a good one to begin this series of surveys is not its loud triumphs and miseries but its revitalization and reshaping of English; here, for the first time, the emergent language can be quoted to give immediate pleasure and information. I said at the outset that the age would be allowed to 'speak for itself', and this must be done in its own language, Middle English.

There are difficulties here. First, our language was fragmented into regional dialects of equal status (though literary dialects already obtained, and must often have swamped local usage); thus, genius being a thing of wilful geographical occurrence, various different dialect forms will have to figure in these pages, and if we were foolhardy enough to tinker with them (say, to cast them all into Chaucer's tongue) we would destroy the poetry of their rhyme, alliteration, and syllable-counting. Secondly, even within a fairly consistent dialect area, there was no standard spelling; it is dismaying for a modern reader to find *though* in one manuscript line and the utterly archaic *þouȝ* in the next. Nor are there any grounds at all for our 'normalizing' the spelling here—there was no norm, and the only safe course is to adhere to the manuscript and trust the scribe's sincere attempt to describe the sound he heard. So I have retained all the manuscript forms, of which the most irritating are v for u (especially in initial letters), u for v (especially in medial letters), and the rarer j for i. Two new letters must be mastered by the reader unfamiliar with Middle English: þ and its capital Þ, ȝ and its capital ȝ; þ (called *thorn* and often written th) is the hard or soft *th* sound of Modern English, and ȝ (called *yogh* and often written gh) is initially *y* and medially and finally a rasping sound something like that in Scots *loch*. I have rightly made a concession to students of language and literature (though I would not have done so if this book were intended for students of palaeography); I have changed the originals to the present-day style of capitalization and punctuation.

After every quoted passage, and even every phrase, stands a version in Modern English; these are not meant to be polished, but to be as nearly literal as makes a decent idiomatic rendering. Further, they are not meant as a substitute for the original whereby the original can be ignored as hard and odd; it is vital to the whole purpose of this book that the Middle English passages should be read carefully and with growing enjoyment, if possible aloud, and therefore some help towards hearing the language is given in the section on its shape. It is hoped that by the end of the book the not inaccurate judgment will be reached in the reader's mind that much of the quoted material is pretty close to our own standard dialect (and indeed, much of it *is* that East Midland that Chaucer and Wyclif helped to establish). It may also be felt that the vocabulary is by no means unknown to us, though the more northerly poets produce some unrecognizable words and in all areas the use of supposedly familiar words proves to be vastly or delicately different from our own practice. But with Chaucer we shall feel comfortably at home; much of his vocabulary of over 8,000 words (Shakespeare needed 24,000) is still with us, and the 4,000 Latin (and later Romance) loans among these, of which about 1,000 are new to him *as far as records go*, have mostly kept their connotations to this day. As English returned to its own, the people conferred Anglo-Saxon surnames on most of their sons, so that the stated shape of society loses much of the quaintness of an earlier century.

Similarly, Chaucer shared many of our assumptions; again, we keep getting that comfortable notion, as we read him, that he is 'one of us'. Yet the differences should be striking, too, and his exact but limited education, the closed system inculcated by the Church of his day, and the code-bound nature of contemporary society, fix the small gulf between us. The education he received as a well-off vintner's son is likely to have been, and is revealed in his works as having been, the same as he would have received generations before: the primer when he learned to read, the same old encyclopaedias and bad maps, arithmetic (though now with the cypher *0*), the seven liberal arts of higher education, Latin and polite French (to which he personally added Italian), the fairly shallow philosophy of Boethius, some Latin writers, and the Latin Vulgate Bible. For more privileged youths new opportunities were opening in such foundations as William of Wykeham's at Winchester and New College, Oxford; but it would be a delicate task to discern the influence of these endeavours on the surviving vernacular literature.

The Bibliography lists primary sources, the writers themselves; I have not included commentaries as such, being content to let the student discover the writers before they read books about them or, worse, reviews of the books about them. But it must be understood that many of these editions contain excellent introductions and commentaries, and I must also point out the difference between the Oxford (W. W. Skeat) Chaucer and the Cambridge, Mass. (F. N. Robinson) Chaucer, and the desirability of possessing both; it has always struck me that whatever the rights and wrongs of his editorial methods, Skeat demonstrated a good ear in his choice of lines that 'worked' metrically, and since I want readers to know the full joy of hearing Chaucer's poetry I have quoted the Oxford Standard Authors text throughout, and used its line-numbering. But Robinson's lavish notes are essential, and much that is amazingly subtle and expressive in Chaucer will not come alive without their help.

1 : The English Language

Its New Status

For anyone who speaks English, the most exciting thing about the period is not the drums and tramplings of the futile war with France, or the sorry strife of peasants, or the divisions of religious sectaries, but the redemption of our language. This is not the place to detail and document the unhappy and almost incredible story of the decline of English after 1066—the substitution of Norman French for polite speech and officialdom and of Latin for all scholarship and much else, the withdrawal of patronage from the old classical English poetry, and the alien tongue used in schools as the medium of instruction and even among harried English Jews as their vernacular; but one or two earlier commentators may be cited, as showing at least a realization that the national tongue was in danger. Of course, the very use of English, especially when it was rhetorical and witty and shapely, was a defiant and hopeful gesture; but the first real promise of an official English, the English Proclamation of King Henry III (B. Dickins and R. M. Wilson, *Early Middle English Texts*, Cambridge, 1951, pp. 7–9) issued in 1258, died with the death of Simon de Montfort and his cause, which is said to have included in its programme the liquidation of monoglot French-speakers here. Already, in the late eleventh century, a Winchester poetaster (ibid., pp. 1–2) had complained in the old metre of one aspect of the decay, the lack of English-preaching bishops and other teachers; but by about 1200 the earnest and tedious Orm (ibid, pp. 84–5) stressed the usefulness to his countrymen of his gospel paraphrases and exegesis, though without any oblique criticism of the ruling tongue—and it would be quite improper to take his remarkably consistent spelling conventions as an attempt to stabilize and unify the language, or as anything but a help to the reader aloud. A hundred years later, a passage (ibid., p. 14) in the chronicle that usually goes by the name of one of its compilers, Robert of Gloucester, sounds very easy and casual about the problem:

> So that was how England got into the hands of Normandy. And the Normans could not speak anything then except their own speech, and they spoke French as they had done at home, and had their children taught it, too, so that important men in this country who come from their stock all keep to that same speech that they derived from them; because, unless a man knows French, he is thought little of. But humble men keep to English and their own speech still. I reckon there are no countries in the whole world that do not keep to their own speech, except England only. But it is a well-known fact that it is good to know both, because the more a man knows the more deserving he is.

Others, however, felt more restive, and in the same period, round about 1300, a blunter Northerner spoke frankly of the anomalous situation. The unknown author of *Cursor Mundi* began his Prologue with some grave literary criticism of the edifying or fribble tales that people were reading or having read to them, and not surprisingly he soon continues with these linguistic strictures (O. F. Emerson, *A Middle English Reader*, London, 1905 etc., pp. 133–4):

> Efter haly kyrces state
> Þis ilke bok it es translate,
> Into Inglis tong to rede,
> For þe love of Inglis lede,
> Inglis lede of Ingeland,
> For þe commun at understand.
> Frankis rimes here I redd
> Comunlik in ilk a sted;
> Mast es it wroght for Frankis man—
> Quat is for him na Frankis can?
> Of Ingeland þe nacioun,
> Es Inglis man þar in commun.
> Þe speche þat man with mast may spede,

Mast þarwith to speke war nede.
Selden was for ani chance
Praised Inglis tong in France;
Give we ilk an þare langage,
Me think we do þam non outrage.
To lauid Inglis man I spell . . .

[This same book is translated, in accordance with the dignity of
Holy Church, into the English tongue to be read, for love of
the English people, the English people of England, for the
common people to understand. I have normally read French
verses everywhere here; it is mostly done for the Frenchman—
what is there for him who knows no French? As for the nation
of England, it is an Englishman who is usually there. It ought
to be necessary to speak mostly the speech that one can best
get on with. Seldom has the English tongue by any chance
been praised in France; if we give everyone their own language,
it seems to me we are doing them no injury. I am speaking to
the English layman . . .]

This protest is so eminently reasonable, with none of the vengeful-
ness that would have excluded its ten very useful French words,
that it is amazing that more was not being officially or popularly
done for the language.

But there was a half-century silence, and then all the occasions
of emancipation seem to come at once. Before we consult the
historian of this change, John Trevisa, it may be said clearly that
the factors which he does not mention wholly corroborate his
thesis: a South-Western deed of 1376, in British Museum Harley
Charters 45.A.37, is 'the oldest private legal instrument' surviving;
the Mercers' Petition to Parliament, of 1386, is our oldest piece of
parliamentary—sometimes, indeed, unparliamentary—English; the
oldest English wills in the London Court of Probate are of 1387,
and will soon emerge from their barbarous formula of 'French
with English subtitles' into an honest all-English jargon; the
oldest returns in English of the ordinances, usages, holdings, etc.,
of the gilds were made in 1389, principally for London, Norwich,

and King's Lynn. These vital developments, a new vogue for talking English, and the first instances of English in the law-courts and for the King to open Parliament, guaranteed its survival more surely than a hundred Chaucers could have done; Trevisa shows interest only in speech, in the education of young gentlemen, and in the ugliness of the Northern dialect, but his statement is perhaps the most exciting by any historian of the language.

Born at Crocadon in St. Mellion, Cornwall, he had crossed the Tamar 'into England' and gone up to Oxford; despite a fellowship of Exeter College, his career there was stormy even to ejection for 'unworthiness'—which may mean the taint of Lollardy—, and he eventually became Vicar of Berkeley (Glos.) and chaplain at the Castle, with a canonry of the collegiate church of Westbury-on-Trym later. His lifework was translation from Latin: he gave the English in their vernacular the biggest encyclopaedia and the biggest history he could find, and in a style that made few concessions to elegance and many to clarity, explaining 'hard' words and even pairing new borrowings with familiar native stems to bring out the meaning. When he records a dialogue between a lord and a cleric (surely Berkeley and himself) they discuss translation, and the lord wisely chooses prose as the medium rather than the too-easy verse which was current. Trevisa died in 1402, and lies in Berkeley church.

In the course of his 1387 rendering of the chronicler Ranulph Higden, monk of Chester, who had died in 1364, he first translates as follows (Emerson, op. cit., pp. 224—5):

As hyt ys yknowe houȝ meny maner people buþ in þis ylond, þer buþ also of so meny people longages and tonges. Noþeles Walschmen and Scottes, þat buþ noȝt ymelled wiþ oþer nacions, holdeþ wel nyȝ here furste longage and speche, bote ȝef Scottes, þat were som tyme confederat and wonede wiþ þe Pictes, drawe somwhat after here speche. Bote þe Flemmynges þat woneþ in þe west syde of Wales habbeþ yleft here strange speche, and spekeþ Saxonlych ynow. Also Englyschmen, þeyȝ hy hadde fram þe bygynnyng þre maner speche, Souþeron, Norþeron, and Myddel speche in þe myddel of þe

lond, as hy come of þre maner people of Germania, noþeles
by commyxstion and mellyng, furst wiþ Danes and afterward
wiþ Normans, in menye þe contray longage ys apeyred, and
som vseþ strange wlaffyng, chyteryng, harryng, and garryng
grisbittyng. Þis apeyryng of þe burþtonge ys bycause of twey
þinges. On ys for chyldern in scole, aȝenes þe vsage and manere
of al oþer nacions, buþ compelled for to leue here oune
longage, and for to construe here lessons and here þinges a
Freynsch, and habbeþ suþthe þe Normans come furst into
Engelond. Also gentil men children buþ ytauȝt for to speke
Freynsch fram tyme þat a buþ yrokked in here cradel and
conneþ speke and playe wiþ a child hys brouch; and
oplondysch men wol lykne hamsylf to gentil men, and fondeþ
wiþ gret bysynes for to speke Freynsch, for to be more ytold of.

[As is it realised how many kinds of people there are in this
island, there are also the languages and dialects of so many
people. Nevertheless Welshmen and Scots, who are not
mixed with other nations, pretty well keep their original
language and speech, unless the Scots, who were at one time
confederates with the Picts and lived with them, incline somewhat towards their speech. But the Flemings who live on the
west side of Wales have abandoned their foreign speech and
speak quite Saxonly. Also, though Englishmen had from the
beginning three kinds of speech, Southern, Northern, and
Middle speech in the middle of the country, according as they
came from three kinds of people in Germany, nevertheless
by mixing and mingling, first with Danes and afterwards with
Normans, in many cases the language of a district is impaired,
and some practise strange stammering, chattering, snarling,
and grating tooth-gnashing. This impairing of the native
tongue is because of two things. One is that children in
school, contrary to the usage and custom of all other nations,
are compelled to drop their own language and to construe
their lessons and their other things in French, and have done
so since the Normans first came to England. Also gentlemen's
children are taught to speak French from the time that they

are rocked in their cradles and can talk and play with a child's trinket; and up-country men want to liken themselves to gentlemen, and try with great effort to speak French, so as to be thought more of.]

This is a glum situation indeed, and it is only wryly amusing to see that last phrase reiterating from Robert of Gloucester the human frailty of keeping up with the Delarues. But now Trevisa interposes a passage of his own:

Þys manere was moche y-vsed tofore þe furste moreyn, and ys seþthe somdel ychaunged. For Iohan Cornwal, a mayster of gramere, chayngede þe lore in gramerscole and construccion of Freynsch into Englysch; and Richard Pencrych lurnede þat manere techyng of hym, and oþer men of Pencrych, so þat now, þe ȝer of oure Lord a þousond þre hondred foure score and fyue, of þe secunde Kyng Richard after þe Conquest nyne, in al þe gramerscoles of Engelond childern leueþ Frensch and construeþ and lurneþ an Englysch, and habbeþ þerby avauntage in on syde, and desavauntage yn anoþer. Here avauntage ys þat a lurneþ here gramer yn lasse tyme þan childern wer ywoned to do. Disavauntage ys þat now childern of gramerscole conneþ no more Frensch þan can here lift heele, and þat ys harm for ham and a scholle passe þe se and trauayle in strange londes, and in meny caas also. Also gentil men habbeþ now moche yleft for to teche here childern Frensch.

[This custom was much in use before the first plague, and is since somewhat changed. For John Cornwall, a grammar master, changed the instruction and construing in the grammar school from French into English; and Richard Pencrych learned that kind of teaching from him, and other men from Pencrych, so that now, in the year of Our Lord 1385, the ninth of the second King Richard after the Conquest, in all the grammar schools of England children are dropping French and construing and learning in English, and have as a result an advantage on the one hand and a disadvantage on the other.

Their advantage is that they learn their grammar in less time than children were accustomed to do. The disadvantage is that now grammar school children know no more French than their left heel, and that is bad for them if they have to go overseas and travel in foreign countries, and in many other cases, too. Also gentlemen have now largely stopped teaching their children French.]

This wonderful parenthesis admittedly stops short of great penetration or great accuracy. It will be seen that he ascribes the change partly to the upheavals of the Black Death of 1348–49, but mainly to the teaching methods of two men with patently Cornish names; we are asked to believe, by a Cornishman with a Cornish name, that two others from his Duchy were largely responsible for the redemption of what wasn't even their native tongue, since all three must originally have been Keltic-speaking! Even if this is not an early example of Cornish nationalism (and as it happens, their good work at Oxford is verifiable), he is perhaps a little imperceptive in supposing that the speech habits of a nation will be much affected by how the privileged learn their Latin. But then, with remarkable prescience and a jolly joke, he sees the typical English tourist on the Continent with no language but his own; and the passage closes with a more convincing reason for the decay of French.

Trevisa next reverts to Higden and to his surprise that our native tongue is so diverse in sound, when Norman—a 'comlyng' [*parvenu*] from another country—has one standard sound when spoken properly in England. He flattered it: it was fragmented by his time, and Chaucer's note on his prioress's speech,

> . . . Frensh she spak ful faire and fetisly
> After the scole of Stratford atte Bowe,
> For Frensh of Paris was to hir unknowe,

[She spoke French very nicely and elegantly, according to the school of Stratford le Bow, because the French of Paris was unknown to her] could be both a gentle criticism of her insularity and an unkinder hint that her little convent of St. Leonard was not so very fashionable. In another brief interpolation, Trevisa points out that there are as many different kinds of French in France as there are of English in England, and thereafter copies wholesale from Higden a rather obvious statement that Easterners talk more like Westerners (after all, they were neighbours) than Northerners talk like Southerners, and that *Mercii*, the Midlanders, understand the flanking dialects, Northern and Southern, better than Northern and Southern people understand each other. The next bit, some more gratuitous criticism of the Northern dialect, started its career from the pen of the Southerner William of Malmesbury before 1125, was disloyally adopted by the Northerner Higden of Chester, and then found its way back to the south with Trevisa:

Al þe longage of þe Norþhumbres, and specialych at ȝork, ys so scharp, slyttyng, and frotyng, and vnschape, þat we Souþeron men may þat longage vnneþe vndurstonde. Y trowe þat þat ys bycause þat a buþ nyȝ to strange men and aliens, þat spekeþ strangelych, and also bycause þat þe kynges of Engelond woneþ alwey fer fram þat contray.

[All the language of the Northumbrians, and especially at York, is so sharp, piercing, rasping, and amorphous, that we Southerners can hardly understand it. I reckon that this is because they are near outlandish men and foreigners, who speak in foreign tongues, and also because the kings of England always live far from that area.]

The theory that the king could greatly influence common speech is idealistic; but it is certainly not without point that by 1399 we had a king, a usurper by popular choice, who spoke English as his first language; his son Henry V had so little French that he could not even woo in it, as Shakespeare makes clear.

It must be emphasized here that whereas the glory of the language in this half-century, and the renaissance of English letters, rests securely in Geoffrey Chaucer, William Langland, John Gower, the unknown poet of *Sir Gawain and the Green Knight* and *Pearl*, and the founders of our prose, the foundation of the ordinary language must be sought in its official use. The one great document in this context is certainly that in which the Mercery of London petitioned Parliament in 1386 (Emerson, op. cit., pp. 232–7); would that our officialese had retained the clarity and frankness of this pioneer piece!—though mercifully the occasions for such fiery pleading have grown rarer. Briefly, Nicholas Brembre, with the Grocers and Fishmongers backing him, and by the use of force, has made himself Mayor of London contrary to the rules of election. (We know also that he was of Richard II's party, was knighted for his adherence, and was hanged in 1388.)

For in the same yere the forsaid Nicholus, withouten nede, ayein the pees made dyverse enarmynges bi day and eke bi nyght, and destruyd the Kynges trewe lyges, som with open slaughtre, somme bi false emprisonementz; and some fledde the citee for feere, as it is openlich knowen. And so ferthermore for to susteyne thise wronges and many othere, the next yere after the same Nicholus, ayeins the forsaide fredam and trewe communes, did crye openlich that no man sholde come to chese her mair but such as were sompned, and tho that were sompned were of his ordynaunce and after his avys. And in the nyght next after folwynge he did carye grete quantitee of armure to the guyldehalle, with which as wel straungers of the contree as othere of withinne were armed on the morwe ayeins his owne proclamacion, that was such that no man shulde be armed; and certein busshmentz were laide that, when freemen of the citee come to chese her mair, breken up armed cryinge with loude voice 'Sle, sle!', folwyng hem, wherthourgh the peple for feere fledde to houses and other hidynges, as in londe of werre adradde to be ded in commune.

[Because in the same year the aforesaid Nicholas, unnecessarily and in defiance of the peace, caused various armings by day and also by night, and destroyed the King's loyal subjects, some by open slaughter, some by unjust imprisonments; and some fled the city because of fear, as is plainly known. And so, in order still further to maintain these wrongs and many others, the year following this same Nicholas, contrary to the aforesaid freedom and the loyal commons, had it openly proclaimed that no man was to come to choose their mayor save such as were summoned, and those that were summoned were by his arrangement and of his opinion. And during the subsequent night he had a great quantity of arms and armour carried to the guildhall, and with them strangers from the environs as well as others from within the walls were armed next morning contrary to his own proclamation, which was that no man must be armed; and certain ambushes were laid which, when freemen of the city came to choose their mayor, leaped up armed and shouting with a loud voice 'Kill, kill!', and pursuing them, for which reason the people in fear fled to houses and other hidingplaces, dreading to be killed all together as if in a country at war.]

Thus the mayoralty and other offices were being held as if by 'conquest or mastery', and anyone who raised any objections was impeached and imprisoned; the Mercers especially had been the object of threats, and Nicholas had declared that twenty or thirty of them deserved to be drawn and hanged. His creature Nicholas Exton, obtruded into the mayoralty the year after, burned the book of good customs called 'Jubilee'; clearly, everything that the strong 1381 mayor John Northampton, Draper, had stood for had now been reversed, and it may not be too fanciful to connect the strength of this prose with the style of John Wyclif, whom Northampton (backed by John of Gaunt) had supported. Certainly the compiler is more nearly lost when he has no bright thread of narrative to guide him, and the purely legalistic passages can be stodgy and asyntactical. He does not leave his theme without a joke—a pun (on *brembre* = 'bramble') arising from an already sustained metaphor: 'sithen this wronges biforesaide han ben used as accidental or comune braunches outward, it sheweth wel the rote of hem is a ragged subject or stok inward, that is, the forsaid brere or Brembre.' [. . . since these wrongs aforementioned have been used as secondary or ordinary branches externally, it clearly shows that the root of them is a ragged subject or stump internally, that is, the aforesaid briar or Bramble.]

The 1389 gild returns (ed. Toulmin Smith, *English Gilds*, Early English Text Society No. 40, London, 1870), just as revolutionary in their way of being the beginnings of trade union English, show a measure of charm, simplicity, and stateliness, that will offset for us the civic unrest of Brembre's régime. A brief one from Norwich (ibid., p. 27), devoid of the fines and threats and ale and swear-words that disfigure some of them, puts its rules as follows:

And a bretherhode þer is ordened of barbres, in þe site of Norwyche, in þe worschep of God and ys moder and Seynt Johan þe Babtis, þat alle bretherin and sisterin of þe same gylde, als longe as xij persones of hem lyuen, þey schulen offeryn a candel and to torches of wax; and þis light þey hoten and a-vowed to kepyn and myntenyn, and þes oþer ordenances þat ben vnder wreton, vp-on here power and diligence, in worschepe of Crist and ys modyr and Seyn John Babtis; and þe to torches schul bien of xl *lib*. weyght; and alle þe bretherin and sisterin schullen offeryn þis candel and þe to torches eueri ȝer a misomere day, and þey herin here messe at þe heye auter atte charunel in Cristis Cherge, and eueri brother and sistir offeryn an *ob*. wyth here candel and here to torches, in honour of God and Oure Lady and Seynt Johan þe Babtis. And þe to torches, eueri day in þe ȝer, scullen ben light and brennynge at þe heye messe at selue auter, from þe leuacioun of Cristis body sacrid, in til þat þe priest haue vsud. This bien þe names of þe men þat ben maystris and kepers of þe gyld:

Philippus Barbur	And þis men han in kepynge
Jacobus Barbir	for þe same light, ij*s*. in here
Thomas Barbyr at Prechors	box.

[And there is ordained a brotherhood of barbers, in the city of Norwich, to the honour of God and His mother and St. John the Baptist, to the effect that all brethren and sisters of that same gild, as long as twelve of them are alive, must offer a candle and two wax torches; and they promised and vowed to keep and maintain this light and these other ordinances which are written below, to the best of their power and diligence, to the honour of Christ and His mother and St. John the Baptist; and the two torches must be of 40lb. weight; and all the brethren and sisters must offer this candle and the two torches every year on Midsummer Day, and they are to hear their mass at the high altar at the mortuary chapel in Christ Church, and every brother and sister is to offer a ½d. with their candle and their two torches, to the honour of God and Our Lady and St. John the Baptist. And the two torches, every day of the year, must be alight and burning at the high mass at this same altar, from the elevation of Christ's consecrated body until the priest has finished. These are the names of the men who are masters and keepers of the gild:

Philip Barbur	And these men have in
James Barbir	keeping for this same light
Thomas Barbyr at the Blackfriars.	2/- in their box.]

It has been just as well to study a document so ordinary and unsophisticated before proceeding to our next subject, the new shape of the language; it is clear that the clerk had no vested interest in retaining etymological spellings—the three quasi-surnames at the end prove otherwise!—, and we may presume that he similarly had neither an academic hankering after archaic grammar nor a poet's savour for older forms. So it is interesting to see how much (it is in fact comparatively little) of the older grammatical inflexions survive in this text, and to bear it in mind when we come to consider the highly educated and poetical practice of Chaucer. The verbs appear to keep a present indicative plural ending in -n (schulen, ben), a present subjunctive plural ending in -n (? herin, and ? the third instance of offeryn), a preterite plural ending in -n (hoten—if this really is a preterite; but the stem vowel is unsatisfactory), and an infinitive ending in -n (the first two instances of offeryn, kepyn, myntenyn); when we see that the preterite participle wreton also bears an -n, which we retain in written, it will become even more obvious that the -n inflexion has too many functions, is not unambiguous, means almost anything, and thus means almost nothing: *herin* and the third *offeryn* could equally be infinitives depending on the previous *schullen*. The nouns are much like ours of the present day, though the 'strong' -*s* plural and the genitive singular are in every case -*es* or -*is*; the 'weak' -*n* plural of *bretherin* is still recognizable, though the analogous *sisterin* is extinct; there is no clear case of a dative singular noun in -*e* after a preposition, and the first *gylde* is contradicted by *gyld* at the end. The adjectives are perhaps more conservative: *alle* may bear the plural inflexion -*e*, and every one in the 'weak' position after the definite article appears to bear the correct 'weak' inflexion -*e* (though *same* always bore an organic etymological -*e* anyway): *same* twice, *heye* twice. Thus partially equipped, let us consider the shape in which this newly vigorous language existed.

Its New Shape

THE Middle English language of 1350–1400 is in its structure largely the derivative of a highly inflected ('synthetic') language called Old English, and largely the origin of a slightly inflected ('analytical') language called Modern English. Old English, especially in its delineation of case in nouns and adjectives by a change of inflexion, and by even more complicated changes for tense, mood, number, person, and even voice, all contained within one protean verb, was of an elaboration akin to that of Latin; Modern English has sloughed most of these inflexions—far more than French in the verb, though in adjectives it is richer than French by normally having an inflected comparative and superlative, and in nouns slightly richer in its inflected possessives and technically its datives like 'give *the boy* the book'. But the changes have been huge; the hundred shapes that a Latin verb stem can adopt, and the fourteen or so of Old English, are now matched by a 'strong' verb such as *sing, sings, sang, sung,* and *singing* (the last now irritatingly used for both present participle and verbal noun) or a 'weak' (nay, feeble in this case) verb such as *put* (for present, past, and past participle), *puts, putting*. And so English has become 'opener': its pages are littered with *of, to, may, might, will, would, do, did, have, had*; whether this confers any benefit of expressiveness or euphony is a point that we shall have to consider.

The path to this state of affairs has not been taken by national choice, the will of the people, or some special judicious reasoning; even the loss which is no loss, grammatical gender, lapsed gradually and not by legislation. Four factors, at least, contributed to the decay of inflexions: the prevalence of *-e*, or *-e-* + a consonant, in the Old English system; allied with this, a tendency early to make other inflexional vowels conform to this *-e*; an emphasis on the stem vowel, reducing the inflexional vowel to a blurred neuter sound shown by *-e*, but approximating to the final *ə* sound of 'Ver*ə*'; and the neighbourhood of two other languages, Old Norse and Norman French. The influence of Norse was bound to be strong, since it shared so many stems yet differed in so many inflexions; thus in the North, where Norse stock had settled, a happy form of pidgin, more or less stems only, could gain ground as a *lingua franca*—certainly the first surviving Northern Middle English texts show a very precocious shedding of inflexions. French, which had opened out vastly from its roots in Latin, would affect the syntax in its escape towards *of* and *to*, and in the use of auxiliary verbs. Thus by Chaucer's early days in the South-East an odd state of affairs had arisen concerning the inflexion *-e*:

In nouns, it stood (though it sometimes fell) for the dative singular of old masculine and neuter strong nouns; for the nominative and accusative singular of these nouns when they derived from forms with an etymological final vowel; for all four cases singular, including the genitive, of most old strong feminines; and for the nominative singular of old weak nouns, and the genitive singular of some that had been feminine. In adjectives, it stood for the plural accompanying a plural noun; for all occurrences of adjectives that derived from forms with an etymological final vowel; and for all adjectives when in the 'weak' position after a definite article, demonstrative, possessive, or hypothetical vocative *0*. It also turned adjectives into adverbs, where we now normally use *-ly*. In strong verbs, it stood for the first person singular present indicative; for all persons singular of the present subjunctive; for all persons singular of the preterite subjunctive; often, for the infinitive (which was 'properly' -en); for the second person singular preterite indicative; and often, save in the North, for the preterite participle (which was 'properly' -en). In weak verbs, the same applied, though the second person singular preterite indicative had -est, and the preterite participle was in a dental or a dental + -e; in addition, the first and third persons singular preterite indicative had a dental + -e.

This is a formidable tally; and it will be seen that a paradoxical situation had arisen whereby -e (as with the far less equivocal -n which we saw earlier) defined almost everything and therefore satisfactorily defined almost nothing. By the end of the century and Chaucer's death, it had very reasonably almost vanished; but before we congratulate ourselves on its disappearance along with many an -n and other 'complications', let us reflect on what we may have lost.

It has been inappropriately said that 'English is degenerating into monosyllabification', and it is certain that our present strings of ugly little words, bounded by stop consonants, bump into one another in a very cacophonous way. To exhibit the words HAND LIGHT SOCKET/ENGINE SUMP/OIL DRAIN on a British Railways shunting engine is pardonable and even has a grubby aptness, but such concatenations of consonants in speech or rhetoric are unpleasant and difficult. An early contemporary of Chaucer might well say and write 'Þe goode laddes wenten faste to þe blake hille'; every -e here is operative and must be sounded, however lightly, giving a total of fifteen syllables. Our own version would have nine—'The good lads went fast to the black hill'; it sheds the -e of the plural adjective, the adverb, the weak adjective, and the dative singular noun, along with the -en of the preterite plural and the -e- in laddes. But it is no easier for being so much shorter; the tongue must perform gymnastics in which a slovenly speaker will probably further elide the -t of went and the -t of fast, whereas the Middle English version has a flow, a lilt, a cadence, that make it supremely easy to say.

To this argument against cacophony we can add another, though less confidently, against loss of expressiveness. In all honesty, nothing can be said in favour of grammatical gender (still the curse of French and German), and probably nothing for the weak adjective; but various lost riches, such as a real dative for a recipient, might still be handy, and the effective passing of the subtle subjunctive is a real loss. When we are told that

> Arthure wolde not ete til al were serued
> (*Sir Gawain and the Green Knight*, 1.85),

we are tempted to render it as 'Arthur would not eat till all were served', but *al* is in fact singular, and *were* subjunctive singular; it is not that everyone ate, and then Arthur willingly fell to, but that he was waiting until that hypothetical moment when 'everyone would be served'. A slight gain only?—perhaps so, but it must be remembered that our auxiliary verb system, now all-important for any suppleness our verbs can possess, is in ruins, and anything to make it more precise would be a boon. Even in this quoted line, *wolde* really has the meaning 'was willing to', not just the casual 'would' as if expressing a future-in-the-past, but observe what we do with it now: 'She would visit her grandmother every day' (= *used to visit*); 'The king would be dead before the year was out' (= *was going to die*); 'I would like' (or is it 'I *should* like'?—we can never be certain); and so on. Add to this the gross over-use of *do* in its many meanings, and of the other small aids to expression, and it will be found that Chaucer's idiom, however much it was 'diseased' with inflexions, has a neatness and a precision that we have surrendered. Inflexions do not make the acquisition of a language harder; an illiterate Albanian peasant juggles with the moods indicative, subjunctive, optative, admirative, imperative, and infinitive, and the (to us) deplorable system of postfixing the definite article, and a Welsh baby picks up (often concurrently with English) a system whereby words change their endings, their middles, *and their initials*. Every time we say 'taller' and not 'more tall' we should be thankful that we did not sacrifice *this* luxury as well.

But, alas, most of the inflexions we are left with are hardly worth having. The hiss and buzz of final -*s* (a hiss only after *p*, *t*, *k*, *f*, and the unvoiced *th*, but otherwise really a -*z*) is our chief link with our inflexional past, but it is unfortunate that it marks plural nouns and singular verbs, and equally unfortunate that it marks plural nouns and genitive singular nouns and (with a fatuous final apostrophe, as if something were missing) genitive plural nouns, whence a trail of modern mis-spellings; it is also in uneasy neighbourhood with feminines in -ess, abstracts in -ness, adjectives in -less, and many other sibilants. I am arguing that our language would be more euphonious and precise if we had extended the 'weak' noun plural in -*en* and retained Chaucer's third person singular present indicative in -*eth* (which was still conferring beauty in 1611, when the Authorized Version used it solely). And though the half-century under review greatly simplified the inflexional system, it remained a far more powerful weapon than that with which we are now equipped in our wisdom and our misfortune.

One other argument against the dropping of inflexions must be briefly mentioned. Anyone familiar with Latin will know how effectively the order of words can be disarrayed for emphasis, because their relationship to one another is made clear by their terminations; nothing so extreme can now be exploited in English, though in speech we emphasize by intonation or gesture. But even in Chaucer's time the inflexional system had so far decayed that any kind of radical disarray would have looked tortuous, and we must hunt further back before we find such examples as that of the wolf arriving at the well where the fox is trapped in a nether bucket:

He com to þe putte, þene vox iherde (Dickins and Wilson, op. cit., p. 66);

despite the inversion, the latter clause means 'heard the fox', because *þene* is masculine accusative singular, and accusative only. Such pliancy of syntax is a small benefit, and our real regret for lost endings must be based on the claims of clarity and beauty; any loyal citizen trying to sing 'Frustrate their knavish tricks' could sigh for a return to Chaucerian English.

We have had to consider somewhat lengthily the flux in which final -*e* found itself, because we shall never be able to read Chaucer or his contemporaries aloud, and achieve their music, unless we know when the -*e* is to be pronounced as a syllable and when not.

To clear some certain ground: Chaucer obviously liked 'feminine' rhymes, the double rhymes of stressed + unstressed syllables (like *sōte/rōte* at the very start of *The Canterbury Tales*), and at a line-ending we shall be safe in sounding every final *-e*; on the other hand, in mid-line an *-e* is elided before a word beginning with a vowel or with the *h-* of an unstressed word—thus 1.2 of the *Tales* falls into eleven syllables:

The droght(e) of March(e) hath perced to the rote,

a good line save that the weak *to* has to bear a stress. A line with a masculine rhyme would have ten, five iambs or a trochee and four iambs. But it is with a medial *-e* before a consonant that the difficulty occurs.

Chaucer's usage here is partly a matter of grammar. If we look through a latish (? 1396) poem, *The Envoy to Bukton*, its 32 lines reveal the following capricious pattern of behaviour on the part of medial words with an *-e* before a consonant:

Retaining the -e: highte (1st singular preterite indicative), *bounde* (preterite participle), *thilke* (etymological *-e* going back to Old English *-a*), *bewayle* (infinitive), *worse* 1.17 (if accepted as adjective, *-e* going back to Old English *-a*; but strictly an adverb, and *that* had ended in *-s*), *worse* 1.18 (the adjective), *teche* (infinitive), *sende* (1st singular present indicative), *matere* (Old French *matere*, and the stress here retained on the second of the three syllables), *graunte* (3rd singular present subjunctive).

Dropping the -e: answerde (3rd singular preterite indicative), *wolde* (3rd singular preterite indicative), *wedde* (infinitive), *have* (infinitive), *these* (demonstrative plural), *Experience* (the *-e* from Old French), *were* (3rd singular preterite subjunctive).

This is disappointing, especially in that the infinitive, which could still bear an *-en*, could have even its final *-e* treated so casually; and it is a mere coincidence that the 1st and 3rd persons of the indicative exhibit different standards. But even as late as this in Chaucer's career ten such *-e*s are retained to seven discarded, and if we go back to a somewhat earlier poem, *Truth*, we shall find in its small compass of 28 lines a pattern more helpful. There are five imperatives singular with *-e* in this vulnerable position (*dwelle*,

stryve, *Daunte*, *leve* twice), and all save *Daunte* must be pronounced as one syllable only; in the case of ten other imperatives
singular (*Savour*, *Werk*, *Tempest*, *Know*, *look*, *thank*, *Hold*, *lat*,
Draw, *pray*), Chaucer or his scribe did not even trouble to write
an -*e*, and it is clear that here was a part of the verb which, through
colloquial use and a natural emphasis of the stem vowel, early lost
its inflexion. *Truth* contains four nouns which, even in their
nominative singular, keep a spelling -*e* that went back to an Old
English final vowel (*wele*, *crokke*) or had developed since Old
English (*trouthe*, *reste*); each of these must be sounded as a disyllable—a surprise to us, who mistakenly tend to look on the
nominative as not being a case at all in the same sense as the
genitive *man's*—, and the scribe has written a number of others
where the organic -*e* will elide with the following word: *hate*, and
envye, *beste*, and *Vache* (from Old French). Thirdly, the behaviour
of the infinitive here is unequivocal: of the six infinitives (apart
from *be*), *rede*, *redresse* and *lede* are to have their -*e* sounded at the
end of the line, *delivere* and *sporne* have it written but elided, and
bihove has it obviously sounded before a consonant. So far, then,
this little poem suggests two grammatical functions where -*e* must
remain in reading, one where it must be silent; we must take such
tenuous evidence little further, but at least it is worth remarking
that one 'weak' adjective after the definite article, in 'the hye wey',
has an -*e* which is written but not real, and the other, in 'His hy
goodnesse', has already lost its -*e*; and that the various dative
singular nouns after prepositions in general have no -*e* supplied,
whereas the first *worlde* has an -*e* that elides with *axeth* and the
second has one which is the fifth syllable of its line.

This indecisive examination of the behaviour of -*e* in poetry has
been necessary before we can consider the sound of our language
in Chaucer's age. Even if we could master Chaucer's use, however,
it would help us only partially in reading other dialects, and it is
certain that in the North the treatment of -*e* was not a decimation
but a massacre. The North was early in shedding its inflexions, and
lucky, too: not in this stride away from synthesis, but in so soon
possessing a dialect formed and stable, with far less tendency
towards doggerel, in which the -*e* was added or docked at will,

c

than in the South. Further, the North had retained (as we shall see in the next section) the native mode of alliterative and unrhymed poetry, which, depending as it did on initial letters and on firm stress-patterns, could be 'translated' easily from area to area when its rhyming rival would have broken down on dialect variants of rhyme and syllable-counting; alliteration could remain stately even within the changing shape of the language. It has been claimed that none, or almost none, of the -*es* in, for instance, the alliterative *Sir Gawain and the Green Knight* is operative; I do not credit this, especially when a clash of stresses results from turning a written disyllable into an actual monosyllable, and many of the lines flow far better if the lilting of the occasional -*e* is allowed, but I admit that there is even less grammatical pattern to the occurrence than in Chaucer. The *Gawain* poet was, however, aware of a real final -*e*; in ll.413–416, one of the rhyming 'wheels' that punctuate the long lines, it comes out clearly, and with a much longer sound than the *ə* in *Vera* which I postulated earlier:

> 'Ta now þy grymme tole to þe,
>   And let se how þou cnokez.'
> 'Gladly, sir, for soþe',
>   Quoþ Gawan; his ax he strokes.

['Now take your grim weapon to you, and show how you strike.' 'Gladly, sir, indeed,' said Gawain, and stroked the axe.]

Here the *to þe* is the equivalent of our 'to thee', and it is plain that the -*e* of the dative *soþe* is, at this point at least, to be sounded as clearly as the 'e acute' of French.

It might be questioned whether we have, at this distance of 600 years, an accurate idea of how Chaucer's poetry sounded. Three factors, at least, give us confidence in our account of his pronunciation. First, those responsible for writing Middle English had no vested interest in retaining historical spellings; totally ignorant of Old English, unpossessed of any current English dictionary, and untrammelled by any 'standard' to be kept to, they wrote what they heard, and had a pretty handy alphabet for the purpose. Paradoxically, we must thank their ignorance for their accuracy; we, despite all our works of reference and our penetrating knowledge of etymology, are using one of the worst alphabets in the world (adjacent to almost the best, Welsh) and very properly spelling on an etymological basis and not on a phonetic one. Secondly, our knowledge of medieval Latin, French, German, Icelandic, Dutch, and other languages, gives us a fascinating criss-cross of borrowed and adapted words and their sounds, an interrelation that must be worked at by linguistic experts at great toil but with a tolerably satisfactory conclusion; a brief and easy example is the Modern French *canif*, early borrowed from a Germanic word like Middle English *knif* (the *i* is long, as in *machine*) and clearly showing that the *k-* was a reality at the time of the loan. Thirdly, we have the evidence of the likely sounds of Old English (a language sharply written and, again, without 'olde' archaizing intentions) and of the known sounds of Modern English; a good example (though lost on people who call themselves Smythe) is that since we say *smith*, and since there is evidence (partly from related Germanic languages) that the Anglo-Saxons said *smith*, then it is highly likely that the Middle English speaker said something very like *smith* as well. In this last category the evidence becomes more slippery; we have a nasty tendency to shorten long monosyllables, but if we know the formulae of the changes that have set in since 1400 we can be on our guard against anachronism when we read aloud.

The first and obvious way to read Chaucer the poet is aloud; the music, mirth and majesty that flow effortlessly from such a reading can alone give him his status as a poet. The normal way for pupil or student to read him has been silently, with the right forefinger in the glossary; from which kind of attention he emerges as a mine of linguistic curiosities, or a social historian, or the father of English humour, but not as a poet. It is my custom to ask sixth-formers applying for admission to read English at the university whether they have ever heard Chaucer aloud; in a few cases the teacher has ventured this treatment—well, how did it sound? The usual answers are: 'Funny', 'Like French', 'Like Latin', and 'Like German'; now these answers cannot all be sagacious, and it is possible even that they are all insensitive and absurd, though each may have a glimmer of accuracy. In a way, 'Funny' is a good description even of Chaucer well read, if it suggests the violent differences in sound between words whose spelling and meaning are alike for Chaucer and ourselves; since his day, the Great Vowel Shift has wrenched and cockneyized our pure long vowels, and we have indulged to the full in a slovenly shedding of those consonants which, by their nature or by their placing next to other consonants, have seemed difficult. So Chaucer's *knight*, with its *k* still sounded, the long *i* as pure as in French and German and sounding like our *ee*, and the *gh* somewhat as in Scots *loch*, will pardonably sound 'funny' to ears accustomed to our short and diphthongized word.

A complete guide to Chaucer's pronunciation would require a pamphlet such as Helge Kökeritz produced in 1954, or the brief essentials on pp. xxx–xxxii of F. N. Robinson's 1957 edition, but a brief statement can be made here. Most of the consonants are easy for us, provided it is remembered that they are always sounded, even in clusters from which we now shrink: *r* initially was trilled, a much prettier sound than the careless top-teeth and under-lip improvisation of today, and may well have been trilled in other positions; *l* is difficult, because we cannot be sure of its effect on a preceding short *a* or short *o*, but to sound these vowels as if they were unaffected will at least be tuneful and consistent; *h* had better be sounded initially when written, though spellings like *ost* for 'host' make us realize that this French word may usually have been unaspirated. The current alphabet was far from perfect, and whereas before *a/o/u* the sounds of *c* and *g* were as *k* and the *g* of our *gas*, before *e/i/y* they were as *s* and *j* (though even here there were exceptions, which will not worry us, such as *get*, *girl*, *give*); further, the ill-contrived spelling *gg* stood for both *g* (as in *pigges*) or *j* (as in *just*); the spelling *gh* (often ʒ at the time) was approximately the *ch* sound of Scots *loch*, though more like the sound of German *ich* after *i/y*; another g, that in *gn*, was sounded initially in such a word as *gnawen* 'to gnaw' but silent in the French termination *-igne*; *ng*, except in the weak ending *-ing*, was perhaps always sounded as in *finger*. Two other consonants were equivocally unvoiced or voiced: *s* was as in *hiss* or (as if a *z*) *his*, and *th* was as in *thin* or *this*, but we shall be fairly safe in sounding them in the form in which we recognize them.

The short vowels are even easier, though short *a* was nearer to German *Mann* than to our *cat*; roughly, we shall be nearly correct in sounding them as Modern English *pat, pet, pit, pot, put* (not the ugly neuter noise of Southern English *cut*), and a short *y* is exactly the same as a short *i* (thus *him* is often written *hym*). But the long vowels will deceive us at every turn:

Long *a* (unhelpfully spelt *a*) had been somewhat 'raised' from the sound in *father*, but had not yet reached the 'e acute' sound in *maker*, and an 'e circumflex' sound as in *'fair'* will be near the mark.

There were two forms of long *e*. The long close *e* (almost 'e acute') was written by a good scribe *ee* and by an indifferent scribe *e*, as in *meeke/meke*, the first syllable of which would be sounded as our *make*; the long open *e* (almost 'e circumflex') was written by a good scribe *ea*, by an indifferent scribe *e*, and by a bad scribe *ee*, as in *beare/bere/beere*, the first syllable of which would be sounded as our *bear*.

Long *i* (unhelpfully spelt *i* or *y*) was the sound in our *machine*, and is never to be diphthongized as in our *mine*.

There were two forms of long *o*. The long close *o* (almost as in our slightly diphthongized *coat*) was written by a good scribe *oo* and by an indifferent scribe *o*; the long open *o* (almost as in our *bore*) was written by a good scribe *oa*, by an indifferent scribe *o*, and by a bad scribe *oo*. The parallel with long *e* will be obvious.

The original long *u*, spelt *ou* or *ow*, remained as in our *soup* or as in Modern Scots *hour* or *flower*; but a long *u* from French (like German *ü*) also existed, and was rendered *u* in words like *vertu*.

The diphthongs are complicated, and scholars are not in agreement on the sounds signified; in general, it will never be wildly wrong to pronounce them as their two members, so that *aw* will sound more like the diphthong in *how*, but whether *ai/ay* and *ei/ey* had fallen together into one sound (perhaps like *eye*) is controversial.

Two other points must be mentioned. A word of several syllables recently borrowed from French will keep its rising accent or have an accent on the stem and on the termination: thus *honourable* will properly rhyme with *table*; and an unstressed *e* will often be silent in a polysyllable between consonants, especially if the second one is a liquid like *r* and *l*.

With this basic knowledge of the sounds and stresses, let us turn to the poem *Truth*, which has the merits of brevity, unfamiliarity, polish, exact metre, linked metaphors, proverbial lore, Biblical references, and a nice joke, all within the compass of its 28 lines. I shall show the long vowels according to best scribal practice, improving on it for long *a* and long *i/y*; I shall also put an apostrophe when a final or medial *e* is to be dropped. For the rest, the student should try to make every line into five iambs, or a trochee and four iambs, with an extra 'feminine' syllable -*e* in each first, third, sixth and seventh line.

> Flee fro the prees, and dwell' with soothfastnesse.
> Suffȳce unto thȳ good, though hit bee smal;
> For hord hath hāt', and clȳmbing tikelnesse.
> Prees hath envȳ', and weale blent oav'r al.
> Savour noa moar' than thee bihoove shal.
> Werk wel thȳself, that oother folk canst reade;
> And trouthe shal deliv'r', hit is noa dreade.
>
> Tempest thee noght al crooked to redresse,
> In trust of hir that turneth as a bal.
> Great reste stant in litel besinesse.
> And eek bee war' to sporn' ageyn an al.
> Strīv' noght, as dooth the crokke with the wal.
> Daunte thȳself, that dauntest ooth'res deade.
> (normally *deede*)
> And trouthe shal deliv'r', hit is noa dreade.
>
> That thee is sent, receyv' in buxumnesse.
> The wrastling for this world' axeth a fal.
> Heer nis noan hoam; heer nis but wildernesse.
> Forth, pilgrim, forth! Forth, beast', out of thȳ stal!
> Know thȳ contree, look up, thank God of al.
> Hoald the hȳ' wey, and lat thȳ goast thee leade;
> And trouthe shal deliv'r', hit is noa dreade.

(*Envoy*)

Therfor', thou Vach', leav' thȳn oald wrecchednesse
  Unto the worlde; leav' now to bee thral.
Crȳ' Him mercȳ, that of His hȳ goodnesse
  Mād' thee of noght, and in especial
  Draw unto Him, and pray in general
    For thee, and eek for oother, hevenlich' meade.
    And trouthe shal deliv'r', hit is noa dreade.

[Flee from the crowd, and live with truth. Be content with your property, though it is small; because avarice brings hate, and ambition brings instability. The crowd is envious, and prosperity is everywhere blinding. Relish no more than you need. Behave well yourself, you who can advise others; and truth will set you free, there is no doubt. Do not agitate yourself to redress everything that is awry, trusting in her who turns like a ball. Great repose is found in the least possible anxiety. And also be careful of kicking against an awl. Do not strive, as the pitcher did with the wall. Subdue yourself, you who subdue the deeds of others; and truth will set you free, there is no doubt. Receive with submission what is sent to you. Wrestling for this world is only asking for a fall. There is no home here; there is only a wilderness. Away, pilgrim, away! Away, animal, out of your stall! Understand what your true country is, look up, and thank God for everything. Keep to the high-road, and let your spirit lead you; and truth will set you free, there is no doubt. Therefore, Vache, leave your old wretchedness to the world; leave off being a slave now. Cry for mercy to Him who in His great goodness made you from nothing, and particularly draw near to Him and pray comprehensively for yourself, and also for others, for a heavenly reward; and truth will set you free, there is no doubt.]

This is a so-called 'minor' poem in the editions; limited in its scope, and perhaps platitudinous in its philosophy (which comes partly from Chaucer's reading of Boethius), it is still a major achievement in its pure music. It may illustrate for us what has been recognized and commented on ever since real study of Chaucer began: his acclimatizing of French words, and his adoption and transcending of French stanza forms. This is a *balade*, in which an exacting rhyme-scheme within each stanza (a b a b b c c, the *b* always feminine), the so-called *Rime Royal*, applies even to its very *sounds* within the whole poem; a further link is by means of the refrain, and the three stanzas of end-stopped lines of general import are given a specific application in the personal envoy, where four of the lines appropriately run on into their neighbours, as if the declamation had suddenly turned to personal and dramatic speech. The friend addressed was, as Miss Edith Rickert convincingly discovered, Sir Philip de la Vache, who was in political doldrums from 1386 to 1390 and may have been sent this poem by way of consolation; he had to accept a joke by which his name ('Cow' literally) was taken up in the words *beast* and *stall*, and possibly in *meade* in the penultimate line: the surface meaning is 'meed, reward', but this would properly be sounded *meede*, whereas the perfect rhyme *meade* means a 'pasture'.

Its New Literature

THE changes so far traced—the recognition of English as the national language, and the simplification of its grammar to a condition stable in the North but molten in the South—were natural processes, the province of ordinary men from artisans to officials; but with them fortunately coincided the unpredictable occurrence of genius. By 1400 Chaucer had acclimatized a variety of French metres and French words; in thinking of the mere shape of what he did, I am setting his achievement at a merely technical level, and this is not the place to elaborate on how he improved on his French sources, brought back from the Continent his own personal Renaissance by his reading of Italian, and founded poetry as we knew it until its recent indiscipline. Gower, a fluent versifier in the three languages of England, produced in his *Confessio Amantis* over 33,000 English lines remarkably consistent in their metric and their spelling, qualities sufficient to make him an authority for those who found his many stories entrancing and were lulled by his pedantic and pedestrian music. These two were the great writers of the Court and London, the cosmopolitan figures who had enough influence to found a tradition, a London 'school' whose continuity would never thereafter be broken. But something very different was happening elsewhere.

It is customary to date the Alliterative Revival in the North and West from 1350, and for the purpose of this book nothing could be more convenient. The alliterative *Alexander* fragments called 'A' and 'B' were written, we are told, about 1350; Humphrey Bohun, Duke of Hereford, had *William of Palerne* taken out of French about 1351, and—whether he hoped for a rhymed and Frenchified verse or not—got from his paid poet an alliterative version; these are narrative poems of 'romance' type, but two speculative and moralizing poems, *Winner and Waster* and *The Parliament of the Three Ages*, came soon after. From then on, alliterative verse formed some fine romances and wrestled with the theological and philosophical intricacies of *Piers Plowman*; it died—as far as record is available—in 1513, when a north-western poet devoted to it a poem on the Battle of Flodden, not long after the Scot William Dunbar had used it for a serious but obscene social satire, *The Two Married Women and the Widow*. Now it is clear to any reader of this body of poetry, a poetry evincing traditional skill and centuried vocabulary, that it is only partly a revival and must be largely a survival. Its basis is the splendidly economical line of Old English, often with only four words, its two halves linked by alliteration of one word with one, or of two with one, scorning rhyme internally or with its neighbours, often running on by enjambement into the following line, and observing a series of careful metrical patterns within itself; to take a well-known name, Cædmon closes his surviving hymn with the line: 'Firum foldu, frea allmectig', where the three *f*s are both the adornment and the substance. Various explanations are given of what happened to this courtly, clerkly, classical poetry at 1066, when the wealthiest patronage of English verse ceased and the best-educated people used French and Latin; but it must be borne in mind that the *surviving* late Old English verse suggests a decadence. In any case, rhyme had begun to occur, and its tinkling foreign charm must have drawn emphasis to the line-ending and thus worked against enjambement. The naive statement that alliteration was pushed out into the highways, the village greens, and the kitchens, must be partly true, and in hands that could not keep to the strict metrical formulae an accretion of extra syllables must have given the line a swollen and desultory shape in which meretricious adornments like internal rhyme and two-two alliteration would occur in an *ad hoc* sort of way; or this verse was a leftover from a supposed 'popular' Old English mode, so popular that it was never committed to expensive parchment and vellum, and leaves no evidence. But, whether 1066 occasioned or confirmed this poetic mode, written records leave us only a silence of nearly 150 years broken by hoarse whispers of archaic doggerel; then, round about 1200, Laȝamon or Lawman, the parish priest of Areley Kings in Worcestershire, gave us his great 16,000-line national epic, in which these features of decay, survival, and new growth, are inextricably mixed. Some of his lines, especially in the heat of battle, have a classical excellence of brevity, with rich and telling alliteration and no trace of rhyme; but most of them admit elements in which the spirit of *Beowulf* is withered—rhyme, assonance instead of rhyme, the rhyming of accented and unaccented syllables as in *king/tiding*, extra syllables that bloat the line and render it nearly formless, slices of mere prose innocent of any metrical adornment, over-alliteration and one-two alliteration, and all the time never a trace of the old surging run-on line.

Laȝamon domesticated at Areley 'with the good knight', who may have patronized this sort of poem; but of other such traditional verse there is now no readable trace for another bleak period of 150 years, and then the Revival bursts in upon us. It has seemed feasible to some that the continuity during those 300 years was by word of mouth, the repetitions of minstrels or of old wives, with Laȝamon merely lucky enough to have some parchment handy: let it be said at once that the first and later examples of the Revival do not look like that kind of creeping growth at all, and do not look like Laȝamon either. *Winner and Waster* and *The Parliament of the Three Ages*, whose purpose is comment, and *Sir Gawain and the Green Knight,* which is ostensibly narrative, are highly educated and exploratory; they show more training, more confidence in their medium, more belief in the special status of the poet, than any of the rhymed verse save Chaucer's. And though they have been labelled a 'native growth', they are aware of French analogues and of the extra subtleties available in the use of French words; the opening line of *Gawain* is a spirited rush in which all four operative words are French: 'Siþen þe *sege* and þe *assaut* watz *sesed* at *Troye*' [After the siege and assault had ended at Troy]. *Gawain* is an original poem in which diverse traditions are brilliantly fused and made interdependent; but it will be agreed that even when there is translation from French involved in an English alliterative poem, the process of adapting the rather trivial octosyllabic couplet to the drum roll of the alliterative line shows far more poetic pressure than its mere adaptation into an English short couplet such as Gower or the young Chaucer could have turned. *Piers Plowman,* freakish in so many ways, stands apart from its fellows in the Revival in the London origin which it claims, in the metrical dislocation of some of its duller passages, and in the seemingly deliberate ugliness of its worst lines: 'And binam hym his mnam, for he ne wolde worche, And ʒaf that mnam to hym that ten mnames hadde.' [And took his talent from him, because he wouldn't work, and gave that talent to him who had ten talents]; but not in its French vocabulary, which is used with assurance and energy. This lonely poem, in which we are asked to believe in a searcher-poet wandering through frustration and sleep to a bald and toothless impotence, is in some respects the crown of the alliterative achievement, scaling like illuminated Gothic manuscripts the height of heavenly mysteries and descending as their borders do to the depravities and fatuities of unregenerate man.

A tenuous oral tradition is unlikely; and a winning and well documented case against it has been brought by Elizabeth Salter in two articles in *Modern Philology* (Vol. 64, Nos. 2–3, November 1966–February 1967, pp. 146–50 and 233–37). While totally rejecting the idea that various provincial barons used, or caused to be used, the alliterative mode to show their defiance of the

Frenchified and even cosmopolitan court, she shows how a group of magnates with West Midland connexions—Bohuns, Beauchamps, Mortimers—were after 1350 variously patrons of alliterative literature or owners of French books related to this literature in theme and perhaps awaiting use as sources or for straight translation. The Berkeleys, Trevisa's enlightened employers, belong here; but above all Mrs. Salter uses John of Gaunt's 1379–83 Register to demonstrate the splendour, the enlightenment, and the patronage, that make *Gawain* a credible narrative and the Revival a deliberate literary movement and not a provincial oddity. Inasmuch as Gaunt had vast holdings in the North and the West Midlands, besides his firm foot-hold at court, he could be regaled at different times and mansions with poetry as different as *Gawain* and the curious tribute that Chaucer paid him in *The Book of the Duchess*. But were there any other unifying factors in our new two-fold literature besides the ears of such privileged patrons as Gaunt? Were *Piers Plowman* and its author such isolated phenomena in London?

Of alliterative literature Chaucer says nothing whatever. On the alliterative habit he puts one comment into the mouth of his parson (whom we are to believe); it is always being quoted as if showing contempt for an uncouth Northernism:

> 'I am a Southren man.
> I can not geste rum-ram-ruf by lettre'

['I am a Southern man. I can't manage tales alliterating rum-raf-ruf'. *Canterbury Tales:* Parson's Prologue, ll. 42 ff.],

but it is conveniently forgotten that the next line is just as sweeping in its condemnation of rhymed verse—

> 'Ne, God wot, rym holde I but litel bettre'

['And, God knows, I consider rhyme only a little better'].

So the parson is merely remembering that poetry is *daemonum cibus*, the food of fiends, that 'song has both good and ill', as the earlier mystic, Richard Rolle, expressed it; and we must rather seek Chaucer's opinion in the use that he made of alliterating phrases and his occasional sharing of a wider alliterative spirit. Certainly there are many pretty lines of this sort to be found in him, and none more artificially effective than 1. 400 of *The Book of the Duchess*, where every stressed word brings out the beauty of the wood in May,

> With floures fele, faire under fete

[with many flowers, lovely under foot]; or he will link the initial letters gnomically, even as we still have a few alliterative proverbs, and thus produces grave lines like *Truth*, 1. 13, 'Daunte thyself, that dauntest otheres dede' [Subdue yourself, you who subdue the deeds of others]; or he will use the idiom for humour, as in the rumbustious 1. 578 of *The Nun's Priest's Tale*, where the whole hamlet turns out to chase the fox, and the line toots with their music—

> Of bras they broghten bemes, and of box

[They brought trumpets of brass and of boxwood]; in *The Knight's Tale*, indeed, the alliterative clash of arms comes so authentically through ll. 2605 ff. that it has been supposed even that Chaucer had attentively heard or read some of the best romances such as the alliterative *Morte Arthure*, a noble poem and one readily communicable to his sympathies. There are just a few lines that suggest his acquaintance with the highly-trained use of very Northern words, and in a context where there is no possibility of his merely imitating Northern speech as he does in *The Reeve's Tale*; perhaps the most striking instance is 1. 1119 of *The Knight's Tale*, 'With knotty knarry bareyn trees olde' [with knotty gnarled barren old trees].

But despite his absention from any overt hostility to the alliterative school, Chaucer had no alliteration at the heart of him: he neither used it emotively, to create a mood, nor found himself using it, willy-nilly or by design, in his moments of excitement and exaltation. The emotive use had been the most hopeful aspect of the mode during its 300 years 'underground'; the lovesick poet of *Alysoun* in MS Harley 2253 conveys his pangs and despairs by wonderfully tuneful and effective strings of suitable initial letters, mainly gentle and poignant liquids: two close-knit patches each with five *w*s, and *l*s everywhere, with sundry *r*s and *y*s; the *Gawain* poet, in Chaucer's own lifetime, conveyed the passing of the seasons, the very proper regret of a poet that the grain and the year should fall and die, and his lifting hope that out of this a spring should return, by subtle groupings of lovely sounds—*w*, *l*, *gr*, *r*, *y*, *w*:

> Wroþe wynde of þe welkyn wrastelez with þe sunne,
> Þe leuez laucen fro þe lynde and lyȝten on þe grounde,
> And al grayes þe gres þat grene watz ere;
> Þenne al rypez and rotez þat ros vpon fyrst,
> And þus ȝirnez þe ȝere in ȝisterdayez mony,
> And wynter wyndez aȝayn, as þe worlde askez.

[Fierce wind from the sky wrestles against the sun, the leaves loosen from the tree and alight on the ground, and all the grass that was green before grows grey; then everything that rose in the beginning ripens and rots, and thus the year runs in many yesterdays, and winter returns, as the world requires. *Sir Gawain and the Green Knight*, ll. 525–30]

The sporadic occurrence of alliteration as the outcome or the means of strong inspiration is something now rather far from our practice; we tend to be post-Tennysonian about the whole subject, and to think of 'The moan of doves in immemorial elms' as a line little felt and greatly decorated. To the medieval religious writer things may genuinely have seemed far otherwise; Thomas of Hales, in his *Love-Ron* of the mid-thirteenth century, preaches a brilliant and chilly negative sermon about the transience of human beings and their loves, reduces even the comely Absolom and the pious King Henry III to the value of a 'herring', and suddenly turns to something positive and warm and lasting, the love of Christ. For ninety-one lines he has sustained his poem by an exacting stanza-scheme rhyming *abab

abab*, by some lovely nature similes, by other proper adornments such as antithesis and chiasmus, and even by the haunting internal rhyme of

'Vnder molde hi liggeþ colde'

[under the earth they lie cold], without recourse to alliteration; but the new thought excites him (or reminds him that he must excite his reader), and Christ is conveyed to us as one

> of mode mylde,
> Of lufsum lost, of truste treowe,
> Freo of heorte, of wisdom wilde.

[gentle of spirit, of lovely desire, faithful in trust, noble of heart, boundless in wisdom.] Then the thrill passes; the advantages of loving Christ are described theologically and systematically, and no alliterative moment recurs.

The two great schools of poetry thus existed side by side, aloof but respectful; for a third current manner of composition, however, Chaucer had only scorn, and expressed it in the first great English parody. We must examine *Sir Thopas* in some detail, since it exhibits, far more entertainingly than its originals, their strutting attitudes and their absurd hero-worship, their primness and yet their mindless spilling of blood, their bluntness and yet their swooning sentimentality, their careful catalogues and yet their haphazard dropping of tags and dead phrases. This moth-eaten verse, by comparison with which Chaucer is a modern and seems to have felt it, is now styled 'tail-rhyme' because of the short chiming-in lines, the *caudae* or 'tails' in a rhyme-scheme *aabccb* (continuing *ddbeeb*, if you wished or could contrive, or even further, until your stanza ground to an end), the *b* lines having three stresses and the others four. To say that Chaucer guyed this metre is very apt; two of the narratives that he had in mind had as their invincible heroes Guy of Warwick and Bevis of Southampton, and indeed it seems that it was normally English figures, legendary or real, who had received this kind of treatment. Chaucer, casting himself in the character of minstrel to entertain his fellow pilgrims, begins as if cautiously:

> Listeth, lordes, in good entent,
> And I wol telle verrayment
> Of mirthe and of solas,

> Al of a knyght was fair and gent
> In bataille and in tourneyment.
> His name was Sir Thopas.

[Kindly listen, lords, and I will tell you a true story of joy and diversion, all about a knight who was handsome and noble in battle and in joust, and whose name was Sir Thopas.]

This, with its enticing alliteration in the opening phrase, its monotonous pairs in ll. 3, 4, and 5, its child-like 'all about' in l. 4, and the colloquial omission of the relative in the same line, is still pretty innocuous until the very last word; but in an age when lapidary lore was great, and the physical and ethical and spiritual efficacy of precious stones was devoutly consulted, the topaz was a yellow gem worn by girls to protect their chastity: the hero is Sir Cissy, for all his prowess.

It is never too early, in the worst romances, to make wild claims for your protagonist. So in the second stanza we are told that he was born in a distant country: the appetite for exotic fiction is whetted, only to be dulled immediately by 'In Flaundres, al biyonde the see' [in Flanders, right over the sea]—again the child-like 'all', to express the nearest bit of the Continent. In fact, it was in the manor-house at Poperinghe, where his father, a very noble man, was lord of the region by God's grace; by God's grace, indeed—we know, and Chaucer's audience must have known, that this lord was an abbot, so that Thopas had made a very irregular start in the world. Next, his face and his splendid physique; though he has the bread-white skin of a delicate girl, and the conventional alliterating lips 'red as rose', his complexion is suddenly said to be like dyed scarlet and, with a bathos still inexplicably funny, the stanza ends with the claim that 'He had a lovely nose'. Keeping up the suggestion of his name, his symbolic colour is seen as yellow: his mane of hair and beard are like saffron—a cook's and grocer's colour, not a knight's; but, on a less homely note, the lure of foreign parts gives him shoes from Cordova, trunk-hose from Bruges, and a robe paid for in Genoese coins. When he hunted and hawked, he committed the gross solecism of carrying the goshawk appropriate to a mere yeoman; with equal indiscretion, he practised the yeoman's and working-man's pursuit of archery, and lowered himself to wrestle professionally for a prize ram. Yet, with that easy contradiction which tail-rhymers always allowed themselves, he was the perfect knight and the worthy object of maidens' love:

> Ful many a mayde, bright in bour,
> They moorne for him, paramour,
> Whan hem were bet to slepe;

[Very many girls, radiant in their chambers, long passionately for him, when they'ld be better off asleep]

even here, after the fulsome alliteration, there is a joke, and a profoundly caddish one—love was its own reward, and the love of such a knight an ennobling passion, so the pretended minstrel is speaking quite out of turn in blaming these lovelorn maidens for their lonely vigils. With a fine renunciation of their company, and the typical wasted and empty couplet of the tail-rhymer—

> And so bifel upon a day,
> For sothe, as I yow telle may

[And it so happened one day, honestly, as I can assure you]

—, Thopas decided to ride out; he 'got on' his grey steed (no leaping or striding aloft, as Gawain and his green adversary do), and away to go, 'pricking'—spurring, that is—six times in the next forty-five lines but questing quite purposelessly. First, he encountered 'many wild beasts', but only bucks and hares, and in his galloping north and east 'almost had a nasty accident'; the flora was all grocery again—liquorice, cloves, nutmegs (digression on how to use nutmegs), as if some new-rich grocer knight was the subject of the parody; and the fauna was the sweet-singing sparrow-hawk and woodpecker, a lucid moment for the genuine song of the thrush, and the wood-pigeon with her 'loud and clear' voice which strikes us nowadays as a muffled cooing. He was thrown into love-pangs 'all' when he heard the thrush, and spurred as if he was crazy; here Chaucer rises to a joke of visionary daftness—the horse 'sweated so much that you could have wrung him out', and

D

the knight, exhausted by the terrain (which was 'soft grass'), flopped down in a glade and surprisingly gave his horse what sounds like his nose-bag instead of letting him browse. And so he dreamed of a fairy love, the pursuit of whom occupies the rest of the poem; it is a marvellous performance, and the finest piece of literary criticism that English had yet produced—the little *b* lines delicately thrown away on tautology and tags, the vague imagery of the tail-rhymers accurately summed up in the take-your-pick simile of his bridle that 'shone like the sun—or like the moonlight'.

This long digression on a seemingly outworn mode has been necessary, because this 'olde' idiom continued to the end of the century and beyond; but it also shows how much we owe to Chaucer for his exact metrics, his choice of *le mot juste*, and his responsible attitude to his calling.

2 : Wars

Europe

THE conduct of our foreign affairs from 1350 to 1400 was disastrous and disgraceful. Whatever views we may hold on Edward III's divine right to the throne of France, his attempts to enforce it were disfigured by massacres of helpless French citizens, by crippling levies on his own people, and by neglect of an England reeling from the Black Death (not yet called *Black*) and subsequent visitations of plague and famine; it was not even crowned with any lasting success. The Hundred Years War, smouldering at the half-century in a deceptive lull, was aflame again by the mid-1350s, and in 1356 the Black Prince (not yet called *Black*, either) routed the French at Poitiers and took their King prisoner; yet nearly all our French holdings had been lost by 1375. The victory went to a prince in the prime of life, and seemed to repeat his dash and chivalry at Crécy; but Crécy, where archers on foot had beaten armed knights, had numbered the days of feudalism, and the prince's chivalry was withered and tainted by the time he had indiscriminately massacred at Limoges. Of course, the caddish sentiments which I have just expressed did not find their way into the histories and eulogies of the time, but we shall come across a few lines of melancholy realization.

Now there exists for this period a composed English chronicle, no literary masterpiece but often good history, with a point of view (not always to our taste), an ability sometimes to comment, and often a vividness enhanced by quotations in direct speech and a few imaginative phrases; this is the *Brut* or *Chronicles of England*, which starts with Troy and with the thirty-three daughters of a mythical Diocletian and runs on well into the fifteenth century. Its many manuscripts—English, French and Latin—were epitomized (though still running to 607 pages) by F. W. D. Brie, whose

second volume (*The Brut*, Part II, London, 1908) contains nearly
sixty pages to our purpose. It will be well to follow its course
immediately with the war in mind, returning to it later for domestic
matters; and it is no bad guide, since the compiler occasionally
shows a nice sense of what was going on, of the 'movement' and
not just the event. We can then consider in detail what literary use
the better authors made of the affairs around them.

After a frightening picture of the Black Death, which left (says
the chronicler) hardly one-tenth of the people alive *and* every new
birth with two 'cheek-teeth' less in its head, he recounts the seafight against the Spaniards off Winchelsea in 1350, when all our
worthy men of arms fought 'manly and stifly' [manfully and
stoutly], took twenty-four ships, and 'had the better' of a bloody
fight. Four years later Edward III came to an agreement with the
King of France that he should receive back his lands and lordships
of the Duchy of Guienne on condition of his relinquishing his
claim to the French throne, and they sent to Rome for a papal bull;
but 'God ordained better for the honour of the King of England,
because, what with the fraud and deceit of the Frenchmen, and the
delay of the Pope and court of Rome, the aforesaid agreements
were quashed and abandoned'—this is typical of the chronicler,
who always puts peace second to honour. Hearing after Whit-
sunday 1355 that the new King John of France had given Guienne
to his son Charles, Edward was very angry and summoned his
son Edward, the Black Prince, whose Guienne was by right, and
bade him repossess it; father and son went on pilgrimage to get
the help of God and His saints, and proceeded to Plymouth with
the Earls of Warwick, Suffolk, Salisbury, and Oxford, a thousand
men at arms and an equal number of archers, and sailed to Guienne.
Later, Edward took his sons Lionel and John, and sailed to Calais;
they made for King John, but hearing of their coming 'he wente
awey wiþ his men & his cariage, cowardly & schamfully fleynge,
wastyng al vitailez ouer al, þat Englisshe men shold nauȝt haue
therof.' [he went away with his men and his baggage, fleeing in a
cowardly and shameful way, destroying all foodstuffs everywhere,
so that Englishmen should not have any of them.] Meanwhile the
Scots for diversionary tactics seized Berwick, though—'blessed be

God!'—the castle withstood them, and Edward returned, got a grant from Parliament of 50/- on every woolsack for six years to defend the realm, and proceeded north. He recovered Berwick easily, and the titular King of Scotland, John Balliol (names and dates are getting confused at this point), gave up the realm and crown to him at Roxburgh—from the nicest of motives, 'considering how þat God dede meny merueylles þingez & gracious for King Edward at his owene will fro day to day.' [observing how God did many marvellous and gracious things for King Edward, just as he wanted them, from day to day.]

During this Scottish digression, the Black Prince, 'like a man inspired by God', was in Guienne, at Bordeaux, threatening the French but making himself popular with 'all the prelates, peers, and important men' of the province; then he set out, ravaging, besieging towns, and capturing many knights. At length the armies met, and after one tough skirmish when he captured two counts they engaged on 19 September 1356 (the chronicler does not say that it was only two days after) at the field of Poitiers with results that are well known and are here catalogued as to prisoners. Above all, the unfortunate King John was led away with every courtesy to Bordeaux, Plymouth, and Westminster. The chronicler is interested in his ransom, set at three million gold crowns, 'and you must understand that a million is a thousand thousand'; other men say another sum, but 'al is on in effecte'. [it all comes to the same thing.] The royal captive was entertained with jousts at Smithfield and a fine St George feast at Windsor, on which he ungraciously commented for scorn 'that he had never seen or heard of such solemn feasts or pomps held or performed by tallies, without the payment of gold or silver.'

On 27 October 1359 Edward set out for Calais again, swearing not to return until victorious. An amicable sojourn with the Duke of Burgundy (who yet had to pay him 70,000 florins to 'spare his men and his people') was interrupted by news that French privateers had sacked Winchelsea and slaughtered all who resisted them, so he turned towards Paris and gave orders 'to destroy and kill by blow and strength of sword those that he had beforehand spared'. Reaching Paris, he divided his troops into

nine armies, with four hundred newly dubbed knights; threats
were delivered at the gates, and even the promise that if battle
were offered, and Edward beaten, he would never again claim the
throne of France, to all of which 'a short and scornful answer'
was returned, so they 'hugely destroyed' the suburbs. The English
also got together a navy, crushed the marauders, and 'skimmed the
sea', taking the island of Caux and inducing the regent Charles's
advisers to ask for peace; but Edward granted nothing save 'truce
for their sea coasts', and marched towards Orleans, destroying the
countryside as he went. But now a terrible storm assailed his
army, so that thousands of men and horses were killed 'as it were
through vengeance'; the chronicler does not use this as a culmina-
tion of disasters and disappointments, but quickly passes on with
a 'Wherefore' to the 'peaceful and final accord' ratified near
'Carnocum'—that is, at Brétigny near Chartres—in May 1360.
The terms are vaguely stated, and the chronicler is happier to get
on with the solemn mass at Paris and the oath taken there by
Prince Charles, matched by Prince Edward's on the Friday after,
and numerous others later. The King returned to London, visited
King John in the Tower, released him (on payment of a first
instalment of 4,000,000 florins—the chronicler has multiplied by
ten), and had him pleasantly escorted home. The treaty was
ratified by the two kings at Calais, with another solemn mass to
follow, and after a Parliament an even more solemn one at Westminster Abbey, graced by the French king's sons and many nobles.
The next few entries are necessarily more peaceful, though there is
mention of the army of various nations led by Englishmen and
called 'a people without a head', who 'did great harm' in France,
and of the similar 'white company' (that is, Sir John Hawkwood's)
who 'did great sorrow' in Lombardy. The Black Prince assumed
the Lordship of Guienne and did homage to his father for it, and
went overseas to Gascony with his wife and children; another
pleasant gathering was the visit of the three Kings of France,
Cyprus, and Scotland, to England—they were greatly welcomed
and honoured (but the chronicler does not mention that David II
of Scotland had been our prisoner until 1357, or that poor John
of France had resumed his captivity here because his hostage son

had broken parole, the ransom was not yet paid, and honour demanded his return). Murmurs of the renewing storm are heard in the note that John de Montfort (an anglophile) beat Charles of Blois at 'Orray' (Auray) in Brittany in 1364, with English help and the loss of only seven Englishmen; but, as usual, the chronicler seems unaware of the political machinations that lie behind this victory. In the same year King John died in his exile at the Savoy, and Edward gave him a splendid funeral before the body was removed to S.-Denis.

Meanwhile another cause of contention was looming, though the chronicler does not help us to see how it would affect England: a knight called 'Sere Bertram Cleykyn' (this is actually Duguesclin!), a good warrior, got 'a great company assembled together' who had been holding some castles and towns of Edward's, and with these *routiers* helped to depose Pedro the Cruel of Castile and put the bastard Enrique of Trastamara on the throne; but Pedro appealed to the Black Prince in Gascony, and was favourably received, though the Prince had many misgivings. The Pope might be affected, and it was only the continual beseechings of Pedro and his friends that made him feel he must assist; but when King Edward assured him by letter that he must proceed against these evil-doers 'who were such enemies to kings' he at once bound Pedro by an oath to maintain the church and restore all that it had suffered, to expel Saracens and other heretics from his realm, and to live honourably with a Christian wife. So to his great victory at 'Naʒers' (Nájera) in 1367, when with his brother John of Gaunt and 30,000 men he beat the usurper and Duguesclin and more than 100,000; as Enrique's forces fled, a bridge gave way, many were drowned or killed, and the leaders were taken—the English losses were 'but a few' to their enemies' 6,000 and more. The end was lugubrious; Pedro, restored to his throne, was soon strangled by the same faction, and many good Englishmen died in Spain subsequently through the 'fflix' [flux]. Nor does the chronicler tell us the real motive of the Prince and his father, which was probably the possession or the neutrality of the Spanish navy; he perhaps genuinely believes all the high-sounding stuff about king and church and chivalry, but in a few years England would be the object of French and Spanish coastal raids again, and he has already mentioned under 1366 the strange naval attack by the Danes in the North Sea and its successful discomfiture.

But now (without any mention of the odious *fouage*, the hearth-tax that so provoked the Gascons and elicited the new French king's sympathy) we are told that the French broke the peace and invaded 'Pountyf' (Ponthieu), taking castles and towns and alleging that the English were responsible for the infringement of the truce. Parliament was consulted as to how best Edward might be avenged, and about midsummer 1369 John of Gaunt took a big force of knights to France, 'where they got themselves only a little honour and reputation', even refusing to give battle; the Earl of Warwick, too, after scaring the French when he landed, did great damage in Normandy but sickened at Calais and died, leaving no knight so noble or valiant behind him. The King, 'by unwise and indiscreet counsel, borrowed a great sum of gold from the prelates, lords, merchants, and other rich men of the realm, saying that it would be spent in defending Holy Church and the realm; but nevertheless it did it no good', and he in fact mustered a big army with tried commanders and returned to France (he was now 57, old by medieval standards). So long as they kept together, the enemy avoided them, but at the onset of winter contention and covetousness split them into different companies; whereas Sir Robert Knollys made his troop safe in a Breton castle, the others were exposed to the fury of the French, who killed and captured many. The Pope came to Avignon to make peace between the kings, but died before achieving anything, and meanwhile a great tragedy was building up at Limoges; galled by the Black Prince's taxes, its citizens revolted and turned to the King of France, so the Prince, on his way home to England, took and razed the city and ordered a general massacre. Then, in broken health and financial difficulties, he returned finally from the wars, leaving Gaunt in Gascony. The King of Navarre came to treat with Edward at Clarendon about the war in Normandy, but to no purpose; Edward asked successive Parliaments for more and more money, and found them restive, but the Pope's ambassadors for peace made no headway with him. His sons Gaunt and Edmund,

Earl of Cambridge, made hopeful dynastic marriages with two of Pedro's daughters in 1372; but a fight with some Flemings at sea, and the capture of twenty-five of their ships laden with salt, was a grievous mistake and caused much bitterness.

Now the French besieged La Rochelle, and when the impious and lecherous Earl of Pembroke was sent to relieve it his force was trounced by the Spaniards on St Mildred's Day, with the loss of 'a huge treasure'; nor could the King raise the siege, since contrary winds prevented him. Gaunt marched from Calais through France to Bordeaux in 1373, but achieved little; and finally in 1375 a truce for two years was concluded at Bruges (though the chronicler either does not know, or does not see fit to mention, how little of France was now left to us; and Gaunt's interest was divided, since he was anxious to ascend the throne of Castile in right of his wife). The truce came just at the wrong time for the Duke of Brittany and his English allies, who were doing well; and the castle of S.-Sauveur, which had withstood a long siege, was absurdly handed over to the French; the wicked Earl of Pembroke was seized for ransom by Duguesclin on the road between Paris and Calais, while on his way home, and died in France. So, with Edward asking the 1376 Parliament for more money for defence, and them refusing, and the death of the Black Prince, the reign wound to its gloomy end in 1377; the chronicler senses the disaster to the realm of the loss of the Prince, 'Whos name & fortune of kniȝthood, but yf it had bene of anoþer Ectour, al men, both Christen & heþen, while he leuyd & was in good poynt, wondred mych, & dred him wonder sore; whos body is worshipfully beryed at Crycherche of Caunterbury.' [All men, both Christian and heathen, marvelled greatly at his reputation and success in knighthood while he lived and was in good health, more than at anyone unless it had been a second Hector, and they feared him very grievously; and his body is honourably buried at Christ Church, Canterbury.)

Some manuscripts now interpose a chapter on Edward III's character; no fault is found in it on the grounds of goodness, resolution, clemency, gravity, piety, charity, patience, medium stature, cheerful countenance, generosity, and much else; he built interesting buildings, and he was 'wise in expenditure' (!). But it is admitted, and elaborated for a quarter of the chapter, that he was lecherous in his old age and thus hastened his death. We have reached 1377 and the coronation of the eleven-year-old Richard of Bordeaux, son of the 'good' Prince and grandson of the 'good' King; apart from this lost background, no hint is given of the boy's inadequacy, and it is to the credit of the various copyists that they do not show themselves wise after the event by at once depicting the deplorable bathos of his reign—thus the impression of white-hot contemporary record is maintained. Foreign affairs were much less exciting after Edward's death, and the chronicler shifts his main emphasis to the desperate deeds at home, but a thread of warfare darkens the remaining twenty-three years of the century.

In the third year of the new reign, we are told, the French galleys were back, sacking, killing, and burning, in seven of our ports—Winchelsea, Rye, Hastings, Portsmouth, Southampton, 'Stormore', and Gravesend. Despite the minatory interlude of the Peasants' Revolt and the great earthquake, the Bishop of Norwich in 1383 led his impious and abortive 'crusade' against the Flemings; but, in fact, it was on behalf of one of the Popes against his French-backed rival, and the next bit of 'foreign policy' recorded had the same drift—the marriage of Richard to the Emperor Wenceslas's sister Anne of Bohemia instead of to a French-backed Valois princess. The chronicler, by concentrating on her welcome, and London's minstrelsy for her at Blackheath, makes it sound merely romantic; and Bishop Despenser's encounter with his supposititious enemies before Dunkirk is magnified to 'a great battle' in which 'a great multitude' of Flemings were killed, though he admits that the siege of Ypres was a failure and that, as in Spain, many of the English died of 'þe flyx'.

In the Peninsula, Edmund of Langley, Earl of Cambridge and later Duke of York, the King's uncle (who would survive all his brothers and their broils), was helping the King of Portugal with an English force to victory against the King of Spain, 'blessed be God and His gracious gift! Amen.' An exotic visitor to Richard's 1384 Christmas at Eltham was the King of Armenia, dispossessed by the Turks and in exile; he expected help from Richard (which suggests the almost legendary fame of English arms), and had a sympathetic and compassionate hearing, but the Council advised the King that 'if he wanted to give him any money, it would be well done; and as for his people, to travel so far to distant lands would be a great jeopardy.' Thus the King contented himself with presents of gold, silver, riches and jewels, and a commendation to God, and the King of Armenia 'passed again out of England'; the full horror of the inexorable march of the Turks against divided Christendom is lost to the chronicler's view.

The fiasco of Richard's 1385 expedition to Scotland is smoothed over, with the Scots coming down to ask for a truce; but prominence is given to the murder at York of the Earl of Stafford's heir by John Holland, the King's half-brother, and the King's rage and grief at it, to which the chronicler wrongly ascribes his return to London. In Ireland there was a reverse; Edmund Mortimer, Earl of March, lately proclaimed heir apparent (yet how could this be, since no one could know that Richard would die childless?), went over to his lordship in Ireland and settled at one of his castles, 'and þere come apon hym a grete multitude yn buschmentis of wilde Iryschmen, hym for to take and distroye, and he come out ffersly of his castell with his peple, and manly ffauȝt with ham; and þere he was take, and hew al to pecis, and þere he deied; on whose soule God haue mercy! Amen.' [and there came upon him a great force of wild Irishmen in ambushes, so as to catch him and destroy him, and he came fiercely out of his castle with his men, and fought manfully against them; and he was caught there, and hewn quite to pieces, and died there; and may God have mercy on his soul! Amen.] This lively piece of reporting exploits the short sentence to good purpose; much of the narrative is slow-moving, and some repetitious stuff is devoted to insignificant incidents, for example the very next item, the capture by Arundel of a French wine-fleet out of La Rochelle, whereby in London you could have bought a tun of wine for twenty shillings, 'and so we had cheap wine throughout the realm at that time, thanked be God Almighty!' Even after the blow to the King's hopes at Radcot Bridge in 1387, and the judicial murder of his friends, the chronicler devotes a whole gay page to jousts at Smithfield in 1388, with foreign nobles invited and all the seemingly innocent pageantry of white hart badges and golden chains, twenty-four ladies leading twenty-four Garter knights, rich gifts and courteous send-offs—as if not realising how such extravagances were leading the King and his advisers to their final ruin. Gaunt's removal to Spain in 1386 (which also lost us a better brain than Richard's) is depicted as a total success, with the King of Spain coming to terms and giving him 'great wedges' of gold and silver and 'eight chariots' full of jewels, ten thousand marks of gold yearly to be delivered at Bayonne, and himself as a husband for Gaunt's daughter; but 'þe flix' took its toll again. The chronicler gives Richard no praise for the slumbering of the war with France and the truce of 1389 onwards, but still calls him a mighty king and emperor when he goes to Calais to receive his second 'wife', the French Isabella, then aged nine, and there is no hint of the attendant unpopularity of this French union. The King is last seen active a few pages later, when he takes an efficient force to Ireland, is well received, and gets the homage and fealty of the 'chieftains and governors and leaders' of the 'wild Irishmen'; 'and thus he conquered the greater part of Ireland in a short time.' From the blithe wording of this, one would never guess that Henry Bolingbroke had landed at Ravenspur—and of course the chronicler, with little sense of anything beyond scattered events, is confusing us hopelessly by telescoping Richard's rather clever and clement handling of Ireland in 1394–5 with his fatal absence there in 1399.

Now it will be clear to any historian from this digest that the *Brut* gives a fair general picture of our foreign affairs, though often with quite the wrong emphasis and—in a way that makes us trust its jottings as contemporary—no inkling of what is to come. This, I take it, was the kind of history that ordinary Englishmen, as spectators of the international scene, had before them, and its perverse interests probably reflect theirs; it can now be our much more interesting task to see how the vernacular poets of the time treated these events, which they referred to their own purposes of patriotism, satire, moralizing, and the rest. Of directly descriptive material there is very little, as if the conflict hardly touched the

LAURENCE MINOT · 61

poets safe at home; but no one blames Jane Austen for not chronicling the Napoleonic Wars.

First in time, and even in relevance, comes Laurence Minot; as (probably) a Yorkshireman, he had reason to dread the incursions of the Scots, and his eleven surviving poems deal with warlike events in which the English took on variously the Scots, French, Bohemians, Spaniards, Flemings, and Genoese. Only his last two poems fall within our scope, and they are not his best, but in them his jingoistic patriotism, his hatred and scorn for all foreigners, and his elaborately rhymed and alliterated verse, with the fifth line of each stanza picking up the fourth, labour solidly on; to him, obviously, the isolated status of England, its new nationalism and the creaks in the strong structure of feudal society, were real and welcome. Look for no strict fairness here, no compassion for the fallen foe; brutality, vengeance, and silence about English reverses, are the rules in Minot. The dialect of these poems is Northern, and the singer's or reciter's art is strongly flavoured with alliterative phrases of long tradition which defy literal translation, and many other idioms which need a gloss; in the first poem, for instance, the 'dale' to which the warriors are 'driven' is the grave, and 'þe waniand' is 'the waning of the moon' and hence an unlucky time. The subject is that which we noticed first in the *Brut*, the victory over the Spaniards off Winchelsea in 1350:

How King Edward & his menȝe
Met with þe Spaniardes in þe see.

I wald noght spare for to speke, wist I to spede,
Of wight men with wapin and worthly in wede,
Þat now er driuen to dale, and ded all þaire dede,
Þat sail in þe see-gronde fissches to fede.
    Fele fissches þai fede, for all þaire grete fare;
    It was in þe waniand þat þai come þare.

Þai sailed furth in þe Swin in a somers tyde,
With trompes and taburns and mekill oþer pride.

Þe word of þo weremen walked full wide;
Þe gudes þat þai robbed in holl gan þai it hide.
  In holl þan þai hided grete welthes, als I wene,
  Of gold and of siluer, of skarlet and grene.

When þai sailed westward, þo wight men in were,
Þaire hurdis, þaire ankers, hanged þai on here.
Wight men of þe west neghed þam nerr,
And gert þam snaper in þe snare; might þai no ferr.
  Ffer might þai noght flit, bot þare most þai fine,
  And þat þai bifore reued þan most þai tyne.

Boy with þi blac berd, I rede þat þou blin,
And son set þe to schriue, with sorow of þi syn.
If þou were on Ingland noght saltou win.
Cum þou more on pat coste, þi bale sall bigin.
  Þare kindels þi care; kene men sall þe kepe,
  And do þe dye on a day and domp in þe depe.

3e broght out of Bretayne 3owre custom with care.
3e met with þe marchandes and made þam ful bare.
It es gude reson and right þat 3e euill misfare,
When 3e wald in Ingland lere of a new lare.
  New lare sall 3e lere, Sir Edward to lout;
  For when 3e stode in 3owre strenkith 3e war all to stout.

[How King Edward and his company met the Spaniards on the sea. If I knew how to do it properly, I would not abstain from speaking of valiant armed men, fine in their armour, who are now hurled to death, and all their deeds perished, sailing on the seafloor to feed the fish. They feed many fish, for all their great show; it was at an unlucky time that they came there. They sailed out into the Zwijn in summer-time, with trumpets and drums and plenty of other proud things. The fame of those warriors spread far and wide; the goods that they had stolen they hid in the hold. They have hidden great riches in the hold, so I believe—gold and silver, and scarlet and green cloth. When those valiant men of war sailed westward they hung their brattices and anchors up on high. Valiant men from the west approached nearer them, and made them stumble into the trap; they couldn't get any further. They couldn't move any further, but there they had to finish, and then they had to lose what they had filched before. Boy with your black beard, I advise you to desist, and at once betake yourself to confession, with sorrow for your sin. If you were in England you wouldn't have any success. If you come to that coast any more, your worries will begin. There's trouble all ready for you there; bold men will detain you, and put you to death and dump you in the deep. You came out of Brittany and diligently exacted your customs. You met merchants and stripped them completely. It is very right and proper that you should come to disaster, when you wanted to learn a new lesson in England. You'll learn a new lesson—bowing to Sir Edward; because when you were upright in your strength you were much too haughty. J. Hall, *The Poems of Laurence Minot*, Oxford, 1914, No. X]

We see here Minot's tendency to leave his ostensible subject and reminisce; the Spaniards had indeed been piratically exacting 'customs', followed by murder, on English merchantmen, and his more than Kiplingesque anger is justified. He likes, too, to mock at the pomp and riches of a doomed enemy; and if Hall is right in identifying the boy with a black beard as the noted Genoese pirate Blackbeard, who had fought against us at Sluys, or as Egidio Boccanegra, who later defeated us off La Rochelle, and not simply as a typical swarthy Spaniard, then Minot's unashamed personal invective is rampant as well.

The last of his poems is of rather less interest and fire. It concerns the English capture of Guisnes in 1352, which does not appear in the *Brut*; the town was won by a ruse during a truce, and Minot admits it as a personal feat on the part of the Calais archer called John of Doncaster, who with thirty companions sneaked over the ditch and the walls, killed the guard, and dispersed the garrison. The style is elliptical and allusive, with heraldry and religion and sardonic jokes; the poet can hardly conceal the fact that he is making a lot out of little: Doncaster was in fact an utterly mercenary adventurer, who traded the town to Edward simply because he was the highest bidder.

How gentill Sir Edward with his grete engines
Wan with his wight men þe castell of Gynes.

War þis winter oway, wele wald I wene
Þat somer suld schew him in schawes ful schene.
Both þe lely and þe lipard suld geder on a grene.
Mari, haue minde of þi man; þou whote wham I mene.
   Lady, think what I mene; I mak þe my mone.
   Þou wreke gude King Edward on wikked Syr John.

Of Gynes ful gladly now will I begin.
We wot wele þat woning was wikked for to win.
Crist, Þat swelt on þe rode for sake of mans syn,
Hald þam in gude hele þat now er þarein!
   Inglis men are þarein, þe kastell to kepe;
   And Iohn of France es so wroth, for wo will he wepe.

Gentill Iohn of Doncaster did a full balde dede
When he come toward Gines to ken þam þaire crede.
He stirt vnto þe castell withowten any stede;
Of folk þat he fand þare haued he no drede.
   Dred in hert had he none of all he fand þare.
   Faine war þai to fle, for all þaire grete fare.

A letherin ledderr and a lang line,
A small bote was þarby, þat put þam fro pine.
Þe folk þat þai fand þare was faine for to fyne;
Sone þaire diner was dight, and þare wald þai dine.
   Þare was þaire purpose to dine and to dwell,
   For treson of þe Franche men, þat fals war and fell.

Say now, Sir Iohn of France, how saltou fare
Þat both Calays and Gynes has kindeld þi care?

If þou be man of mekil might, lepe up on þi mare,
Take þi gate vnto Gines, and grete þam wele þare.
    Þare gretes þi gestes, and wendes with wo.
    King Edward has wonen þe kastell þam fro.

3e men of Saint Omers, trus 3e þis tide,
And puttes out 3owre pauiliownes with 3owre mekill pride.
Sendes efter Sir Iohn of Fraunce to stand by 3owre syde.
A bore es boun 3ow to biker, þat wele dar habyde.
    Wele dar he habide, bataile to bede,
    And of 3owre Sir Iohn of Fraunce haues he no drede.

God saue Sir Edward his right in euer ilka nede,
And he þat will noght so, euil mot he spede;
And len oure Sir Edward his life wele to lede,
Þat he may at his ending haue heuin till his mede. AMEN.

[How the noble Sir Edward, with his great machines and
valiant men, won the castle of Guisnes. If this winter had
passed, I could quite believe that summer would display himself in very bright woods, and that both the Lily and the
Leopard would gather on one field. Mary, remember your
man; you know whom I mean. Lady, think of what I mean;
I make my complaint to you. Avenge good King Edward on
wicked Sir John. Now I shall be very glad to begin on Guisnes.
We well know that the dwelling was hard to win. Christ, Who
died on the cross for the sake of man's sin, keep in good health
those who are now in there! Englishmen are in there, to guard
the castle; and John of France is so angry that he will weep
for anguish. Noble John of Doncaster did a very brave deed
when he came up to Guisnes to teach them their rudiments.
He hurried into the castle without any horse; he wasn't at all
afraid of the people that he found there. He had no fear in
his heart of anyone he found there. They were eager to escape,
for all their great show. A leather ladder, a long rope, and a
little boat were lying handy, and saved them trouble. The

E

people that they found there were eager to give in; their dinner was soon ready, and they wanted to dine there. It was their intention to dine there and stay, because of the treason of the Frenchmen, who were false and cruel. Say, Sir John of France, how are you going to get on, now that Calais and Guisnes have trouble ready for you? If you are a man of great strength, leap on your mare, make your way to Guisnes, and greet them well there. Greet your guests there, and go away miserable. King Edward has won the castle from them. You men of Saint Omer, pack up for the time being, and put out your flags in your great pride. Send for Sir John of France to stand by your side. A boar is on his way to attack you, and he certainly dares to stay. He certainly dares to stay and await battle, and he has no fear of your Sir John of France. God preserve for King Edward his right in every time of need, and whoever doesn't agree, bad luck to him; and may He grant Sir Edward to lead a good life, so that at his passing he may have heaven as his reward. Amen. ibid., No. XI]

Strong meat as this is, the initial couplet is quite misleading, and the digressions sound evasive; further, the pretty line about the Lily and Leopard is obscure, since the 'field' could predict a battle between France and England or a joint coat of arms to be worn by Edward when successful in his claims.

This promise of rich record by partisan poets is not fulfilled; however much events abroad may have moved writers in Latin or French, or composers of perishable oral verse in the vernacular, very little remains to us in English after Minot. Langland, despite his eye for what was deplorable, wrote little of the war, and that in his riddling way; it took Professor J. A. W. Bennett's discovery, that Liar's detention among minstrels and messengers for 'half a year and eleven days' corresponded exactly to the 1359–60 campaign, to make some slight sense of *Piers Plowman* B. Passus II, l. 228. But this campaign, the terrible Black Monday storm of which the chronicler spoke, and the ineffective peace at Brétigny, weighed on Langland's mind, though he adapted the facts to the mouth of the villainess Mede when she addresses Conscience:

'In Normandye was he nouȝte noyed for my sake;
Ac thow thiself sothely shamedest hym ofte,
Crope into a kaban for colde of thi nailes,
Wendest that wyntre wolde haue lasted euere,
And draddest to be ded for a dym cloude,
And hiedest homeward for hunger of thi wombe.
Without pite, piloure, pore men thow robbedest,
And bere here bras at thi bakke to Caleys to selle.
There I lafte with my lorde, his lyf for to saue.
I made his men meri and mornyng lette.
I batered hem on the bakke and bolded here hertis,
And dede hem hoppe for hope to haue me at wille.
Had I ben marschal of his men, by Marie of heuene,
I durst haue leyde my lyf and no lasse wedde
He shulde haue be lorde of that londe a lengthe and a brede,
And also kyng of that kitthe, his kynne for to helpe,
The leste brolle of his blode a barounes pere.
Cowardliche thow, Conscience, conseiledest hym thennes,
To leuen his lordeship for a litel siluer,
That is the richest rewme that reyne ouer houeth.'

['In Normandy he—the King—was never harmed for my
sake; but as for you, you really shamed him often, by creeping
into a hovel because your finger-nails were cold, thinking that
winter would last for ever, fearing to die because of a dark
cloud, and hurrying home because of the hunger in your
stomach. You robbed poor men pitilessly, you thief, and
carried off their brass on your back to sell in Calais. Whereas
I stayed with my lord, to preserve his life. I cheered his men
up and put a stop to their miseries. I patted them on the back
and fortified their hearts, and made them dance for joy at the
thought of having me all to themselves. If I had been the
commander of his men, by Mary of heaven, I'ld wager my life,
and no smaller pledge, he would have been lord of that land
from one end to another, and king of that country, to the great
advantage of his relatives—the smallest brat in his family
would be equal to a baron. You, like a coward, Conscience,

advised him the other way, to give up his lordship for a little silver, though it is the richest realm that the rain falls on.'
B. III. 188 ff.]

Not surprisingly, Langland was incensed by the struggle of Pope with anti-Pope, and condemns the action of a Pope 'who should help all people, and sends men to kill those that he should be saving' (B. XIX. 426–7); this is a plain reference to the Great Schism, the resort to arms, and Urban's 1381 declaration of a crusade against Clement. The corrupt Doctor at Conscience's table is allowed to speak with cold realism when he says that 'all the arguments in the world, and the strength of valiant men, cannot confirm peace between the Pope and his enemies, or make peace between two Christian kings satisfactory to both peoples'— after which, he pushed the table from him (B. XIII. 173–6); when the C-text of *Piers Plowman* came to be written, the 1389 truce with France had begun, and the line about the kings was omitted.

There is a sincere statement of pacifism, too, in Conscience's speech before the King and Mede, neatly interwoven with the law against civilians' carrying weapons:

> Alle þat bereth baslarde, brode swerde or launce,
> Axe other hachet, or eny wepne ellis,
> Shal be demed to the deth but if he do it smythye
> Into sikul or to sithe, to schare or to kulter—
> *Conflabunt gladios suos in vomeres, &c.*

[Anyone who carries a dagger, broad sword, lance, axe, hatchet, or any other weapon, shall be condemned to death unless he has it forged into a sickle, scythe, ploughshare, or coulter—*They shall beat their swords into ploughshares, &c.* B. III. 303 ff.]

The thoughtful Gower, again, has little to say about the war abroad. In his little-known poem in praise of peace, written to Henry IV at the very end of the century and of his career as a poet, and very slight by comparison with his *Confessio Amantis*, he affirms that a king may take up arms to claim his rightful heritage, but soon goes on to paint war very earnestly as the source of all wrongs: the priest slain at mass, the virgin violated, the city ruined, the law nullified, poverty, toppled fortunes, the best endeavours forced to begin all over again; in fact, the only legitimate target for knightly arms is the Saracens, 'who are hateful to Christ'. (G. C. Macaulay, *John Gower's English Works*, Oxford, 1901, II, pp. 481–492) In his main poem, however, he speaks more gently of them; the lover asks whether it is lawful to cross the Great Sea and war against the Saracen and kill him, and gets the answer,

> Sone myn,
> To preche and soffre for the feith,
> That have I herd the Gospell seith;
> But forto slee, that hiere I noght.
> Crist with his ogne deth hath boght
> Alle othre men, and made hem fre,
> In token of parfit charite.

[My son, I have heard that the Gospel speaks of preaching and suffering for the faith; but I have not heard that it speaks of killing. Christ with His own death has bought all other men, and made them free, in token of perfect love. ibid., *Confessio Amantis* III. 2490–2496]

A different and very entertaining way of deprecating this holy warfare is seen in Book IV. 1608 ff., where the confessor speaks of the kind of lover who took up arms in strange lands abroad, and did doughtily in honour of his lady, crossing the Great Sea, fighting on land and on shipboard, raiding in Prussia or Rhodes or Tartary, until heralds cried, 'Valiant, valiant, see where he goes!' —and then he gave them gifts of gold and clothing, and his reputation spread until it reached her ears, and it occurred to her that she should yield to his suit, so self-sacrificing was he for her sake; and the confessor asks the lover if *he* is idle in this respect. He gets a lovely answer: 'Yes, father, and I always was'; the lover goes on to point out, with refreshing candour and enlightenment,

That me were levere hir love winne
Than Kaire and al that is therinne;
And forto slen the hethen alle,
I not what good ther mihte falle,
So mochel blod thogh ther be schad.
This finde I writen, hou Crist bad
That noman other scholde sle.
What scholde I winne over the se
If I mi ladi loste at hom?
Bot passe thei the salte fom
To whom Crist bad thei scholden preche
To al the world and His feith teche;
Bot now thei rucken in here nest
And resten as hem liketh best
In al the swetnesse of delices.
Thus thei defenden ous the vices,
And sitte hemselven al amidde.
To slen and feihten thei ous bidde
Hem whom thei scholde, as the Bok seith,
Converten into Cristes feith.
Bot hierof have I gret mervaile,
Hou thei wol bidde me travaile:
A Sarazin if I sle schal,
I sle the soule forth withal,
And that was nevere Cristes lore.
Bot nou, ho ther! I seie nomore.

[that I had rather win her love than Cairo and everything that's
in it; and as for killing all the heathen, I don't know what
good might come of it, although so much blood were shed.
I find it written that Christ commanded that no man should
kill another. What would I win overseas if I lost my lady at
home? But let those whom Christ commanded to preach to
all the world, and teach His faith, cross over the salt foam;
as it is, they crouch in their nest now, and relax just as pleases
them best in all the sweetness of luxury. Thus they forbid us
the vices and themselves sit right in the middle of them.

They command us to fight and kill those whom, as the Book says, they should be converting to the faith of Christ. But I am very surprised at the way they want to tell me to expend my energy: if I kill a Saracen, I really kill the soul as well, and *that* was never Christ's teaching. But stop there, now! I'm not saying any more.]

Chaucer is equally interesting, though without this humanitarian attitude, on the subject of 'proving' yourself abroad. In *The Book of the Duchess* (ll. 1024 ff.) the knight in black is made to commend his dead love because she did not

> sende men into Walakye,
> To Pruyse and into Tartarye,
> To Alisaundre, ne into Turkye,
> And bidde him faste anoon that he
> Go hoodles to the Drye See,
> And come hoom by the Carrenare,
> And seye, 'Sir, be now right ware
> That I may of yow here seyn
> Worship, or that ye come ageyn!'
> She ne used no suche knakkes smale.

[send men to Wallachia, Prussia, Tartary, Alexandria, or Turkey, and give him strict instructions that he should at once go with his head bare to the Dry Sea, and come home through the Kara-Nor, and say, 'Sir, be very careful now that I may hear honourable reports of you, before you come back!' She didn't go in for little tricks like that.]

The knight represents John of Gaunt mourning his first wife Blanche, and he had already had some military experience of the routine sort against France and even some distinction in Spain; but curious adventures *in partibus infidelium* were left to professional soldiers like the knight in *The Canterbury Tales*, who had returned, battlestained and with no sign of riches save good horses, from a chivalrous lifetime spent not only 'in his lord's war' in Europe, but at campaigns and sieges in Alexandria, Prussia, Lithuania, Russia, Granada, Algeciras, Benmarin in Morocco,

Lyas in Armenia, Attalia in Asia Minor, the Mediterranean, Tlemcen in Algeria, and Turkey. Robinson helps us to see this catalogue as a credible record of campaigning from about 1343 onwards, very probably including service with the brilliant Pierre de Lusignan, King of Cyprus.

But on the French wars, perhaps quietly approving of Richard's pacifist policy, Chaucer is singularly silent; after all, he had served in them—briefly and ingloriously. As a member of the expedition of 1359–60, he was captured near Rheims and ransomed on 1 March 1360, King Edward contributing a generous £16. But the war is never his theme, however much one may choose to find echoes of the servitude and grandeur of military life in the tale told by the knight; a nasty reference to a related campaign, however, is in his *Envoy to Bukton*, where he warns his widower friend that

> Experience shal thee teche, so may happe,
> That thee were lever to be take in Fryse
> Than eft to falle of wedding in the trappe.

[Experience will teach you, perhaps, that you would rather be captured in Frisia than fall again into the trap of marrying.]

The Frisians did not ransom their own men when they were captured in war, and butchered their prisoners; but Chaucer's seems a flippant way to express a contemporary outrage. However, he makes more serious use of the horrors of his age in three of the four modern 'tragedies' inserted into the *Monk's Tale*, those of King Pedro of Spain, Pierre de Lusignan, and Bernabò Visconti. As Robinson points out in his notes, Chaucer could have heard a lot about Pedro at first-hand, since Gaunt had fought at Nájera and married Pedro's daughter, his wife Philippa Chaucer was for a time attached to the new Duchess's household, and other written and oral sources were available. Certainly he gives no hint of Pedro's cruel streak that gave him his nickname; the first eight lines call him 'noble' and 'worthy', and execrate his brother for murdering him with his own hand, and the other eight criticize Duguesclin (not by name, but heraldically, with his black eagle on silver) as the author of the plot, and Oliver Mauny (not by name, but punningly as a 'wicked nest', *mau ni* in Old French, and with a reference to Charlemagne's noble Oliver) as its abettor. Pierre de Lusignan, King of Cyprus, gets only eight lines; he had been at the English court in 1363, and, as we have seen, Chaucer's knight (who may have been real) had probably served with him, but Chaucer simply mentions his winning of Alexandria and his assassination abed in 1369, attributed here to his lieges' jealousy of his prowess. As for Bernabò Visconti, his niece was married to Chaucer's former employer Lionel, Duke of Clarence, and his daughter to Sir John Hawkwood, and Chaucer may have met him in Milan in 1378; the single stanza devoted to him jumps from the epithets 'God of delight and scourge of Lombardy' to his death in prison, ending with the flat and bewildered line

But why, ne how, noot I that thou were slawe.

[But I don't know why or how you were killed.]

Although Chaucer does not see fit to sing the French wars, their realities of both pomp and blood glare through a tale of very different times and climes; the knight in *The Canterbury Tales* uses for circumstantial details in his story a wealth of material that would be familiar to him from his campaigns. As his formal warriors assemble, they are accompanied by a rich disarray of steeds, palfreys, harness, goldsmithry, embroidery, steel, bright shields, head-armour, horse-trappings, gold helmets, hauberks, coat-armour, lords clad on their coursers, knights of retinue, squires, spears being nailed and helmets buckled and shields strapped and thongs laced, foaming steeds gnawing golden bridles, armourers rushing around with files and hammers, yeomen on foot, common people with short sticks, pipes, trumpets, kettle-drums, clarions to 'blow bloody sounds in the battle' (ll. 2495 ff.). This is enthusiastic, but all the same somewhat unfelt; 'and the people perished' says Homer at the beginning of the *Iliad*, and a poet such as Chaucer should have seen beyond—and seen through—this costly tinsel to its awful implications for his own generation. The fight that follows is not ugly enough; it enjoys the noises of its own alliteration, and its rigid end-stopped lines are a measure of its unnaturalness:

> Ther shiveren shaftes upon sheeldes thikke.
> He feleth thurgh the herte-spoon the prikke.
> Up springen speres twenty foot on highte.
> Out goon the swerdes as the silver brighte.
> The helmes they tohewen and toshrede.
> Out brest the blood, with sterne stremes rede.
> With mighty maces the bones they tobreste.
> He thurgh the thikkeste of the throng gan threste.
> Ther stomblen stedes stronge, and doun goth al.
> He rolleth under foot as dooth a bal.

[Shafts shiver there on thick shields. He feels the jab through his ribs. Spears leap up twenty feet high. The swords come out as bright as silver. They hew and tatter the helmets. Out burst the blood in grim red streams. They crushed the bones with mighty maces. He thrust through the densest part of the throng. Strong steeds stumble there, and everything goes down. He rolls underfoot like a ball. ll. 2605 ff.]

A far better use of the clamours of war occurs in the Cleopatra section of *The Legend of Good Women*, where the seafight of Actium is depicted with more skilful and subtle alliteration in a framework of enjambed poetry; the facts here could well be from Froissart, or from authentic accounts of the various naval engagements of the era—with the Spaniards off Winchelsea in 1350, at La Rochelle in 1372, or even as early as Sluys—, but the telling is entirely Chaucer's own:

> And in the see hit happed hem to mete.
> Up goth the trompe, and for to shoute and shete,
> And peynen hem to sette on with the sonne.
> With grisly soun out goth the grete gonne,
> And heterly they hurtlen al at ones,
> And fro the top doun cometh the grete stones.
> In goth the grapenel so ful of crokes
> Among the ropes, and the shering-hokes.

In with the polax presseth he and he;
Behind the mast beginneth he to flee,
And out agayn, and dryveth him overborde.
He stingeth him upon his speres orde.
He rent the sail with hokes lyke a sythe.
He bringeth the cuppe, and biddeth hem be blythe.
He poureth pesen upon the hacches slider.
With pottes ful of lym they goon togider.

[And they chanced to meet upon the sea. The trumpet sounds, and shouting and shooting, and they endeavour to attack with the sun behind them. The big gun goes off with a frightful noise, and they dash together fiercely all at once, and down come the big stones from the fighting-tops. In goes the grapnel all full of hooks, among the ropes, and so do the shearing-hooks. This one and that press in with the pole-axe; one starts to escape behind the mast, then out again, and drives another overboard, or stabs him with the point of his spear. One tears the sail with hooks like a scythe. One brings the cup, and tells them to be of good heart. One pours peas on the slippery hatches. They advance together carrying pots full of quicklime.]

Behind battle-poetry of this sort lies the august presence of such poems as the alliterative *Morte Arthure* in Robert Thornton's MS at Lincoln Cathedral (edited by E. Brock, London, 1871 &c.). Even if Chaucer was not in time to be aware of this great and aristocratic poem, it is one of the highest achievements of a school which he carefully imitated at these two points in his work, and a romance which remains tributary to the current wars. The fatuous list of Arthur's conquests in Europe reads much more like Edward III's aims; it includes Holland and Hainault, Burgundy and Brabant, Guienne, Bayonne and Bordeaux, Touraine and Toulouse, Poitiers and Provence, with Flanders and France almost at the top (ll. 30 ff.). His pious yet gorgeous feasts are like Edward's, and his courtesy to foes whom he hopes soon to butcher is unpleasantly like Edward's jousts and feasts for foreigners; the Roman Emperor's envoys are served with peacocks and plovers on golden platters, great swans on silver chargers, tarts from Turkey, and dainties such as 'hedoyne' and 'gumbaldes' which no lexicographer has yet interpreted (ll. 176 ff.). The offences to his honour, to his ancestry, and to that deadliest sin of pride, involve him in wasteful campaigns only too like Edward's, and his knights and under-kings uphold him in his folly (ll. 249 ff.), promising him astronomical figures of armed men and of course involving the Deity in their common endeavour: ' "Ah! Ah!", says the Welsh king, "honoured be Christ! Now we shall fully avenge the wrath of our ancestors!" ' Personal affronts can now be settled by these most Christian knights; the Welsh king, for instance, wants to vanquish a viscount for a villainy at Viterbo (it is hard to re-tell these strange, tight incidents without alliterating). It is even suggested that the coming war will be a good thing, because they have lived too long in peace and plenty. After all the feasting and pleasantry, the Roman messenger and his party are not given a very sporting farewell: he must get from Carlisle to Sandwich in seven days, using Watling Street and no other road, which will come to sixty miles a day ('the sum is but little!'); he will have to spur his horse, and bed for the night just where he stops, tying his steed by the bridle to a bush and 'lodging under a linden'; but

> 'be thow foundene a fute withowte the flode merkes,
> Aftyr the aughtende day, whene vndroune es rungene,
> Thou salle be heuedede in hye, and with horsse drawene,
> And seyne heyly be hangede, houndes to gnawene!'

['if you are found one foot the wrong side of the high-water mark, after the eighth day when terce is being rung, you shall be immediately beheaded, drawn by horses, and then hanged on high for dogs to gnaw!' ll. 461–4]

But they are safe with Arthur's passport, and Sir Cador courteously conducts them to Catterick and commends them to Christ!

Hereafter the marvels and exaggeration begin, the Emperor's summoning of cowed kings and preposterous giants, witches and warlocks mounted on camels; but a sudden return to Arthur (ll. 625 ff.) in the Octave of St Hilary reminds us again of the French wars—the rendezvous arranged at Barfleur, the fleet assembled at Sandwich, a Parliament at York with all its kingly provision for a viceroy, for the continuity of the chancellery, the finances, and the law, and even—if the worst should happen—for the succession. There is a splendid moment when the chosen Modred kneels and begs to be allowed to join the expedition instead, but the King's fatal decision has been made. At Sandwich they ship on to barges horses and grand helmets, steeds with fine trappings, tents and other canvases, splendid shields, cabins, clothing-bags, noble chests, hackneys and their caparisons, and armed horses; as if he has been sticking deliberately to an authentic quartermaster's list, the poet adds, 'Thus they stow in the stuff of very stern knights' (l. 735). The passage immediately following shows a mastery of the technical terms of fourteenth-century seamanship, and an eagerness to use them in detail and in proper sequence; thus the seamen finally haul in the boats, shut the ports, heave the lead on (apparently) the luff, take soundings, look at the lodestar, and carefully plot their course with the needle and lodestone. All this is of far more interest, even if a mainly antiquarian interest, to us than is Arthur's ensuing nightmare, or than the absurd sequence of the gross and lustful giant who has eaten more than five hundred people and as many freeborn 'fawntekyns' [little children]; yet even inside the dismal story of this monster's ravishing and murder of the Duchess of Brittany the poet stays to paint a landscape where

> they roode by that ryuer that rynnyd so swythe,
> Thare the ryndez ouerrechez with realle bowghez.
> The roo and the raynedere reklesse thare ronnene,
> In ranez and in rosers to ryotte thame seluene.
> The frithez ware floreschte with flourez fulle many,
> Wyth fawcouns and fesantez of ferlyche hewez.
> Alle the feulez thare fleschez that flyez with wengez.

[they rode along that river that ran so swiftly, where the trees spread over with noble boughs. The roe and the reindeer ran recklessly there, to run riot in thickets and rose-bushes. The woods were blooming with very many flowers, with falcons and pheasants of marvellous colours. All the birds that fly with wings were flitting about there. ll. 920 ff.]

This string of thirteen *r*s and ten *f*s is exceeded by ll. 1844–67, where there are four adjacent lines alliterated on *s*, then two on *c*, two on *f*, six on *s*, six on *b*, and four on *c*; comic at times to our ears, such sounds may have a dreadful appropriateness, as when the giant's seasonal supper is of seven male children 'Chopped in a charger of chalk-white silver' (l. 1026).

We should not pursue this myth much further, but it is interesting to see the tension of Arthur's incredible fight with the giant relieved by a cool and gentlemanly joke: he had told two of his friends that he was going on a pilgrimage, and when they attended on him that evening and found him exhausted near his dead victim, Sir Bedivere observed that this was a funny sort of saint to seek and enshrine in silver; it was amazing that the Lord allowed him in heaven, and if all saints were like that he hoped *he* would never be one (ll. 1162–1169). This interlude over, we hear of misdoings by the Emperor of France that sound perilously like the behaviour of Edward III and the Black Prince, though in Arthur's mind it is the trespassing, rather than the 'confounding of the commons', that is so heinous. Huge numbers are involved in the consequent battle, and the British kill fifty thousand, besides taking prisoners whose ransoms could include in one case 'sixty horse-loads of silver by Saturday' and in another 'chariots charged chock-full with gold'; but Arthur holds that it is not fitting for a king to accept a ransom—a curious remark to make against the background of Edward III's treatment of John of France (ll. 1549 ff., 1579 ff.). In further conflicts the ludicrous conventions of the age are displayed as if with commendation: riding boldly into a strategically prepared trap, challenging to single combat, boasting of one's imminent feat, taunting with doubtful ancestry, scorning to retreat even from overwhelming odds 'for dread of any dog's son in yonder dim woods', reminders of their lord's generosity in treasures and gold and greyhounds and big horses, dubbing of knights before the fight is engaged, and the leader kissing the corpse of the first casualty and swearing vengeance. In the event, it is frankly admitted that the new knights were not much good, and had to be rescued; how much of this fair-play warfare is based on facts is doubtful, and the tide of it can in one line not just change but ebb completely—'Fifty thousand folk were felled at once', in view of which carnage, and of all the mighty prisoners taken, it seems to us ungracious of King Arthur to upbraid the general, Sir Cador, for losing fourteen knights (ll. 1922 ff.)! The fights grow sillier, the dignity of the individual lines not amounting to a convincing picture; only a grim humour relieves the carnage—Arthur cuts the giant Golapas in two at the knees, adding, 'Come down and talk to your mates! You're too tall by half' (ll. 2126–7), the wicked captives are shaved (with warm water) by a team of barbers in tents (ll. 2330 ff.), and the bodies loaded on camels and on an elephant for transit to Rome have to be reported as Arthur's arrears of tribute (ll. 2342 ff.)!

Arthur's ambitions grow boundless: relaxing in Luxembourg, he plans annexation of Lorraine, administration of Lombardy, and trouble for Turkey; but he will always protect papal lands and 'spare the spiritual' (ll. 2396 ff.)—let us not go too far and see all this as a caricature of Edward, who would surely not have made fun of his knights as Arthur does with Sir Ferrere presently, saying that he would be afraid if a fly landed on him. The poet can now (ll. 2464 ff.) display his technical knowledge of siege warfare; they invest Metz, spy out the suburbs, skirmish a little and have a brush with the sentinels, break down some barriers, destroy a barbican, and win the drawbridge, but at the great gates the garrison is able to withstand them, so they pitch camp and prepare their artillery for a regular siege. Gawain wanders off from the camp (in a way that sounds blameworthy) to find adventure, and finds it for a hundred lines of gentlemanly single combat with a bloodthirsty battle to follow. Metz falls to an assault of commonplace ghastliness; movable towers, primitive wooden 'tanks', men scaling the walls, pellets hurled by torsion, minsters and *maisons-dieu* smashed to the ground, churches and chapels pulverized, stone steeples lying in the streets, chambers and chimneys and big houses and plaster walls all in ruins. Despite the exultation of all this, 'the torment of the people was pitiful to hear', and the ladies, led by the Duchess, kneel to Arthur for mercy, which is granted and, when the city has been entered, chivalrously upheld. Next, with the same tedious and highly-wrought brilliance, the poet takes his hero over the Alps to the conquest of Lombardy, Tuscany, and eventually Rome itself, but an enormous dream and its unfavourable interpretation announce the decay of his fortunes, and soon Sir Cradok, journeying from Britain in the guise of a pilgrim, tells him of Modred's treachery and the pagans that have overrun his country. He hastens back to Britain and wins a complicated but closely itemized sea-battle, and then turns to Modred's forces on land; but Gawain, after initial successes, rashly takes a little band into the midst of sixty thousand men, and is soon offering no other apology or promise save that they will shortly be supping with Our Saviour along with prophets, patriarchs, and apostles. What he achieves before being cut down is conveyed in exciting and nimble words of intrinsically monotonous content yet a joy to watch in manipulation; even Modred mourns for him, and repents his own cursed destiny. So to Arthur's revenge, the pursuit of Modred, the last battle, the exchange of fatal blows, and the Passing; a poet can hardly go wrong with this scene, and it is perhaps not fanciful to see the old, tired, disappointed Edward here, handing on his crown to the boy Constantine even as to the boy Richard, assuring the succession, sedulous in dying with the right words on his lips, buried with all the pomp and holiness of the ages, the strange cult within it summed up in the colophon *Hic jacet Arthurus, rex quondam rexque futurus.*

Now Chaucer wrote a whole poem on a war: *Troilus and Criseyde* depicts (to see it perversely) the old alliance of Mars and Venus, the sharpening and extra meaning of young love when the cleaving hand of a war is always imminent; we hear, with no more than interest, of the young man's prowess and knighthood and, with perhaps a little misgiving, of the lady's awkward possession of a traitor father; but the delicate process of Troilus's winning her so occupies our minds that we feel that herein lies all the splendour and the sadness, that the war is in every way something outside the walls. It is a long time asserting itself; but suddenly Criseyde is to be exchanged for a useful warrior who has fallen into Greek hands, and this is harsh—yet still not a threat of wounds or widowing or unfathering, sack or massacre. When her escort to the Greek camp gets his plain mind to work on her weakness, he uses the war, the threat to Troy, in fact the sure fate of the city, and hers is an added weakness now, 'with few women, among the strong Greeks' (V. 688); yet Troilus sounds still like the young man-about-town, telling his solicitous mother, brothers and sisters that the only thing wrong with him is to do with his heart, and no urgency in his military duties seems to possess him. His sister Cassandra has something cogent to say, though of course she was doomed to suffer everyone's unbelief, and it is not until Book V. 1546 that the war sounds importunate, when Fortune

> Gan pulle awey the fetheres brighte of Troye
> Fro day to day, til they ben bare of joye.

[started to pull away the bright feathers of Troy, day after day, until they are stripped of joy.]

Hector is killed in the next stanza; any medieval reader could see forward to the catastrophe in this, since Hector was the perfect hero, and of course our kinsman—for were not the British descended from Brutus the Trojan? We were always on the side of the Trojans; to use an idiom from a very different work, they may have been wrong but romantic, but the Greeks were right but repulsive. Troilus's fiddling with his dying love-affair is pathetic after this, and his death comes casually in one line.

Margaret Adlum Gist, in her *Love and War in the Middle English Romances* (Philadelphia, 1947), has some very interesting conclusions, based on her reading of about a hundred romances, on the medieval justification of war and on actual conduct on the battlefield; her final opinion (p. 190) is justly scornful—that the lawlessness and beastly cruelty in this class of fiction is no exaggeration, and that the idealism, depicted only as 'quixotic and superficial gallantry', is 'a matter of showmanship and

F

histrionics'. It will be more inspiring to end with the inscription
that John de Cobham affixed to the eastern tower of the court-
yard gatehouse at his castle of Cooling in Kent, when he obtained
leave to crenellate it in 1381; it was to resist the inroads of the
French, and the inscription was graced with a remarkable piece
of craftsmanship in copper, the lettering in black enamel on white,
the imitation seal and cords duly coloured:

> Knouwyth that beeth and schal be
> That I am mad in help of the cuntre.
> In knowyng of whyche thyng,
> Thys is chartre and wytnessyng.

[Know, all who are and shall be, that I have been made to help
the country. In acknowledgement of which fact, this is charter
and witness.]

Scotland

We may now briefly consider Scotland. It must first be emphasized that the hugely predominant language there was English,
in its Northern dialect form, and the fertile Lowlands and the
populous towns were the abode of English-speaking descendants
of Angles; there was no intrinsic barrier of race or speech, as
there was in the case of Wales, and a Scots courtier could call a
Gaelic highlander or islander 'Irish' as if more alien than an
Englishman. The puny numbers of Gaelic-speaking people had
almost no traceable influence on the language and literature of
the rest of Scotland, and even the far north used a version of
Norse, and not Gaelic. But Edward I, Hammer of the Scots, had
driven a wedge between the two kingdoms and had forced the
Scots into a position rather novel in Europe—nationhood. His
unpardonable interference in Scots affairs, and his bad deeds of
pillage and death on the fair soil of Scotland, had roused Wallace
and Bruce to truceless enmity and to final triumph; but the first
flush of all this was forgotten by 1346, when King David II became
England's prisoner at Neville's Cross. Thereafter the Auld Alliance
with France, so dangerous and profitless to Scotland despite the

chivalric tinsel of it, was resumed, and with it the pattern of Border cruelty exemplified in those two eminent ballads *The Battle of Otterbourne* and *Chevy Chase*, where a talented Scot and a more pedestrian Englishman see a wasteful slaughter of 1388 from their respective points of view. (The two poems are conveniently together in W. Beattie, *Border Ballads*, Harmondsworth, 1952, pp. 34–49.) Douglas and Percy, brave, sporting, noble, doomed, are given that plausible background of heightened realism by which the ballad beguiles us: after Douglas's burnings in the Tyne valley and near Bamburgh, along with 'three good towers on Roxburgh fells', and his colloquy with Percy at the walls of Newcastle, the same technique of little bright vignettes, isolated figures as sharply seen as in an illuminated manuscript, takes us on to his stay at Otterbourne. Here we are given the fussy circumstantial detail, no doubt meant to convince us and to heighten the suspense, that those with servants sent their horses out to grass, and those without attended to themselves; Douglas's 'little page' is called a 'liar loud' for warning his master of Percy's arrival, with no apology save for the admission that Douglas had had a dream that seems to confirm it:

> 'I saw a dead man win a fight,
> And I think that man was I.'

His resignation in death, and his modest burial at the bracken-clump, are hardly matched by the Gordons, who soaked their hose and shoes in English blood; but his nephew Montgomery behaves with punctilious courtesy to the beaten Percy, and the Scots account is given a noble ending. *Chevy Chase* is grosser, though it reasonably concedes that the catastrophe arose from a hunt recklessly undertaken:

> 'The child may rue that is unborne
> The hunting of that day.'

Whereafter all is blood and rushing, not even interrupted at the ringing of the evening bell; the principal victims are catalogued, and the survivors numbered—55 out of 2,000 Scots, 53 out of

1,500 English. Only the squire Witherington stands out, and that comically to our ears:

> 'For Witherington needs must I wayle
>   As one in dolefull dumpes,
> For when his leggs were smitten of,
>   He fought upon his stumpes.'

The real beginnings of Scots literature are found in this period, in the person of Archdeacon John Barbour of Aberdeen, an older contemporary of Chaucer and with a fairly well documented life as churchman and statesman; he died on 13 March 1395, and his worn pink sandstone effigy and inscription are still in St Machar's Cathedral at Aberdeen. The purpose of his surviving poem (John Barbour, *The Bruce*, ed. W. W. Skeat, Edinburgh and London, 1893–5) was to chronicle the deeds of King Robert Bruce, and incidentally to praise the current Stewart dynasty; his hero had been dead less than fifty years, and there are eye-witness stories. In fact, when incidents become repetitious and exaggerated, it may be that the sober and well-read Barbour was being led astray by old patriots of addled memory. His narrative does not qualify— by eighteen years—for real inclusion in this period, but his attitude to the English of the 1320s is that of his contemporaries, one of dislike and scorn; even their seeming achievements are depicted with a sting in the tail—thus their glittering hosts before Bannock-burn, with 'pensalis to the vynd vaffand' [pennons waving in the wind], looked as bright as angels (Book XI. 193, Book XII. 426), but the Scots were plain, hardy, and efficient. *Brus* is not great poetry, but it is conscientious history, and it throbs with pardonable patriotism and indignation; its 13,549 lines are in the tiresome short couplet that Chaucer early rejected, the rough '8-and-8' that is still the favourite medium for verse pantomimes. Yet its consistent point of view, its grim and realistic humour, its delight in spring and good women as an intermission from carnage, lift it above mere verse chronicles and isolate it from English work in the same field. Barbour in Book I, just before the highly poetic notion of comparing Bruce's Scots with the Maccabees, refers to his incipient poem as a 'romanys' [romance], and this spirit of a literature newly emancipated has gained for one passage (Book I. 225–36) the doubtful honour of frequent anthologizing out of context:

> A! fredome is a noble thing!
> Fredome mayss man to haiff liking.
> Fredome all solace to man giffis.
> He levys at ess that frely levys.
> A noble hart may haiff nane ess,
> Na ellys nocht that may him pless,
> Gyff fredome failȝhe; for fre liking
> Is ȝharnyt our all othir thing.
> Na he that ay hass levyt fre
> May nocht knaw weill the propyrte,
> The angyr, na the wrechyt dome,
> That is cowplyt to foule thyrldome.

[Ah, freedom is a noble thing! Freedom causes man to have pleasure. Freedom gives man every happiness. He who lives freely lives in comfort. A noble heart can have no comfort, and nothing else to please him, if freedom is lacking; because free determination is sought beyond all other things. Nor may he who has always lived free really know the peculiar state, the anguish, or the wretched fate, that is associated with vile thraldom.]

And the context is odd indeed, since Barbour goes on to compare thraldom with wedlock, as an illustration of how harsh and binding it is; he says he is quoting others, but the remark is a typical cleric's aside against women.

Apart from Barbour, the Scots poets in our half-century were merely feeling their feet; thereafter, when a new start is made with King James I and his poetic successors, there is a noble subjection to Chaucer, despite the cleaving hand of the Edwards, and the Scots dialect is able to exploit a linguistic feature that the observant may have seen and heard in the last quotation—unlike the English of England, Scots was now fully-formed and had shed most of its inflexional system. The operative final -e, so often a source of ignorant puzzlement to readers of Chaucer and of pardonable despair to readers of his English imitators, had been shed; and through this and other factors, including native genius, Scots doggerel is far rarer than English in the fifteenth century.

Wales

In Wales, on the other hand, with its totally different language, the bitter centuries of dispossession and subjection had begun again. Edward I had proved equally a hammer of the Cymry, and the fat-towered castles were both the latest thing in military architecture and the symbol of anglicization. With the slaying of Llywelyn ap Gruffudd, the last reigning Prince of Wales, in 1282, changes set in which were bound to be reflected in literature, especially in a poetry as disciplined and conservative as Welsh had always been. The increased urbanization touched Welshmen rather little; when the greatest poet of them all, Dafydd ap Gwilym, joined the crowd in Bangor Cathedral to see the amazing new organ imported from England, his attention was very quickly and properly distracted from it by sight of a beautiful golden-haired girl. Yet there was no lack of sophistication; with an imaginative leap unknown in the formal or fumbling love-lyrics of England, poets such as Dafydd took the friars' devotion to the Virgin and daringly bestowed it on Morfudd and on others of equal beauty but different colouring, with the corollary that it was a sin to be a nun in springtime. The glade was a church, but its liturgy was not the native wood-note wild of an outlaw—rather, it was in a poetic form as stringent and exacting as any Classical metre, with tightly-packed obligations of alliteration, assonance, and rhyme; and this at a time when most English love-lyrics were either polished by their derivation from French or 'charming' in their innocence and their repetitive simplicity.

The decline of the Welsh princes and nobles had likewise baneful repercussions on the stately and centuried poetry which they patronized; the *pencerdd*, the chief poet, was of course displaced from his proud position as chronicler, prophet, counsellor, and celebrant of his lord in songs of the strictest traditional metres, whereas the household bard, whose object was rather to entertain, and who could use new and freer measures, was more able to adapt his art to a new society where the magnates had less political freedom but more stability in a pacified country. Dafydd belonged to neither class strictly; his family in South Wales was both noble and conformist, using English rule while perhaps secretly despising it, and he fulfilled a role not paralleled in medieval England—that of the pure poet avoiding the economic and political implications of his time, and wandering as a bard with every arrogant right to be heard and feasted and revered, to use the old or the freer metres, or to adapt them. So again the situation is paradoxical: the crushed country has on its roads and in its halls an aristocrat whose self-expression blows where it lists, yet with classical discipline, while the big neighbour allows its Chaucer only the leisured intervals between the jading occupations of a civil servant.

In another respect, too, the conquest had seemed to benefit poetry, or at least to give it a fresh start; civil wars, the silliest and most vengeful of all organized killings, had officially ceased, and the celebration of doom and victory was no longer required of the poet. Dafydd and others could turn from official adulation to frank liking, expressing it in daring similes and highly personal observation; even the despised culture of the common enemy, his mercantile skill that still imposes 'London House' or 'Manchester House' on many a mid-Wales haberdasher's facia, is pressed into poetic service, as when Morfudd has an eyebrow of 'du Llundain' [London black] and the fluffy thorn-stems look like linen-drapers' shops in 'Sieb Lundain' [London Cheapside]. But of a shared culture there is no sign, and a Welsh extremist might be forgiven for seeing Dafydd and his fellows as the product of elevated Welsh bardic training, of Norman intermarriage, of the continental *clerici vagantes*, of the love-songs of Provence, and even of the pilgrimage to Santiago (whither we know that his friend Gruffudd Grug resorted).

Just as Dafydd's love-poetry is frank and impudent, without a trace of coyness or of regret for adulterous passion, so his delineation of Nature is sharp and new and delighted; these subjects were the essentials of his poetry, and those who find him unserious for his lack of political and social comment misjudge him totally. Another poet of the half-century, Iolo Goch, had more respect for the officialdom of the changing society, though it was partly his consciousness of the poet's deserts that made him praise the table (and the music and seating-arrangements) of the good Bishop Ieuan of St Asaph; he has similar praise for Owain Glyndwr's hospitality at Sycharth—but Glyndwr's revolt would end the century in 1400, giving the lie to that picture of peaceful resignation which I have been building up. Regrettably, Iolo Goch stooped to praise deeds of blood in the French wars, and to flatter Edward III for his brutal siege of Berwick; but in a nobler mood he wrote with lavish craftsmanship a long tribute to the ploughman, a subject unthinkable in contemporary England unless it were pressed into allegorical service.

This digression on Welsh literature, necessarily brief and without illustration, will—if nothing else—serve to exhibit the new isolation of England and the freedom that literature can enjoy from seemingly intolerable pressures; though in both the cultures a genius, Chaucer no more than Dafydd ap Gwilym, was the central figure.

3 : Domestic Affairs

FORTUNATELY, the *Brut* is not just an excited record of wars and foreign adventures; it is much fuller and sounder on domestic affairs, and though even here it must be amplified for us by more thoughtful and privileged historians in other tongues, such as Walsingham and Froissart, it has many interesting and persuasive details in which it can exploit its use of the vernacular.

Its half-century begins with Edward's new coinage in his 26th regnal year; a penny, a fourpenny groat, and a twopenny half-groat, but—in a manner still familiar—of less value than the old sterling by 5/- in the pound. Next year there was a great dearth of victuals, so that it was called the dear summer, and in 1351, in which the only 'good' news was the raising of Henry, Earl of Lancaster, to be Duke, there was drought—'no rain' at all—from March to July, so that nearly all the crops came to nothing, men and beasts were diseased, food ran short, and this normally plentiful island had to send abroad for supplies. Two years later, Edward 'by his wise and discreet counsel' transferred the staple of wool from Flanders to England, it and all its 'liberties, franchises and free customs' being settled in Westminster, Canterbury, Chichester, Bristol, Lincoln, and Hull. (There were in fact fifteen staple towns, including some in Wales and Ireland.)

The Lancaster house were much in the chronicler's mind, and the next domestic items, against a background of war, begin with the marriage in 1359 of John of Gaunt, the King's third surviving son, to his cousin Blanche, daughter of the recently-created Duke (a marriage that soon gave him his title and inspired Chaucer to write a memorial poem on her); the Mayor and aldermen of London held three-day jousts, and the King 'privily, with his four sons Edward, Lionel, John and Edmund, and nineteen other great lords, held the field honourably'. In the same year, eyewitnesses declared that blood came out of the tomb of the executed Thomas, Earl of Lancaster, 'as fresh as the day he was done to death', but the chronicler does not try to call him a martyr and saint, as one faction did. The happening reminds him that the King at this time piously chose his tomb—at Westminster, near the shrine of the Confessor.

By all accounts, there was an abundance of natural phenomena of the more awful sort, and it was easy for a chronicler to treat them as portents in times so disturbed; ours seems to avoid this, though the juxtaposition of strange visitations with fearful inhumanities and sufferings can be suggestive. After King John of France's release from captivity, we are told that men, animals, trees and houses were destroyed by sudden tempest and violent lightning, '& the deuel appered bodyly in mannis liknes to myche peple as they went in diuerses pleces in the cuntre, & spake to hem.' [and the devil appeared in bodily form, in the likeness of a man, to many people as they went about in different parts of the country, and spoke to them.] After the Westminster Parliament when the terms of the Treaty of Brétigny were published, and the solemn mass in the Abbey, there was an eclipse of the sun at midday in Ascensiontide, followed by another drought that caused a barrenness of grain, fruit and hay, and in late May 'a sanguine rain, almost like blood', in Burgundy and 'a sanguine cross, from dawn to prime', at Boulogne, which was seen by many and afterwards moved and fell into the sea. Worse was to follow: in both England and France, dwellers in flat and treeless country said that two castles suddenly appeared, out of which came two hosts of armed men, one in white and one in black, which engaged, and the white overcame the black, but the black then took heart and beat the white, after which they returned to their castles and the whole apparition vanished. And then there was a pestilence which especially carried off men, so that their wives took husbands from among strangers and 'ignorant and simple men' and, 'forgetting their own honour and birth', married people of low degree and little reputation. This is immediately followed in the chronicle by the death of Henry, Duke of Lancaster, and (rather tactlessly) by the wedding of Prince Edward, the heir apparent, to Joan of Kent after her tangled matrimonial adventures; there is no hint of her here as 'the Fair Maid of Kent'. Then comes the elevation of John of Gaunt to the Duchy of Lancaster in 1362, of his elder brother Lionel to the Duchy of Clarence (also in right of his wife), and of young Edmund to the Earldom of Cambridge, and the departure of Prince Edward for Guienne; but meanwhile the terrible storm of 15 January 1362 had occurred, on 'St Maurice's Day, about evensong-time', when up started so fierce a south wind that 'he broke and blew down to the ground high houses and strong buildings, towers, churches, and steeples, and other strong things; and all other strong structures that stood still were so shaken with it that they are still, and always will be, the feebler and weaker while they stand; and this wind lasted without stopping for seven continual days.' This was followed by 'such waters, in hay time and in harvest time, that all work in the fields was greatly hindered and left undone.' But the year had one hopeful spot: 'hit was ordeyned in þe Parlement þat men of lawe, bothe of þe temporall & of Holy Chirche lawe, fro þat tyme forth shold plede in her moder tunge.' [it was ordained in Parliament that men of law, both civil law and that of Holy Church, should from that time onwards plead in their mother tongue.] Next year the elements grew cruel again: a hard frost lasted from late November to mid-March, so that tilling and sowing were prevented by the hardness of the earth.

The fortieth and forty-first regnal years of Edward III are given as a strange jumble of incidents. Edward the Black Prince's son Edward was born (but died aged seven); Richard of Bordeaux, his second son, was born; the payment to Rome of Peter's Pence was stopped; and Nature staged some dreadful spectacles. So much rain fell in hay time that it rotted and destroyed the corn and hay; there were sparrow-fights all over the country, and countless multitudes of them were found dead in the fields; a plague of a type never before known killed men who had retired to bed in good shape; and smallpox raged. The birds continued to give dark and ambiguous warnings; on the sand of the Scottish sea, many men saw for three consecutive days two eagles, one from the north and one from the south, which cruelly and strongly fought and 'wrestled' together until the southern one had the victory and tore the other with his bill and claws, and then flew back to his own region. Just afterwards, it was seen before sunrise, and also on 30 October, 'þat meny sterres gaderid togedir on an hepe fel doun into þe erþe, levyng behind hem fery bemes in manere of lightnyng, whos flaumes & hete brent & consumed mennys cloþes & mennys here, walkyng on þe erþe, as hit was seen & knowen of meny a man. And 3et thilk northren wynd, that is euere redy & destinat to all evell, fro Seynt Katerins even til iij dayes aftir lost good wiþoute nombre vnrecouerable. And in þese same dayes þer fill & comen also such lightnynges, þundres, snowe & hayl, þat hit wastede and destroyed men, bestes, houses and trees.' [that many stars gathered together in a group fell down to the earth, leaving behind them fiery beams like lightning, whose flames and heat burned and consumed the clothes and hair of men walking on the earth, as was seen and acknowledged by many men. And also that same north wind, which is always prompt and bound for every evil, from the eve of St Katherine until three days after wasted goods without number irrecoverably. And during the same period there happened and came also such lightning, thunder, snow and hail as to lay waste and destroy men, animals, houses and trees.]

A great comet in March 1367 (he calls it 'Stella Comata') between the north and west coasts was followed by the marriage of the Duke of Clarence in Milan and his untimely death, and by the death in 1369 of Blanche, Duchess of Lancaster, the occasion of Chaucer's *Book of the Duchess*. Worse news comes in the latter year: a great pestilence of men and animals, the corn destroyed by wet and a bushel of wheat costing forty pence, and the death of good Queen Philippa. The King, after giving her a noble funeral at Westminster Abbey, 'with great expense and honours', held a Parliament and asked the clergy for a three-year 'dime'; but they put it off until the following Easter; by 1371 he was asking them in Parliament for another subsidy, which they granted after a general convocation. At the same Parliament, lords hostile to the men of Holy Church obtained the removal of the Chancellor, Treasurer, and Clerk of the Privy Seal, who were bishops, and their replacement by laymen—one of the chronicler's villains, the Earl of Pembroke, was among the ringleaders; in this atmosphere, it is not surprising that a papal embassy to the King achieved nothing. His June Parliament at Westminster in 1372 lasted only eight days, and churchmen summoned to it by writ numbered only four bishops and four abbots; it considered rumours of treason on the part of merchants of London, Norwich, and various other places.

But now a long altercation occurred with the Pope, whereby 'the King sent him certain ambassadors, asking them that he should leave off meddling in his court with the holding and reservation of benefices in England, and for those who were chosen for bishops' sees and dignities to be confirmed in the free and rightful enjoyment of them'; other points concerned the archbishops and metropolitans, and the interests of the King and the realm. The Pope replied cautiously; and after the vacancy and filling of the sees of York, Ely, and Worcester, it was agreed that the King should not in future 'write against' those who were chosen at cathedral elections, 'but rather help them to their confirmation by his letters; and this statute was kept, and produced great profit and good. And in this Parliament the King was granted a dime of the clergy, and a fifteenth of the lay fee.' In June 1374 William Whittlesey, Archbishop of Canterbury, died, and the Christ Church monks wanted a cardinal to succeed him; the King was so angry that he intended to exile them, and they had to buy back his favour, but neither he nor the Pope nor the cardinals would consent to their request. In August deliberations began at Bruges, and lasted for almost two years; it was at last agreed that the Pope should not deal with the reservation of benefices in England, and that the King should not grant benefices by his writ called *Quare impedit*, but nothing was decided about the aforementioned elections, '& þat was ywyted & put oppon certeyn clerkes, the whiche raþer supposed & hoped to be auaunced & promoted to bysshopriches which þey desired & coueyted by þe court of Rome þan by eny eleccions.' [and that was blamed on and attributed to certain clerics, who expected and hoped to be advanced and promoted to bishoprics that they desired and coveted rather by the court of Rome than by any elections.] The doomed Simon Sudbury was translated from London to Canterbury, the Bishop of Hereford to London, and the Bishop of Bangor to Hereford; the chronicler seems to love these details. The heat that summer was so great that it brought a pestilence in its train, and many died in England and abroad; the Pope, at the instance of an English cardinal, sent two bulls granting the repentant and shriven dead six months' remission. A curious detail of information at this point is the death, and honourable burial at Tewkesbury Abbey, of Edward, Baron Despenser, 'a worthy and bold knight'; his monument still stands, and is altogether deserving of the chronicler's digression, since his wife commemorated him in the exquisite fan-vaulted Trinity Chapel, with his armoured figure kneeling above in a little tabernacle, his face turned in prayer towards the high altar.

The long reign slumped to its close. In the 1376 Parliament (the chronicler does not call it 'Good', but at least says that it was the biggest seen for a long time) the King again asked for a massive subsidy for the defence of the realm, but the commons answered harshly that 'þey were so oft, day be day, ygreued & charged wiþ so meny talyagez & subsidies, þat þey myȝte no longer suffre non such berþes ne charges; and þat þey knewyn & wisten wel þat þe King had ynov for sauyng of hem & of his reaume, yf þe reaume wher wel and trewly gouerned, but þat it had be so long euel ygouerned by euel officers þat the reaume myȝt neither be plenteuous of chaffare and merchaundise ne also wiþ richesse; & þese þinges þey profered hemself, if þe King wold, certeynly to preue & stonde by. And if it were found & proued after þat þe King þan had nede, þey wold þen gladly, euery man after his power and state, hem wold helpe & lene.' [they were so often, day after day, harassed and oppressed by so many taxes and subsidies, that they could no longer suffer any such loads or charges; and that they knew and fully realized that the King had plenty for the protection of them and of his realm, if the realm was properly and truly governed, but that it had been so long badly governed by wicked officials that the realm could abound neither in trade and merchandise nor in riches; these facts they offered themselves to prove for certain, and stand by, if the King was willing. And if it was subsequently found and proved that the King was then in need, they would then, every man of them according to his power and rank, help him and lend to him.] The particular authors of this corruption were soon revealed; Lord Latimer, who was the King's Chamberlain, and Alice Perrers, who was the King's mistress 'for a long time'. The chronicler, now showing his very reasonable point of view, blames these two above all others for misleading the King; the 'wise, . . . true, and . . . eloquent' knight Piers de la Mare, the speaker, was their outspoken enemy, trusting in the support of the Black Prince, but with the death of the Prince Dame Alice managed to get him condemned to life imprisonment in Nottingham Castle, and he spent two years there.

The kind of anarchy that was always near the surface is shown in the horrific account of how the tenants of the Earl of Warwick attacked the Abbey of Evesham and its tenants, 'wounded and beat their men, slew many of them, went to their manors and manor-houses and did great damage, broke down their game-parks and enclosures, burned and slew their wild animals and chased them, broke the dams of their fishponds, let the water from their ponds, stews and rivers run out, took the fish away with them, and did them all the harm they could; to such an extent that that abbey, with all its members and appurtenances, would have been permanently destroyed, if the King had not the sooner helped it and had regard for it'—this last clause has muddled syntax behind which it is just possible that there is criticism of the King for tardiness. The Earl was ordered to desist and reimburse, and various lords and other friends on both sides restored peace; but the chronicler makes something more of this local flare-up— 'it was said' that because of it the King would not be governed by the lords in his Parliament, but made his son John of Gaunt the governor of the realm. But he got the money he wanted out of Parliament: the lay fee of fourpence out of every man and woman over fourteen, known beggars excepted, twelvepence out of every beneficed or promoted churchman, and fourpence out of all those not promoted, the four orders of mendicant friars excepted. The fatherless Prince Richard was created Prince of Wales, Duke of

Cornwall, and Earl of Chester; and 'the Cardinal of England' (Simon Langham, formerly Archbishop of Canterbury) was smitten with a palsy after a meal, lost his speech, and died four days later. In the closing days of the reign, Sir John Munsterworth was drawn, hanged, and beheaded, for enormities of treason, his quartered body sent to the four chief towns of England, and his head set on London Bridge; he had appropriated sums given to him by the King and Council for the wages of soldiers, and when he feared exposure fled to the King of France and swore to bring a Spanish navy to destroy England: 'But rightful God, to whom no pryvite is vnknowe, suffrede hym ferst to be shent and spilt or that he sholde so trecherously & falsly his leige lord, the King of Engelonde, and his peple and his reaume—in the whiche ground the same Iohn was bore—thourgh bataill destroye, or bryng his cursed purpose aboute.' [But righteous God, to Whom no secret is unknown, allowed him first to be disgraced and ruined before he could so treacherously and falsely destroy in battle his liege lord, the King of England, and his people and realm—in which land he had been born—, or bring about his accursed purpose.] With this resounding sentence, the knighting of young Richard at Windsor, King Edward's death at Sheen, and his burial in Westminster Abbey, the dark clouds gather about the new reign.

This will be a convenient point at which to consider the not considerable literature commenting on these twenty-seven years, since the home affairs of the next reign will be far more complex and will inspire a more varied body of writings. Our period begins propitiously, with a lavish and surprising poem, not quite finished at 503 lines: the debate between Winner and Waster, confidently dated 1352. Nothing but complete quotation and comment would really do justice to a poem so inaccessible to the modern mind, but a digest must be attempted. The poet begins as does the equally unknown writer of *Sir Gawain and the Green Knight*, with a reference to our supposed origins in Brutus of Troy; but it is only an 'abverb clause of time' since when many odd things have happened, but none so odd as now. We are having to deal with smartness and self-will and wiliness, the ties of friendship are slack, and no western gentleman dares send his son south (not surprisingly, the poem is in the West Midland dialect); it's obvious that the world is coming to an end—what with wild waves, hares making their nests on hearths, and upstart lads marrying ladies. Equally noticeable, from the point of view of this first poet of the 'alliterative revival', is the fact that lords used to welcome minstrels who could compose new poetry; but now mere youths 'without chinweeds', who never strung three words together, are valued for their chatter and their jokes. So in this mood of tiredness and disappointment he says that he wandered by himself in the west and lay down in a delightful landscape with the hot sun on him; but the noise of birds singing and tapping bark, and of a bubbling brook, kept him from a 'nap' until it was near nightfall, and then the dream came. He is in a lovely green meadow, with a range of hills a mile long locking it in; in woods on either side are two armies arrayed for battle and already in troops. The dreamer knows that the 'prince' can put things right, and prays, until he sees a pavilion on the crest of a cliff, decorated with English golden roundels, each one surrounded by a blue garter inscribed in blue and gold 'Hethyng haue the hathell þat any harme thynkes' [Honi soit qui mal y pense]—so this is a clear reference to the recently founded Order of the Garter, with whose motto (in French) *Sir Gawain and the Green Knight* closes. With a hasty prayer for the king, he goes on to describe the herald who guards the tent, shaggy like a wild man of the woods and with twisted locks, but helmeted and hatted, with his crest of a long, lithe, staring leopard made of gold, and his tabard quartering the arms of France and England, the fleursdelys and the leopards, with pearls and silk as well. Further inside he could see a handsome king with a golden crown, sceptred and on a silken bench, in tunic and mantle as brown as a berry (like his beard) and embroidered with birds and blue garters, and with a belt picked out in wildfowl trembling in fear of falcons; and he reflects that this king must be a great hawker along the river-banks. King Edward (for we are left in no doubt of his identity) speaks to a splendid and trusty warrior standing near, reminds him of the obligations of his knighthood, and tells him to part and stay the two hosts. The Black Prince (for, again, it is obviously he) waits only to gird

G

himself in leg-armour, gorget and stomach-armour, his arms in steel rings, and plate-armour buckled on, with a close-fitting jupon, and his famous Arms for Peace (the three great wing-feathers of the ostrich) embroidered on it back and front; since his errand is peaceful, he has no shield or helmet, and he carries nothing but a branch he has torn off—even as the Green Knight enters Arthur's hall with a holly-branch. The poet is struck by his combination of sense and youth (he was in fact twenty-two in 1352, and Crécy was behind him).

The Prince delivers the King's message, that the peace must be kept; and then, conveniently, we are enabled to see the two armies through *his* eyes instead of through the poet's. On the one side are people not only from England and Ireland but from France, Lorraine, Lombardy, Spain, Westphalia, and the Hanseatic League. Six main banners head them—those of the Pope, the lawyers, and the four orders of friars—, and others betokening wool and wine and the rest of the merchants' marks. The heraldry here enhances what the poet has to say, and does not disguise it; this western provincial speaks with complete boldness, and on the delicate subject of the nation's economy, with his king set in the middle to hear what could be a painful and embarrassing debate. For this first host are the Winners, and the foreigners among them are a direct reference to the tolerant policy of King Edward towards merchants from abroad.

Ranged against them, says the Prince, in a mere four lines, is a body of soldiers, squires and bowmen, who sound plainer but equally resolute; these, it will turn out, are the Wasters. Their summons before the King produces two spokesmen, who significantly agree on the King's merits:

> He clothes vs bothe,
> And hase vs fosterde and fedde this fyve and twenty wyntere.

[He clothes us both, and has fostered and fed us these twenty-five years.]

So these two follow the Prince and fall down on their knees before the King, who welcomes them equally and calls for wine; the poet gets a share, too, and it blears his eyes, but with the familiarity of the best minstrel tradition he asks for a fill-up before going on with his next 'fit'.

Now begins the debate proper. If we are people of ordinary prudence, we may assume at the outset that Winner is right and Waster is wrong; it is not quite as simple as that—the former at his worst hoards, forestalls and sends prices soaring, uses the bribery and corruption that we associate with Mede in *Piers Plowman*, affects his countrymen by a Free Trade Policy as Edward had in 1351, and secures the profits of this fiscal policy to the King in his capacity as protector of foreign merchants. Whereas on the one hand this wealth was dangerously amassed, on the other the thriftless or luckless were selling up their ancestral estates and living for the day; it is noticeable that their army is all of men-at-arms, the tired soldiers expecting a grateful country to give them a living, yet faced with the disgusting rise of a new merchant class who had stooped to trade—and it must be borne in mind that the Black Prince himself was always bedevilled by debt. Sir Israel Gollancz, in his edition of the poem (Oxford University Press, 1930), fills in this urgent and perhaps even desperate background for us, calling the King himself 'Waster *par excellence*' and 'Winner *par excellence*'; the poet is bolder than his fulsome praise of the King has suggested.

The shifting course of the debate (which is nicely analysed in John Speirs, *Medieval English Poetry: The Non-Chaucerian Tradition*, London, 1957, pp. 277 ff.) leaves our judgment poised; even if we conclude that Winner is a bad and repulsive arguer who doesn't make the best of his better case, the poet is very fair and leaves the King with a nice compromise to work out, since the claims of both economy and expenditure are by right strong. At Winner's opening speech we learn to dislike him even while we largely agree: he pinches and scrapes, and then Waster is prodigal. With an appeal through essentials, corn, he tears into Waster for his neglect of husbandry; and his neglect goes beyond tillage: 'Downn bene his dowfehowses, drye bene his poles' [His dovecots are down, and his fishpools are dry]; he has sold his tools, and a few weapons do instead—but it's his horses and hounds that run

away with his money. And all this, observe, is through Pride
(l. 230).

But Waster can trot out a sin, too, though he does not name it
at this point: Avarice.

> When thou haste waltered and went and wakede alle þe nyghte,
> And iche a wy in this werlde that wonnes the abowte,
> And hase werpede thy wyde howses full of wolle sakkes—
> The bemys benden at the rofe, siche bakone there hynges,
> Stuffed are sterlynges vndere stelen bowndes—,
> What scholde worthe of that wele, if no waste come?
> Some rote, some ruste, some ratones fede.

> [When you have tossed and turned and stayed awake all night,
> and all the worldlings who stay with you, and when you have
> packed your wide buildings full of woolsacks—the beams bend
> at the roof, such bacon is hanging there, and sovereigns are
> stuffed into steel boxes—, what should become of that wealth,
> if there were no waste? Some would rot, some rust, and some
> feed rats. ll. 248–54]

Winner spares nothing for the poor, and has sold his soul into
hell. So the speaker is not just a Waster—he has some sense of
the circulation of money, and he is made the vehicle of two
biblical sentiments: the proneness of treasure laid up to contract
moth and rust, and the voice that said to the man with the cram-
med barns, 'Thou fool'.

Winner now counters with an accusation of excesses that
include a third Deadly Sin, Gluttony. The self-indulgence reaches
its peak in a loud tavern, with everyone ready with a bowl to blear
Waster's eyes, and women crowding round, as if Lust is being
included, too:

> Then es there bott 'fille in' & 'feche forthe', Florence to schewe,
> 'Wee-hee'and 'worthe vp', wordes ynewe.

> [Then there's nothing but 'fill up' and 'fetch out', for Florrie
> to appear, and horse-noises and 'come up', and words in
> plenty. ll. 281–2]

But Waster should remember to be prudent

> For þe colde wyntter and þe kene, with clengande frostes,
> Sythen dropeles drye in the dede monethe;

> [against the cold, keen winter, with its clinging frosts, and then
> the dropless drought in the dead month. ll. 275–6]

the poetry that arises from this flyting-match is often far beyond the demands of the satire. Unless Waster gets his labourers to till and fence and rebuild and clear, he is for the fire; behind this lies the pressing shortage of labour consequent on the war, the Black Death, and social upheavals, and the 1351 Statute of Labourers, which had tried to tackle the problem, must have been in the poet's mind. Winner has even been talking to a 'clerk', and this regard for the weather forecast tells him that 'there is greater cold to come' (l. 293), which looks like a reference, after the event, to the bitter winter of 1352–3.

But this is answerable. Waster points out that his feasts and parties benefit the poor in a way pleasing to the Prince Who made paradise and Who would prefer wealth shared to wealth huddled and hidden and wrapped in coffers, or carted off by friars, when Winner has gone, for the plastering and painting of their walls and pillars. In fact (and here comes another sin), Waster would like Winner to be drowned in the deep sea (no drought down there!) along with ember days, eves of saints' days, Fridays, the Saturday fasts for the Virgin, and his brother Wanhope, who is Accidy or Sloth, that faithless Despair which makes the fifth of the seven. This speech, of course, would be considered a little naughty in its jettisoning of pious acts; but Waster in the course of it gives his approval to the kindly 'mind-ale', the feast commemorating the deceased a month after his death. He reaches the climax of his speech with some bitter personal invective against 'Scharshull', that Lord Chief Justice Shareshull who at the January parliament of 1352 had attacked riotous young nobles as 'disturbers of the peace', and—perhaps revealing the sin of Wrath—begs the King (ll. 319–23) to let them begin battle. But Winner has a trump-card to end the 'fit', an unfairly elaborate catalogue of the typical Waster feast, which may tentatively be of use to the social historian; there is even a kind of frothy poetry made out of it, and its cumulative effect sounds damning until it is observed how Winner is unconsciously showing the last of the sins, Envy, and consoling himself with thoughts of another's ruin—this kind of food burns your bowels inside. Gross as the menu sounds, it is in fact paralleled and even exceeded by surviving bills of recommended fare, in which, furthermore, the courses were punctuated by 'subtleties', models in paste and jelly and so forth of scenes as elaborate as the Visitation of the Blessed Virgin to St Elizabeth, brought in to encourage the pampered feasters to proceed. Anyway, Winner says that Waster and his friends tuck into the following (ll. 332–56): boar's head with bay-leaves on it, broad buck-tails in broth, venison and frumenty of wheat boiled in milk, rich pheasants, baked meat, chopped-meat pies, chickens grilled on the coals, roast with rich sauces, splendid spices, kids cut along the back, quartered swans, ten-inch tarts, birds on the spit, barnacle-geese, bitterns, snipes, larks, linnets covered in sugar, woodcocks, boiling hot woodpeckers, teals, titmice, rabbit broth, sweet custards, expensive pasties and pies, and what they call mawmeny 'to fill your maws'—twelve plates at a time between two men! All Winner is used to is salt Martinmas beef, a few vegetables, and perhaps a hen for the householder; and the proud blaring of Waster's trumpets offends him, too. All this mouthwatering fare seems too much for the poet, who again asks for a fill-up before proceeding to the final 'fit'.

It is Waster's turn again, and he has a grave charge to make: when there is a good harvest sent by God, Winner is in despair, because the price of grain comes down, and disappointed in his hope of a hard year he will hang himself. To this unnatural impiety is added his disregard for a fixed social order; does he want lords to live as lads, prelates as priests, proud city merchants as village pedlars? Waster assigns to the privileged classes bitterns and swans, bacon and beef to the rest; ruddy wheat to the one, the 'roughness of rye' to the other; good broths to the one, 'grey gruel' to the other—always a share for the poor. Furthermore, if it were not for hawking and hunting and fishing (and the feasting that follows), there would be such repletion that no one would care to work for a master; so whoever wants to win wealth must find a waster. The mention of the poor now gives Winner his cue; a far greater upset to the social order is made by landowners who impoverish themselves by selling their ancestral estates, their woods of oak and ash, and all but sprouts and saplings, to glut their wives' vanity with furs and silk saddles and splendid rings. In the good old days gentlemen liked to take their visitors out to their woods and coverts for a little hunting, but now everything has been sold up so that people can be in the fashion with trailing sleeves and ermine trimmings; it is all in scandalous contrast with the Blessed Virgin, who fled from her country on an ambling ass, with no more pride than a Child in her bosom and a broken halter that Joseph held in his hand. Whether this last is meant as an example of the mean Winner's humbug the poet does not make clear, but Waster ignores it, telling him in effect to mind his own business about what other people pay for their luxuries; if a knight treats his sweetheart well, she will be an inspiration to him in battle. Winner gets no joy out of his winnings, which the devil and the executors will dispense at his deathbed; so let's have a short life and a gay one.

The ending—the King's judgment—is strange. Winner must go and domesticate with the Pope of Rome (he was in fact at Avignon); the cardinals will welcome him, and give him silken sheets and fine food, but he must return at once when the King summons him. Gollancz points out that this linking of high finance with the papal court will suit Clement VI, who died on 6 December 1352, but hardly his more rigid successor, so that this is another help in dating the poem. Waster's lot is equally satirical; he must go to London, where wealth has wings, and get a room in Cheapside with a wide window to spy out any rich stranger coming into town, then offer to take him to an inn, get him drunk on Cretan wine, introduce him to the eatables in Bread Street and Poultry, provide a soft seat and a tablecloth, and generally hoodwink him. Another flurry of birds, eight edible varieties, ends these instructions, but the King makes a remark unworthy of his prudence when he adds, 'The more you waste your wealth, the more Winner loves you'—perhaps so, but the debate has produced some valid arguments, and the King's judgment has proved to be no more than a sarcastic suggestion of where these two imperfect creatures best belong. He turns finally to Winner, with instructions to attend him when he is at war abroad; he will dub him knight, give gold and silver to loyal lieges, and then return to Cologne, where the Three Magi are entombed.

It will be clear that this poem is one of the most topical surviving from its age. Speirs wants to see further into it, with the birds having their origin in the assemblies of humans dressed as birds in fertility rituals, the basis of the poem in pageantry, and the atavistic elements of flyting, pre-Christian drama, drinking rites, the wild man, the upsets of Nature and order, and the conflict of Youth with Age. But if we expect the eulogy of King Edward III to be conveyed in his final verdict, we shall be disappointed; as so often in medieval debates, the decision must be ours, and the King can content himself with a speech of mere ridicule.

After the fireworks of *Winner and Waster*, the 112 lines on the death of King Edward III in the Vernon MS (R. H. Robbins, *Historical Poems of the XIVth and XVth Centuries*, New York, 1959, No. 39) are flat and repetitive, and without any hint of the King's failings. The stanzaic form, with its rhymes arranged ababbcbc and in lines of four stresses, could have lent itself to a chronological treatment of the King's victories and other high points of his long reign, but instead a moralizing tone is adopted, and the existence of a refrain brings each stanza dully back to some variation on the idea that 'what is seldom seen is soon forgotten'. Thus two stanzas are thrown away on platitudes about fickleness, though at the end of them 'he who was our greatest asset' appears; the next eight stanzas then present and develop the conceit of 'an English ship' which his people once had, noble and with a high topcastle, dreaded throughout Christendom, tough and enduring in battle and in storm; its rudder steered it incomparably, but now they are parted and forgotten. Whether the sea was rough or 'demure', the ship made good havens.

Þis goode schip I may remene
  To þe chiualrye of þis londe.
Sum tyme þei counted nouȝt a bene
  Beo al Ffraunce, Ich vnderstonde.
Þei tok and slouȝ hem with heore honde,
  Þe power of Ffraunce, boþ smal & grete,
And brouþt þe king hider to byde her bonde;
  And nou riht sone hit is forȝete.

[I may compare this good ship with the knighthood of this
country. At one time they did not give a bean for all France,
so I believe. They captured and slew with their hands the
forces of France, both great and small, and brought its king
here to endure their bondage; and now it is forgotten straight
away.]

It had a trusty mast and a big, strong sail, as well as a barge that
did not give a cleat for all France; it was a trusty shield for us.

Now an explanation of the rather obvious allegory begins.
The rudder was not made of oak or elm; 'it was Edward the
Third, the noble knight'. The Prince, his son, kept up the helm of
the rudder, and was never 'scoumfited' [discomfited] in fight; the
King sailed and rowed properly, and the Prince feared nothing.
The swift barge was Duke Henry of Lancaster, of whom the *Brut*
approved; here emphasis is laid on his 'allegiance'—the return to
royal favour of the House of Lancaster—and his eagerness to
chastise the foe. The ship's mast signifies the 'good commons',
who kept the war going throughout by their grants of goods and
money, and the wind that blew the ship so prosperously was good
prayers, 'I'll tell you that plainly' (but devoutness is thrown out
now, and good deeds forgotten).

So far the poem is bad history but fair panegyric. Now a new
idea starts in the poet's mind, and he tries to prophesy good for
the new king's reign; it is probable that he was writing in 1377,
just after Edward's death and not long after the Black Prince's,
but he suppresses his melancholy and his apprehensiveness in
another conceit—of the boy Richard as a shoot or scion of the
same stock and its root. He hopes, and prays to Christ, that the

boy will hold his enemies underfoot; if only the shoot were fully grown, and had sap and pith, he would probably be recognized as a conqueror of many countries, because he is active and nimble, toiling and sweating in arms. So the poet urges everyone to lift up the head of this shoot, and support it until it is fully grown; the French can boast and brag, and threaten us scornfully, and if the English are disloyal and sluggish they may forget the lesson of the previous reign. 'And therefore, good sirs, have mind of your doughty king, who died in old age, and of his son Prince Edward, who was the fount of all courage'; with the present diminution of their fame, the poet obviously trembles for the realm —and with prescience.

Some of the most eminent comments on Edward's reign, though confined to the latter part of it, were made by Langland. Even if Mede the Maiden is not a caricature of Alice Perrers, the whole of her dealings with the King in Passus II–IV should be read carefully as a frank statement on the corruptions of the royal court and the courts of law; its humour—Mede mounted on a newly-shod sheriff, Falsehood on a juryman trotting gently, Flattery on a daintily caparisoned sycophant—cannot conceal Langland's indignation, and this part of the poem at least has a decisive and 'happy' ending, since Mede is overthrown and the King makes all manner of good resolves.

The combined effect on labour of the Black Death and the 1351 Statute of Labourers is actively remembered in B Passus IV. 309 ff. While beggars and tramps grow mightily finicky about their food, labourers with only their hands to live by won't eat yesterday's vegetables or drink penny-ale or take a bit of bacon— it has to be fresh meat or fish, fried or baked and oven-hot (in fact, *chaud* or *plus chaud*, in French!), for fear they get a chill on their stomachs. They grumble unless they get high wages, cursing the time that they were born to be labourers, and even cursing the King and his council for their oppressive laws about workmen; the only statute they jumped to was Hunger's, when *he* was their master. The end of this Passus, which follows immediately, contains a dire prophecy advocating hard work; its references seem to be to the pestilence in 1376, the eclipse of the sun in 1377, the dearth in the same year, and the ascendancy of Alice Perrers ('a maiden has the supremacy').

The Death itself (in its various visitations) is movingly described in B. XX. 99 ff.:

> Deth cam dryuende after, and al to doust passhed
> Kynges and knyȝtes, kayseres and popes;
> Lered ne lewed, he let no man stonde,
> That he hitte euene, that euere stired after.
> Many a louely lady, and lemmanes of knyghtes,
> Swouned and swelted for sorwe of Dethes dyntes.

[Death came dashing after, and pounded quite to dust kings and knights, emperors and popes. He left no one standing, cleric or layman, but hit him so squarely that he never stirred again. Many lovely ladies, and knights' sweethearts, swooned and died in agony at Death's blows.]

And its effect on parishes—their poverty and depopulation, their bare living for the clergy that remained—is mentioned in the Prologue, ll. 83–6, where the clergy give up the struggle and hope to live by singing for simony in London. The plague, of course, recurred, and it is not always certain that the 1348–9 visitation is the one being discussed; but there is a plainly dated reference to the 1362 outbreak in B. V. 13 ff., when Reason tells the whole kingdom that 'these pestilences were just because of sin, and the south-west wind on the Saturday evening was obviously just because of pride and for no other reason'; this was the wind that so impressed the writer of the *Brut*, and it also figures impressively in a fifteenth-century carol, obviously touched up long after 1362, in British Museum MS Sloane 2593 (R. L. Greene, *A Selection of English Carols*, Oxford, 1962, No. 73):

> Thynk, man, on the dere yeres thre.
> For hunger deyid gret plente,
> Powre and ryche, bond and fre;
> Thei leyn dede in every way.

Thynk, man, on the pestelens tweye.
In every cuntre men gnnne deye;
Deth left neyther for lowe ne heye,
  But lettyd hem of here pray.

Deth is wonder coveytous.
Quan he comit to a manys hous,
He takit the good man and his spows,
  And bryngit hem in powre aray.

After cam a wyndes blast
That made many a man agast.
Stefve stepelys thei stodyn fast;
  The weyke fyllyn and blewyn away.

Many merveylis God haght sent
Of lytenyng and of thunder-dent.
At the Frere Camys haght it hent
  At Lynne toun, it is non nay.

Lytenyng at Lynne dede gret harm
Of tolbothe and of Fryre Carm;
Thei stondyn wol cole that stodyn wol warm.
  It made hem a wol sory fray . . .

[Think, man, of the three expensive years. A great number of
people died of hunger, poor and rich, bondmen and freemen.
They lay dead on every road. Think, man, of the two plagues.
Men died in every region; death did not desist for humble
people or important ones, but kept them from their winnings.
Death is amazingly covetous. When he comes to a man's house,
he takes the householder and his wife, and reduces them to a
wretched state. Afterwards came a blast of wind that made
many men terrified. Tough steeples stood firm; the weak ones
fell and blew away. God has sent many marvels in the matter
of lightning and thunderbolt. It took hold of the Carmelite
Friary in the town of Lynn, there's no denying that. Lightning

did great damage at Lynn to the tolbooth and the Carmelite Friary; those who stood very warm now stand very cold. It gave them a very nasty fright.]

Here, the two epidemics will be those of 1348–9 and 1361–2, the windstorm that of 15 January 1362; the three lean years are harder to fix, but we have seen that the *Brut* mentioned several such. What is mysterious about this vengeful poem, however, is that there is no record of the two specific disasters at King's Lynn, and the ancient Carmelite steeple is known to have fallen on 9 April 1631; Greene supposes that the writer may have belonged to a rival mendicant order, especially the Franciscans, whose 'tough steeple', tall and octagonal, is still a graceful feature of that lovely town.

The *Brut* does not record the dry April of 1370, but Langland's character Activa Vita, who makes lovely bread, remembers with relish the shortage, and the demand for his goods, 'in a dry April in the year of Our Lord one thousand three hundred twice thirty and ten . . . , when Chichester was Mayor' (B. XIII. 269–71); we know that John Chichester was Mayor until October 1370. Apart from his interest in natural phenomena, Langland also has many scattered comments to make on the happenings of his time; for instance, he mentions merely as an illustration that 'Poverty could pass through the Alton Pass without fear of robbery' (B. XIV. 300–1). He seems to be obsessed with the brigands who pounced out from the woods of Alton, near the Surrey-Hampshire border, on traffic going to and from Winchester; in C. V. 51–4 Peace is robbed while making for St Giles's Down, where the Winchester Fair was held, and the Fair there occurs again in B. V. 205 and C. XIV. 52. With similar topicality, the poet of *Sir Gawain and the Green Knight* lets his hero have a poor time socially in 'the wilderness of the Wirral; few lived there who loved either God or man with a good heart' (ll. 701-2); it had been systematically afforested, but by the late fourteenth century was a haunt of outlaws and other desperadoes. Langland's B. Passus IV is full of awful extortions, money going overseas to fill papal pockets, the good notion of searching would-be pilgrims at Dover for, as it were, infringing currency restrictions, and the anomalous situation of having two Popes; in B. Passus X and XII are aired the perennial problems of whether the King should have supreme power over churchmen, 'benefit of clergy', the Becket theme. Yet it is surprising, from an age so rich in architecture and in ceremonial, how little we know in the vernacular of the conduct and ritual of the church services; *St Erkenwald*, dated very probably in 1386, when the cult of this Anglo-Saxon bishop of London was somewhat strengthened at St Paul's, imagines the pre-Conquest high mass with many handsome lords gathered to hear it 'even as the most important people in the kingdom often make their way there' (ed. Sir Israel Gollancz, London, 1932, 1. 135), but on the aesthetic treats of eye and ear our writers are generally silent.

In the disappointing and worrying time after the death of the Black Prince, with the old King failing and his heir a boy, Langland penned the remarkable re-telling of the old fable in which the rats and mice, wise up to a point, decide to bell the cat (B. Prologue, ll. 146 ff.). Skeat claimed that the rats were 'the burgesses and more influential men' in the commons, the mice the lesser men, the cat Edward III, the kitten Richard II; this would date the passage between 8 June 1376 (the death of the Black Prince) and 21 June 1377 (the death of Edward), and Skeat, seeing a reference to Edward's Jubilee in B. III. 299, further limits it to March-April-May 1377. More recently the cat, who 'came from a court just when he wanted to, and easily pounced on them and caught them as he pleased, played dangerously with them, and tossed them about', has been seen as John of Gaunt, by now a far more effective figure than his father; and the mouse 'who seemed to me to know what's what' may be the speaker, Piers de la Mare, as mentioned in the *Brut*. Thus these are an allegory or parody of the workings of the 'Good' Parliament of 1376; the cat's departure 'catching conies' may either be an obscene reference to Gaunt's amours or a contemptuous glance at his numerous absences. The rat who thinks of the bell is inspired to it by looking at the gold chains and collars round men's necks in London, but his idea remains a dream of no practical fulfilment. The clever mouse is disposed to accept the cat or kitten and not provoke them; but he is glum about the future, and quotes in Latin from *Ecclesiastes* X. 16, 'Woe to that land where a child is king'.

To return to the *Brut*: it must be remembered that we are dealing with a chronicle rewritten, polished, excised, and made 'safe' in the usurping reigns after 1400, so that the picture of the new King is harsh. Richard of Bordeaux, now aged eleven, was crowned at Westminster Abbey in 1377, but in the following year the building witnessed an ugly sacrilege; Lord Latimer and Sir Ralph Ferrers were claiming, against two squires called Hawley and Shakell, a noble prisoner, the Count of Denia, taken in Spain, and finding Hawley at mass before St Edward's shrine they killed him there and threw Shakell into the Tower, until the King 'granted him grace'. The fourpenny poll-tax of 1380, to be paid by every man, woman and child over fourteen, proves to be the prelude to the rising of 1381, 'which they called *hurling time*' (we now call it the Peasants' Revolt). The chronicler's account is admirable as a narrative, and must be read in full:

And þei of Kent & of Essex madyn hem ij cheveteynez to rewle & gouerne þe compayne of Kent & of Essex: þat one me callid Jacke Strawe and þat oþer Watte Tyler; and þai comen and assembled ham vpon þe Blake-Heth yn Kent. And apon the Corpus Christi day and after, þei comen doune ynto Southwerk, and brekyn vp þe prison hous, þat is to wite, þe Kingis Bench, and þe Marchalsy, & delyverde out alle þe prisoners. And so þe same day þei comen ynto London, and þere thay robbyd þe peple and slowyn alle alyens þat þay myȝt fynde yn þe cyte and aboute þe cite, and despoiled alle her godez, and made havoke. And on the Fridai next aftir, þat was on þe morowe, thei comyn vnto þe Tour of London, and the King beyng þereyn, þei sette out of þe Tour þe Archebishop of Caunturbury, Maistir Symond Sudbery, and Ser Robert Halez, Pryour of Saint Johnes, and a Whit Frere þat was confessour vnto King Richarde, and brouȝt ham vnto þe Tour Hill; and þere þay smytyn of her hedys, and comyn ayen to London, & slowyn mo peple of men of lawe, and oþer worthi men yn dyuers parteyez of þe cite. And þanne went þai to the

Dukez place of Lancastre, beyonde Saint Mary Stronde, þat
was callyd Savoy. And þere þei deuoured & destroyed al þe
godez þat þay myȝt fynde, and bare ham away, and brent vp
þe place. And þanne aftir þey went to Seint Johnes without
Smythffelde, and destroyed þe godes, & brent vp þat hous, and
went to Westminster, and so to Sent Martynez þe Graunt,
and made hem go out of þe sayntwarye, alle þat were þereynne
for eny maner of gryth, and þanne come vnto þe Temple, and
to alle oþer ynnez of men of lawe, & dispoyled ham and
rebbed ham of her godez, and also taare hir bokis of law.
And þai come to London, and brake vp the pryson of Newgate,
& droff out alle þe prisoners, felons, & oþir of bothe countres,
and alle þe peple þat was withynne ham, & destroyed alle þe
bokis of bothe countres; and þus þay contynued forth, both
Saturday and Sonday, vnto þe Monday next folowyng, yn alle
hir malice & wickydnesse. And þanne on the Monday King
Richard, with his lordez þat were with hym þat tyme, and
with þe Meire of London, William Walworth, þe aldermen &
þe commynez of þe cite, come ynto Southwerk to here &
know þe entencion of þese rebellis and misgouerned pepil.
And þis Iak Straw þanne made an oyes in þe felde, þat alle þe
pepyl of accorde schulde come nere & here his clamour and
his crye and his will; and þe lordez, and the Mayre and þe
aldermen, with the communialte, hauyng indignacion of his
covetise and falsnesse, and his foule presompcion, . . . anon
William Walworth, þat tyme beyng Mayre, drew out his
knyff and slow Iack Straw, and anon ryȝt þere dede smyȝt
of his hed, and sette it vp apon a spereschafte; and so it was
bore þrouȝ London, & set on high vpon London Brygge.
And anon alle þe rysers and mysgouernyd men were voyded
and vanysched, as hit hadde not byn þay.

[And those from Kent and Essex made themselves two ringleaders to rule and govern the company from Kent and Essex;
one was called Jack Straw, and the other Wat Tyler; and they
came and assembled on Blackheath in Kent. And on Corpus
Christi day and the day after, they came down into Southwark,

and broke up the prison house, that is to say, the King's Bench, and the Marshalsea, and delivered all the prisoners. And so the same day they came into London, and there they robbed the people and killed all aliens that they could find in the city and its suburbs, and plundered all their goods, and made havoc. And on the next day, the Friday, they came to the Tower of London, where the King was, and took out of the Tower the Archbishop of Canterbury, Master Simon Sudbury, and Sir Robert Hales, Prior of St John's, and a White-friar who was confessor to King Richard, and brought them to Tower Hill; and there they cut off their heads, and came back to London, and killed more people from among the lawyers, and other worthy men in different parts of the city. And then they went to the Duke of Lancaster's place beyond St Mary-le-Strand, which was called Savoy. And there they devastated and destroyed all the goods they could find, and carried them away, and burnt the place up. And after that they went to St John's outside Smithfield, and destroyed the goods, and burnt up that house, and went to Westminster, and so to St Martin-le-Grand, and made all those who were inside the sanctuary for any kind of immunity leave it, and then came to the Temple, and to all the other inns of the lawyers, and pillaged them and robbed them of their goods, and also tore their law-books. And they came to London, and broke up Newgate Prison, and drove out all the prisoners, felons, and the rest, from both countries, and all the people who were inside, and destroyed all the books of both countries; and thus they continued, both Saturday and Sunday, until the Monday following, in all their malice and wickedness. And then on the Monday King Richard, with his lords who were with him at that time, and with the Mayor of London, William Walworth, and the aldermen and commons of the city, came into Southwark to hear and find out the aims of these rebels and misgoverned people. And this Jack Straw then made an *oyez* in the field, so that all the people of good will should come nearer and hear his clamour and his shouting and his will; and since the lords, and the Mayor and aldermen, along with

H

the commonalty, were indignant at his covetousness and dis-
loyalty, and his vile presumption, . . . at once William Walworth, the Mayor at that time, drew out his knife and killed
Jack Straw, and at once right there had his head cut off, and
set it up on the shaft of a spear; and so it was carried through
London, and set high up on London Bridge. And at once all
the risers and misgoverned men had disappeared and vanished, as if it had not been they at all.]

Lively and persuasive as it is, this account is unfair to the boy
King; he showed incredible bravery in the face of the mob, and
achieved one of the few personal triumphs of his erring reign. On
the other hand, the account of the aftermath will suppress the
treachery and cruelty to which he perforce had to lend himself.
A small point, perhaps, is that it was Tyler and not Straw who
was so opportunely struck down by Walworth; a poem shortly
to be quoted has the same error, and the Latin chronicler Knighton
curiously notes that there has been a change of name to that of
Straw. No earthly reason is quoted for the murder of the Archbishop and of Treasurer Hales; they were, in fact, closely tied
up with the execrated poll-tax (which, by the way, was not new to
1380). Nor are we permitted to hear of those little mitigating
features in the behaviour of the rebels—their safeguarding of the
absent Gaunt's family at the Savoy, the prohibition of plunder;
indeed, the chronicler makes it sound as if loot were one of their
chief purposes. Luckily, there exists a big literature of the Revolt
in English, which we can call upon, and very full treatments in
the Latin of Knighton, the *Chronicon Angliae*, and Walsingham's
Historia Anglicana, and Froissart's French.

The immediate reaction of the King, as far as the chronicler
cares to say, was to make six knights; one was Walworth, of
course, but another was that Nicholas Brembre whom we met in
another context (p. 23) as a bloodthirsty gangster. The King
went back to the Tower, and 'rested himself' until the people had
cooled down; then the hangings began, 'on the nearest gallows in
every lordship throughout the realm of England', in forties and
thirties, tens and twelves, just as they could be caught. There is

no comment on this, no touch of clemency; the chronicler does not even bother to cite, on behalf of abstract justice, the harsh deeds of the rebels at Bury St Edmunds, St Albans, and elsewhere.

In 1382 occurred the great earthquake 'all over the world', with its effect on the minds of the faithful, who feared God's vengeance; its interruption of the Blackfriars proceedings against Wyclif is not mentioned—nor, for that matter, is Wyclif, at any point in his influential life, so that we shall also lose one of the motives or excuses of those who proceeded against Sir Simon Burley and other early Wyclifite sympathizers a couple of years after. Burley is mentioned at this point, as escorting Anne of Bohemia to her marriage with the King; the chronicler does not record the last act of their friendship, when she went down on her knees to the Lords Appellant in an attempt to save his life, and for the moment he is concerned to make the wedding sound a happy intermission and a hope for the future—so that it is tactless of him to point out what became notorious, that 'all her friends who came with her had big gifts and good entertainment, and were well treated the whole time they stayed here'. A treason combat at Westminster ended with the victory of the defendant and the judicial hanging of the appellant; Christmas passed at Eltham, and after the show of arms against the Scots, and the fracas at York involving his half-brother Holland, the King held a Parliament and made two dukes, a marquess, and five earls. They were, politically speaking, a mixed crowd, though the chronicler gives no interesting hint of their loyalties or of the ghastly disasters that some of them would inflict on the King; for whereas the new Duke of York remained ineffective, the new Duke of Gloucester became his nephew's deadly enemy, though the royal train had to suffer for their master; Gaunt's son Bolingbroke got the Earldom of Derby, the beginning of his steady march to the throne; the upstart Michael de la Pole became Earl of Suffolk and Chancellor, to his own speedy ruin. And March, the heir and so near the throne, was meanwhile killed in Ireland; yet all this is announced as if it bore no relation to the next item of home news, the collapse of Richard's court party at Radcot Bridge in 1387, and the ascendancy

of the five Lords Appellant, carefully named and titled here—
Gloucester, Arundel, Warwick, Derby, and Nottingham. They
were moved, says the chronicler, by the wickedness and inefficiency
of the King's council, of which the three leaders at once fled
overseas, and never returned; but Tresilian the Justice, Brembre,
and others, were charged with treason and drawn from the Tower
to Tyburn to be hanged and have their throats cut; old Burley,
who was a Knight of the Garter, and Sir John Beauchamp and
Sir James Berners, were merely given the favour of going on foot
to Tower Hill and dying under the more honourable axe. The
impassive tone of this account, and its one-sidedness, turn us
against the writer as both historian and human being, and he
forthwith proceeds to his whole page of gush about the Smithfield
tournament of 1388. But another treason combat at the Palace of
Westminster, with its gory end of the accuser; Gaunt's absence in
Spain; an unfortunate Christmas at Woodstock, where the good
Earl of Pembroke was killed jousting in the park; and a sordid
scuffle in Fleet Street between a baker's man and a yeoman of the
Bishop of Salisbury, into which were drawn the constables and
the Bishop's household, then the Mayor and sheriffs on the one
hand and the Bishop and the Archbishop of York on the other,
and finally and absurdly the King himself; —all these incidents
sound (and are perhaps meant to sound) ominous. Summoning
the Mayor and sheriffs to Windsor, the King rebuked them 'fulle
foule' [very foully] and deposed them; by putting in his own
'warden and governor of the city', and replacing him after a month
for being 'so tender and gentle' to the citizens, he at least left it in
the hands of 'good men' until the election of the next mayor, but
maliciously moved all his courts to York—the Chancery, the
Exchequer, the King's Bench, and the Common Pleas. Yet after
six months, finding the arrangement inconvenient, he moved
back to London, and the citizens received him rapturously. The
Mayor and the chief citizens had a collection made, in hopes of
regaining his grace and their liberties and franchises, but it was
Queen Anne's prayer that moved him to grant what they asked,
at Sheen in Surrey. Two days later, the Mayor and his train met
the royal party on the heath between Sheen and London, and

brought them to the gate of London Bridge, where they gave Richard 'a milk-white steed' superbly turned out, and Anne a white palfrey with the same caparison of white and red, 'and the conduits of London ran white and red wine, for all kinds of people to drink'. Between St Paul's and the cross in Cheapside they had a high scaffold with many angels, and melodies and songs; and an angel was swung down from the top to put crowns of gold, jewels, and pearls, on the heads of the King and Queen; finally, at Westminster Palace they gave him two costly silver-gilt basins, and sued for his love and their rights, which he had confirmed by letters patent. The Queen, and other good aristocrats, begged him on their knees to grant all this, which he graciously did, and the citizens went home. But the empty triumph of jousts at Smithfield, when the English nobles beat their Scots challengers, was followed by a loss to the King personally, and probably to the nation as a whole: the young Queen died at Sheen, and was taken back along her triumphal road to London and Westminster for burial near St Edward's shrine; 'on whose soul Almighty God have mercy and pity! Amen.'

Whatever his grief, he soon remarried, and one of the longest passages in the chronicle is devoted to the ceremony and feasting of this empty and barren nuptials; the little girl was given every outward form of welcome, but is the chronicler sorry for her when he records that she 'was brought to the Tower of London, and there she was all night'? The King's action in marrying her and pledging peace with France was an unpopular show of self-assertion, and the chronicler takes care to mention the stampede on London Bridge, when eleven eager onlookers were trampled to death, and to follow the coronation feast with the King's next arbitrary act. It was, of course, his long-meditated revenge; 'by evil excitation and false counsel, and because of the great anger and malice that he had felt so long against his uncle, the good Duke of Gloucester, the Earl of Arundel, and the Earl of Warwick', he rode out with a body of men, late in the evening of 25 August 1397, to Chelmsford and on to Pleshey, where the 'good Duke of Gloucester was staying. And the good Duke at once came to welcome the King.' Now Gloucester was 'good' in several respects, but mainly as a fighting man and as possessing a decent library; he was ambitious and merciless, and the chronicler's bias against the King is conveyed in his slovenly repetition of this word 'good'. Gloucester was arrested and shipped to Calais, where his mysterious death is dogmatically described as if it were a known fact: while he was asleep, 'anon þei bonde hym honde and foot, & chargid hym to ly stylle; and whanne þai hadde þis do, þey token ij smale tewellys, and made on ham rydyng knottis, and caste þe tewellys aboute þe Dukis nek, and þanne þei token þe fetherbed þat lay vnder hym, and cast hit aboue hym; and þan þei drowen her towellis eche wayez; and sum lay vpon þe fethir bed apon hym, vnto þe tyme þat he were ded, because þat he schulde make non noyse. And þus þei strangled þis worthi Duk vnto the deth, on whose soule God, for His pite, haue merci! Amen.' [at once they bound him hand and foot, and ordered him to lie quietly; and when they had done this, they took two small towels, and made slip-knots on them, and threw the towels around the Duke's neck, and then took the featherbed that was lying under him and threw it over him; and then they pulled their towels both ways; and some lay on the featherbed on top of him, until he was dead, so that he should not make any noise. And thus they strangled this worthy Duke to death, and may God, in His pity, have mercy on his soul! Amen.]

Arundel and Warwick were next seized (though Arundel was on parole until Parliament time), and the lesser men Cobham and Cheyney. The 'Great Parliament' was convened, and for the trial the King ordered a long, large building of timber, 'which was called a hall', with a tile roof and open along both sides. He sent his writs to every lord, baron, knight, and esquire, in every shire of England, ordering them to bring their retinues for the defence of the King against his enemies. Above all, he obtained from his darling palatinate of Cheshire the troop of yeomen and archers whom he took into his own court, on court rations and good wages, as his personal bodyguard; he favoured and trusted them above all others, but they 'soon afterwards turned to the King's great loss, shame, hindrance, total ruin, and destruction, as you shall hear soon after' (we don't). The great muster of the King's

adherents is headed by Derby (Bolingbroke), since the chronicler
—wise after the event—is emphasizing the usurper's tireless loyalty
and patience towards his cousin. The city was packed, and people
were lodged in every house for twelve miles round London. Arundel
was the first to be condemned and, escorted by the Cheshire guard
for fear of rescue, axed on Tower Hill, taking it 'very patiently';
the Austin Friars buried him in their choir. Warwick was spared
for his great age, the lords compassionately packing him off to
perpetual imprisonment on Man; Cobham and Cheyney were
condemned to hanging and drawing, but their sentences, too,
were commuted to life imprisonment when the lords pleaded for
them. The chronicler is again unfair; the King was showing far
more mercy than Gloucester and his henchmen had shown, and
even the execution of Arundel was a piece of clemency in place
of the customary slow death for treason.

Now comes the last deceptive breathing-space. Dick Whitting-
ton was Mayor, and he and the sheriffs kept every gate and every
ward in London well guarded with armed men and archers during
the Parliament. The King created five dukes, and once again
Hereford (Bolingbroke) heads the list; and the rest of his friends
were rewarded with other peerages. But Gaunt died in Holborn,
and the King gave him a fine burial in St Paul's next to his Duchess
Blanche, 'daughter and heir to the good Henry, who had been
Duke of Lancaster' (the chronicler's Lancaster adherence echoes
even in the tomb); next, getting the sequence wrong—for Gaunt
was still alive—, we hear of the dissension between Hereford and
Norfolk, the duel arranged at Coventry, and the King's strange
mishandling of the affair, the exile of both parties, and the exile
of Archbishop Arundel and his replacement by Walden. Stranger
still, 'by the false counsel and imagination of the false and covetous men around him', he countenanced the affair of the 'blank
charters' bearing rich men's seals; as a result, all good hearts in
the realm were alienated from him, and he who had been 'so high
and so excellent a king' was brought to destruction: 'Alas, the
pity of it, that such a king could not see!' The stewardship of the
kingdom was put out to the four royal favourites—the Earl of
Wiltshire, and Bussy (or Bushy), Bagot and Green (later to be

called 'the caterpillars of the commonwealth')—while the King
went off to Ireland; meanwhile Bolingbroke landed, to claim his
Duchy of Lancaster (says the chronicler, unwilling to attribute
any baser motive to him), and Archbishop Arundel with him. The
people flocked to him, Worcester the King's steward broke his
staff as a token of deserting Richard, Wiltshire and the caterpillars were proceeded against (though Bagot seems to have
survived), and the hapless Richard was put in the Tower, then in
Leeds Castle in Kent, and finally in the castle of Pontefract,
where he 'made his end'. Bolingbroke was chosen King for his
'mighty manhood', and he was crowned on St Edward the Confessor's Day at Westminster; titles and bishoprics were distributed,
but poor Richard died starved at Pontefract, 'for he was kept four
or five days without food and drink'. The belief long continued
that he was still alive, and a lot of harm it caused; the new King
had the body wrapped in linen save for the face, so that it should
be recognized, and after obsequies at St Paul's and Westminster
Abbey it was buried at Langley. But the first year of the new reign
was soon disturbed by the conspiracy of a group of nobles, of
which the Duke of Aumale fortunately informed to the King,
and numerous decapitations followed, at Cirencester, Pleshey,
Bristol, and London; Shakespeare, with more taste, mentions
only 'The heads of Oxford, Salisbury, Blunt, and Kent' and
'The heads of Brocas and Sir Bennet Seely'. On which typical note
the century ends.

How did observant writers in the vernacular view the disasters
and the zigzagging policy of this deplorable reign? It is, for our
purpose, all the more regrettable that the one writer who described the polity with any keenness or consistency, John Gower,
had given up the job of reforming by the time he wrote his main
English work; though this is really a clumsy way to describe the
mature subtlety by which he turned from the overt and grim
didacticism of his 30,000 French lines, and the appalled picture of
society and the Peasants' Revolt in his 20,000 Latin ones, to the
cool appraisal that we find in the even bigger English *Confessio
Amantis*. And there was an overlap, since his Latin account of
Richard's 1392 reconciliation with the Londoners is certainly

later than the first draft of the *Confessio*; in the first book of which, as soon as the Prologue is over, he starts with a modest disclaimer:

> I may noght strecche up to the hevene
> Min hand, ne setten al in evene
> This world, which evere is in balance;
> It stant noght in my sufficance
> So grete thinges to compasse,
> Bot I mot lete it overpasse
> And treten upon othre thinges.
> Forthi the stile of my writinges
> Fro this day forth I thenke change
> And speke of thing is noght so strange, . . .
> And that is love. . . .

[I cannot stretch up my hand to heaven or put quite right this world which is always delicately balanced; it is not in my power to achieve such great things, but I must let it pass by, and I must deal with other things. So from this day onwards I intend to change the style of my writings and speak of a matter that is not so unfamiliar, . . . and that is love. *Confessio Amantis*, I. 1 ff.]

It might be thought that the reformer, only ten years off declaring himself old and blind (*senex et cecus*), was mellowing and learning to compromise, that by 1390 it was dangerous to blurt even if you were a bit of a reactionary and blurted in Latin; but in fact his outward behaviour over his great poem took the form of a positive and dangerous political act—having originally called it 'A book for King Richard's sake', adding his delight at meeting him on the Thames and being invited into the royal barge (Prologue, 24 ff.), he in late 1392 or early 1393 rededicated it to Henry of Lancaster, still in apparent favour with the King but already proving his prowess and representing to serious minds the strength and stability that Richard lacked. At the same time, Gower excised the tribute to the King at the very end (VIII. 2985 ff.); he is called 'worthy', one in whom justice has always been found mingled with pity, generosity along with charity; his person displays a king's true qualities, and he is so merciful that he has never sought vengeance cruelly against any of his lieges, whatever fault had been discovered; and thus his position is 'safe, as it certainly ought to be'. We need quote no more of this encomium; it ascribes every due kingly quality to the King, and by 1393 it must have seemed laughably inaccurate. But when it went it took something else with it which we must regret—the farewell to Chaucer; and the motive for this snub is altogether more mysterious. The life records of both poets show something of their contact and even of their friendship; if 'politics' was the issue between them, we know that Chaucer was not of Uncle Gloucester's party and even suffered by its ascendancy, whereas Gower may have turned against the King at this point; if it was religion, we know that Gower was strictly conformist and that (as we shall see later) a tinge of heterodoxy may have adhered to Chaucer; or we may reflect that courts breed envy, and a personal estrangement may have come about. Whatever the cause, the very pretty tribute to Chaucer, spoken by Venus, is a casualty of the revision: pretty, but hardly a piece of solid criticism—Chaucer is Venus's 'disciple and poet', he composed ditties and gay songs in the flower of his youth, and he must compose his testament of love as the crown of his life-work. Unappreciative as this is, the *Confessio* is greyer for its departure.

The form of the poem, and its appeal to stories of high life in various dynasties, allow Gower to explore the subject of kingship and obliquely to offer advice to the dangerous monarch whom he served. For instance, he tells briefly the Story of Codrus, King of Athens (VII. 3183 ff.), who was given the choice of dying in battle or seeing his people discomfited, and chose the former; then he asks, 'Where is there now such another head that would die for the limbs?' And with a choice of vocabulary perilously like the ideal description of Richard in Book VIII, and a sort of *non sequitur*, he wrenches the argument into the need for a king to spare his lieges, to have mercy on his enemies when he might take vengeance, to use victory for the exercise of clemency, and to earn a worthy name by such a reputation. At this point Gower has not long left some abstract pleading for the maintenance of laws by kings; as if with deliberately bald, formulaic simplicity, he writes in good vernacular speech:

> For thing which is of kinges set
> With kinges oghte it noght be let.
> What king of lawe takth no kepe
> Be lawe he mai no regne kepe.
> Do lawe awey, what is a king?
> Wher is the riht of eny thing
> If that ther be no lawe in londe?
> This oghte a king wel understonde,
> As he which is to lawe swore,
> That if the lawe be forbore
> Withouten execucioun,
> It makth a lond torne up so doun,
> Which is unto the king a sclandre.

[Because a thing which is ordained by kings ought not to be hindered by kings. Any king who has no regard for law cannot keep any realm lawfully. If law is done away with, what is a king? Where is the justice of anything if there is no law in the land? A king should fully understand, as being one who is pledged to the law, that if the law is foiled and not executed it turns a land upside down, and that is scandalous for the king. VII. 3071 ff.]

Later in the same book he uses the story of Rehoboam, and his unwise recourse to the advice of young hotheads, to illustrate the need for a king to take good counsel; but the whole seventh book, indeed, is a series of grave theses for the King's attention, on the control of generosity, fidelity to faithful subjects, the curbing of flattery, adherence to absolute justice even at awful personal sacrifice, the exercise of pity, the just war, the preservation of one's subjects as preferable to the destruction of one's enemies, the avoidance of that fleshly lust which has destroyed so many kings, and—perhaps the intended climax—King Lucius's fool, crouched on his stool before the fire and playing with his bauble, who advises his irresolute master that he must not blame his counsellors, since if he were wise he would not have bad ones.

Nor need we wait until Book VII for a serious review of the affairs of state; in the very Prologue of a poem which is to treat of love, this citizen of London, 'the town of New Troy' (l. 37), who had in 1381 tasted something of the sack and riot attendant upon living in Troy, uses five hundred lines to examine the flaws now scandalously apparent in temporal governors, the church, and the commons. Platitudinous as is much of this material, the stuffy nostalgia of the ageing puritan, it has some specific remarks that suggest that Gower had a status of privilege in which he could criticize boldly. All kingdoms are the same in their degeneracy, he says, and 'hevene wot what is to done' [heaven knows what is to be done, l. 141]; the divisions and discord of a realm are seen reflected in external war, of which Gower has a fine unfashionable view—instead of martially speculating on who gets the upper hand, he reflects that in war 'non wot who hath the werre' [no one knows who gets the worst of it, l. 176], and he is writing in character when he depicts the Alexander of Book III as primarily a warmonger. The church gets even more extensive criticism than the secular authorities; not in any Lollard spirit (he hates 'This new sect of Lollardy', l. 349), but in horror at the new pride and simony, the contention and envy that consume the clergy like Etna's fires, the outcome of this at Avignon, the rumours of clerical unchastity, their employment of Sloth as librarian, and their physical participation in wars; in a line of beautiful simplicity, he attributes their lapse to the fact that 'The hevene is ferr, the world is nyh' [The heaven is far, the world is near, l. 261], but he returns to harry them in Book V. 1848 ff., where the timid prelate says 'Life is sweet', Peter's ship almost founders, and cockle is sown in the corn. The commons of the Prologue are dismissed more peremptorily; nothing, really, is said of them save their tendency to break bounds and overflow. Gower's latest critic, J. A. W. Bennett (in *Selections from John Gower*, Oxford, 1968), reminds us that 'the uprising that historians call the Peasants' Revolt . . . was at its bloodiest in Gower's Southwark'; Chaucer saw his friend's suburb in a more cheerful light, as the venue of a pleasant and pious social gathering at the Tabard Inn. But it is time for us to consider whether the civil broils ruffled Chaucer's blandness into expression.

His one clear reference to the dark days of 1381 is at the end of the nun's priest's tale in *The Canterbury Tales*; it is important to observe that the context is light-hearted, scholarly, and assured, with no suggestion of remembered horror. The reference is used simply as a comparison with the noise and bustle of a hamlet as it chases a fox that has snaffled a cockerel:

> So hidous was the noyse, ah, *benedicite*!
> Certes, he Jakke Straw and his meynee
> Ne made never shoutes half so shrille,
> Whan that they wolden any Fleming kille,
> As thilke day was maad upon the fox.

[Oh, bless us! the noise was so frightful that, honestly, Jack Straw and his followers never uttered shouts half so shrill, when they wanted to kill every Fleming, as were uttered that day against the fox. ll. 4583–7]

Nor is the focus on the deep-seated and lasting abuses of the time, the serious and imaginative aspects of the 'industrial relations', but just on an ancillary incident within the whole movement—the isolated massacre of the clever Flemish workers in London by jealous racialists; it is as if Chaucer is concentrating on the sensational story and ignoring the larger issues behind it. But it is probable that when he wrote obliquely he could show far more feeling for the sad times; in the knight's tale, he has already linked with Mars 'the smiler with the knife behind the cloak, the shippon burning with the black smoke, the treason of the murder in the bed' (ll. 1999–2001), and this strong hint of Edward II's death at Berkeley is no more affecting than Saturn's office of 'the drowning in the pale sea, the prison in the dark cell, the strangling and hanging by the throat, the murmur, and the rebellion of peasants' (ll. 2456–9). It has even been suggested that a pun on one of the leading figures in the revolt figures in *Troilus and Criseyde*, IV. 184, when the clamour of the Trojans pleading to have Criseyde exchanged for the prisoner Antenor is likened in its fury to a 'blaze of *straw* set on fire'; and it is significant, as

Robinson shows in his edition, that Chaucer wrenches the mob's demands to the very opposite of what they had been in the accepted histories, and thus makes them much stupider—since the traitor Antenor would be their bane. It has been customary to see an earlier line of the poem, 'Just as our first letter is now an A' (I. 171), as a reference to the more hopeful times that ensued, when Richard married Anne of Bohemia at the beginning of 1382; and with the marginal note *Auctor*, Chaucer in the Oxford scholar's tale obtrudes an attack on the populace for fickleness, as if—say some scholars—contrasting Richard's reception by the Londoners in 1387 with their acceptance of him in 1381.

> 'O stormy peple, unsad and ever untrewe,
>   Ay undiscreet and chaunging as a vane,
> Delyting ever in rumbel that is newe,
>   For lyk the mone ay wexe ye and wane!
>   Ay ful of clapping, dere ynogh a jane!
>   Your doom is fals; your constance yvel preveth;
>   A ful greet fool is he that on yow leveth!'

['O you tempestuous people, unsettled and continually unfaithful, always indiscreet and as changeable as a vane, for ever delighting in any new rumour, because you keep on waxing and waning like the moon! Always full of chatter, pretty dear at a ha'penny! Your judgment is false; your constancy proves to be evil; he who believes in you is a very great fool!' ll. 995–1001]

Whereas Gower sounds choked, and Chaucer reticent, a great number of anonymous writers roundly declared that the age was corrupt, often for their purpose modernizing old tags and lists of abuses: 'uneducated bishop, imprudent king, reckless young man, witless old man, shameless woman' (B.M. MS Harley 913). Or, with all manner of clippings or paddings, they trotted out the old story of the Emperor faced with plague, famine and revolt, who called in four philosophers and received their grave diagnosis; thus an unpublished MS of the late fourteenth century makes them reply as follows:

1. 'Meede in thy lande is domys man.
   Gyle is take for a trewe chapman.
   The grete holt no lawe,
   Nor servauntys kepe noon awe.'
2. 'Wyt in thy lande is tournyd to trechorye,
   Love in lyk wyse to lecchorye,
   The halyday vsed in glotonye,
   And gentris rebuked in velonye.'
3. 'Wyse men of thy land ar forscornyd,
   Wyduys ayenst ther wyl foryornyd.
   The grete men are coveytous & love to be glosed.
   The smale ar bar doun and mys losed.'
4. 'Thy lordys in thy land arn waxe blynde.
   Also kynnysmen to eyther othir been vnkynde.
   Deth is foryete & soone out of mynde,
   And trouthe vnnethe no man may fynde.'

[Bribery in your land is the judge. Guile is accepted as an honest merchant. The great men don't keep to any law, and servants show no respect. . . . Intelligence in your land has turned to treachery, and love in like manner into lechery; the holy day is devoted to gluttony, and nobility is scandalously rebuked. . . . Wise men in your land are despised. Widows are courted against their will. The great men are covetous and love to be flattered. The little men are borne down and wrongly destroyed. . . . Your lords in your land have grown blind. In the same way, kinsmen are unkind to one another. Death is forgotten and soon out of mind, and a man can hardly find anything trustworthy.]

But such generalizations, applicable to any age, are far less compelling than the topical literature of the year 1381, including a prophecy of it and the 'programme' of the chief insurgents. Most medieval prophecies were, demonstrably, composed after the events they prophesied—an altogether efficient way of going about them; but there is reason to suppose that the astonishing unfulfilled one that uses the six faces of the dice (No. 46 in R. H. Robbins, *Historical Poems of the XIVth and XVth Centuries*) is more inspired than the rest, since it never came about. It does its job neatly, and one manuscript obligingly supplies us with marginal clues:

Euermore schalle the ⠒ ⠒ be the best cast on the dyce.
Whan that · beryth vp the ⠒ ⠒ Ynglond schal be as paradice,
And ⠪ and ⠒⠒ set al on oone syde.
Then schal the name of the ⠒ ⠒ spring vonder wyde,
⠶ set aside and ·· clene schent.
Ye schal haue a new king at a new parlement.
⠒ ⠒ schal vp and · schal vndur.
When dede men ryse that schal be moch wondur.
The red rose and the floure-de-lyce the lockes schal vndo.
Yet schal the ⠒ ⠒ ber the pryce, and · schal helpe ther-to.

(I have emended the MS. *vndur* of the penultimate line to *vndo*, for rhyme and sense.)

[The *six* will always be the best throw on the dice. When the *one* supports the *six* England will be like paradise, and *five* and *four* set quite aside. Then the name of the *six* will spread marvellously widely, the *three* will be set aside and the *two* utterly ruined. You will have a new king at a new parliament. The *six* will come up and the *one* will go under. When dead men rise it will be very surprising. The red rose and the fleur-delys will undo the locks. The *six* will still win the prize, and the *one* will help it to happen.]

Whether this could be interpreted without the clues in Trinity College Dublin MS 516 is doubtful; there we learn that the numbers from one to six stand for the king, the *bilingue* (presumably the French-speakers), the traitors, the lords, the churchmen, and the common people, but some dark and riddling statements remain even then.

With the arrival on the scene of John Ball, the mad priest of Kent, a popular literature of revolt sprang up that was epitomized in his persuasive tag

When Adam delved and Eve span,
Who was then the gentleman?

His Blackheath sermon to the rebels, with this specious text, was the crown of a life that had often fallen foul of authority; and the contact of his social preaching with Wyclifite doctrine was one of the arguments that Wyclif's enemies could use. But he had already sent a famous letter to the Essex peasants, in which he quoted—topically, but with no regard for the anti-communist feelings of the author as expressed in B. XX. 271 ff.—the magic name of *Piers Plowman*. He had to speak in a kind of cipher, and even his own identity is masked under a new name, but his former office at one of the York churches of St Mary is mentioned, and Colchester, where we know he had run into trouble:

Iohon Schep, som tyme Seynte Marie prest of ȝork, and now of Colchestre, greteth wel Iohan Nameles, and Iohan þe Mullere, and Iohon Cartere, and biddeþ hem þat þei bee war of gyle in borugh; and stondeþ togidre in Godes name, and biddeþ Peres Plouȝman go to his werk, and chastise wel Hobbe þe Robbere, and takeþ wiþ ȝow Iohan Trewman and alle hiis felawes, and no mo, and loke schappe ȝou to on heued, and no mo.

> Iohan þe Mullere haþ ygrounde smal, smal, smal.
> Þe Kynges Sone of Heuene schal paye for al.
> Be war or ȝe be wo.
> Knoweþ ȝour freend fro ȝour foo.
> Haueþ ynow, and seith 'Hoo!'
> And *do wel* and *bettre*, and fleth synne,
> And sekeþ pees, and hold ȝou þerinne.

And so biddeþ Iohan Trewman and alle his felawes.

[John Shepherd, formerly priest of St Mary's, York, and now of Colchester, sends friendly greetings to John Nameless, and John the Miller, and John Carter, and begs them to beware of treachery among townspeople; stand together in God's name, and ask Piers Plowman to go to his work, and punish Hob the Robber soundly, and take with you John Trueman and all his companions, and no others, and see that you appoint one leader for yourselves, and no others. John the Miller has

I

ground small, small, small. The Son of the King of Heaven
will pay for everything. Beware lest you be in trouble. Know
your friend from your enemy. Have enough, and say 'Whoa!'
And *do well* and *better*, and flee from sin, and seek peace, and
keep yourselves in it. And thus begs John Trueman, and all
his companions. B.M. MS Royal 13. E. ix, fol. 287 r]

Knowing, as we do, the fate of this ill-led rabble, and the ghastly
drawing, hanging and quartering of Ball at St Albans in the same
year, we are bound to feel pity for his simplicity here: the child-
like disguising of names, whereby he becomes Shepherd (= Pas-
tor) and all the participants are called John; the belief that God
is on the side of their ragged battalions; the peasant fear of
townsmen; and the unauthorized and uncomprehending use of
bits of Langland—not only *Piers Plowman*, but the long sections
on *Do Well* and *Do Better*, *Robert the robber* in B. V. 469, and
perhaps even (as Skeat would have us believe) the *sheep* (= shepherd) of the second line of the Prologue and the *Tom True-Tongue*
of B. IV. 17.

Before sending this relatively coherent document, Ball had
addressed 'all manner of men' with encouraging sentiments in a
letter printed by R. H. Robbins (*Historical Poems*, No. 17). In
words akin to the refrain of Chaucer's *Truth*, he urges them to
stand together manfully in the truth, and then goes off into three
little couplets, and a hanging line, on the way the Seven Deadly
Sins are now rampant in the realm; wrath is not mentioned, and
its line may once have rhymed with the last one. But this piety
was no proof against official disapproval of all that he stood for,
and the most eloquent statement on the year's doings is a scornful
attack on the rebels as murderous upstarts; its lines are alternately English and Latin, but the Latin tend to gloss the English,
which can be read independently until almost the very last line,
a little Latin prayer:

> The taxe hath tened vs alle . . .
> The Kyng þerof had small . . .
> Yt had ful hard hansell . . .
> Vengeance nedes most fall . . .

In Kent care began . . .
On rowtes þo rebawdes þey ran . . .
Ffoles þey dred no man . . .
Laddes þey were þere cheveteyns . . .

Laddes lowde they lowght, . . .
The bischop wan þey slowght . . .
Maners down þey drowght . . .
Harmes they dyde ynowght . . .

Iak Strawe made yt stowte, . . .
And seyd al schuld hem lowte . . .
Sadly can they schowte, . . .
Þe wycche were wont to lowte . . .

Hales, þat dowghty knyȝght, . . .
Dolefully he was dyȝght; . . .
There he myȝght not fyght . . .

Savoy semely sette, *heu! funditus igne cadebat.*
Arcan don there þey bett . . .
Deth was ther dewe dett . . .

Oure kyng myght have no rest . . .
To ride he was ful prest . . .
Iak Straw dovn þey cast . . .
God, as Þou may best, *Regem defende, guberna.*

[The tax has ruined us all. The King had little of it. It had a very nasty omen. Vengeance just had to fall. The trouble began in Kent. Those rascals ran in mobs. The fools feared no man. Their chieftains were churls. The churls laughed loudly when they killed the bishop. They pulled down manors. They did plenty of damage. Jack Straw swaggered, and said that everyone would have to reverence them. They who had been accustomed to show reverence were shouting vigorously. That valiant knight Hales was treated dismally; he could not offer fight there. The beautifully built Savoy was, alas! burnt to the ground. They beat down Achan there. Death was their proper due. Our King could take no rest. He was very eager to ride. They threw down Jack Straw. God, as Thou canst best, defend and govern the King. Robbins, *op. cit.*, No. 19]

For a highly partial account, this is surprisingly accurate and detailed, though the Latin has Straw killed at Smithfield, instead of Wat Tyler. The poll tax of 1377, 1379 and 1380–1 is seen as sparking off the revolt, and the King is exonerated from the profits of it. The murders of Archbishop Simon Sudbury, the Chancellor, and of Sir Robert Hales, the Treasurer, are deplored, along with the destruction of manor-houses (and their rolls) and of the Savoy Palace; the King receives some undiluted commendation. The one grudging tribute to the insurgents is the statement that they would not condone looting of riches, which was the crime of Achan at Jericho against the orders of Joshua. A variant manuscript, first printed by T. Wright and J. O. Halliwell in *Reliquiae Antiquae* (London, 1841–3), II. 283, says that 'thus they made their way from Kent to London; that was an evil band. Afterwards they were soon discomfited. Peasants uttered boasts that they must needs be free. Charters were endorsed; they lost their freedom there.'

But whatever one's political views, and however one looked at 1381, it was a sorry time, and never summed up better than by the flinty epigram (often printed, or printed in part, or with the dating mutilated to mean '1391') of which the best version seems to be:

> Man, be war & be no fool.
> Thynk on the ex and on the stool.
> The ex was sharp, the stool was hard,
> The fourthe yeer of King Richard.

[Man, be careful and don't be a fool. Think of the axe and the block. The axe was sharp, the block was hard, in the fourth year of King Richard.]

The aftermath was plague and earthquake in 1382; small wonder that a poet of the Vernon MS composed eighty-eight lugubrious lines on this string of disasters, each stanza ending with the refrain 'a warning to beware'. Of all the minatory marvels, the first cited is the revolt:

> Whon þe comuynes bigan to ryse
> Was non so gret lord, as I gesse,
> Þat þei in herte bigon to gryse
> And leide heore iolyte in presse.

[When the commons began to rise, there were no lords so great, I believe, that they did not begin to be terrified at heart and to put their cheerfulness away in the cupboard. ll. 17–20]

The next is 'when this earth quaked'; again, pride was shaken and 'jollity' forsaken, and they thought of God *while it lasted*, but as soon as it had passed over they grew as evil as they had been before. It made them, for the time being, forget their gold and silver and rush out of their houses, while chambers and chimneys burst, churches and castles were damaged, and pinnacles and steeples crashed to the ground. The poet interprets it all as a warning:

> Þe meuyng of þis eorþe, iwis,
> Þat schulde bi cuynde be ferm & stabele,
> A pure verrey toknyng hit is
> Þat mennes hertes ben chaungable
> And þat to falshed þei ben most able,
> ffor with good feiþ wol we not fare.

[Really, the moving of this earth, which ought by nature to be firm and stable, is an absolutely true sign that men's hearts are changeable and that they are chiefly capable of falsehood, because we are not willing to behave in good faith. ll. 49–54]

The 'three things'—the rising of the commons, the pestilence, and the earthquake—are all tokens of God's vengeance on sin; 'we are so full of sin and sloth that shame has gone over the tops of our heads, and we are lying quite as heavy as lead, entangled in the devil's snare. . . . Many a man would for gain betray his father and mother and all his family. . . . Our money-bag hangs on a rickety nail. . . .' (ll. 67 ff.). Thus here, as so often, the lively interest of material things is sacrificed to the desire to be didactic, and the poem is bloated into generalizations.

We considered above a poem of the type now loosely called 'macaronic', with its lines alternately in English and Latin; in that case the English formed a satisfactory independent poem, but another—assigned on somewhat shaky grounds to 1388—shows the two languages used interdependently and with great rhetorical skill. It was published long ago by T. Wright, in *Political Poems and Songs* (London, 1859), I. 270 ff., and deserves more currency than it has received, though its technical cleverness is not matched by any great wealth of interesting allusions. Its first complaint is of the decay of English manliness, honour and truth, to which have succeeded lechery, sloth and pride. Where once were England's friends, there are now her enemies armed with bow, shield and spear. The fear of God is lacking, and the truth has gone down before whisperers and flatterers. So, 'England, awake now!' The rich are enjoying themselves, and the poor are weary; the church is harmed, and with the general lowering of standards the holy days are given over to sinful pleasures on the part of gentlemen, grooms and boys. The law, whatever experts there may be at Westminster Hall, is grossly maladministered and corrupt, and 'jurors have painted sleeves'. Great damage has been done to the land by usurped power, and 'The King doesn't know everything'. Here there comes another possible suggestion from *Piers Plowman*, the belling of the cat's neck, and a dark joke against Jack (off in remote realms) and Jack Noble (with him), who may stand for Robert de Vere, Earl of Oxford and Duke of Dublin, and for Michael de la Pole, Earl of Suffolk, King's men who were both in lucky exile by 1388. Then the foppish male fashions of Richard's reign are castigated; gallants with empty purses strut around in the new styles, and 'broader than God ever made, their shoulders swell artificially—they are narrow, but they seem broad', because they are not satisfied with God's 'plasmation' of them. They wear wide, high collars, and long spurs on their heels, and their hose are such that they can hardly bend their knees, so that when other men kneel in adoration they stand at their heels for fear of hurting these absurd garments and their long padded toes. The women dress just as extremely, and the poet goes off into a less coherent attack on lovers and drinkers and much else.

The real sufferings of the poor and oppressed could never find expression so long as the abuses of the age were thus funnelled into potted sermons; even the compassion of Langland, who could speak of the woe of women that live in cottages, was perhaps no more constructive than Chaucer's gentle understanding shown at the beginning of his nun's priest's tale, where the poor widow is admittedly oldish, straitly housed, restricted in goods and income, abstemious of necessity in her food, and with a sooty 'bower' (chamber) and 'hall'—these last showing Chaucer's little grin as he compares her cottage with a great castle or manor-house. But the passage continues more hopefully, and with a manly admiration for her regimen; she needed no sauce to help her eat, she was never sick through repletion, she obviated medicine because she had a proper diet and plenty of exercise and a contented mind, she was not prevented from dancing by any gout, and her head was not affected by any apoplexy. Yet it seems as if Chaucer had not the heart to inflict reality upon her; she had three big sows, three cows, a sheep, a yard of eight poultry, and a supply of milk, brown bread, bacon, and the odd egg—and we know that there were a suffering multitude less fortunate than this. The Wyclifite *Piers Plowman's Creed*, once its vitriolic attack on the friars is over and before another graver one begins, interposes a haunting description of Piers as he toils wretchedly at his plough; it is one of the most memorable passages in all Middle English:

> And as y wente be þe waie, wepynge for sorowe,
> I seiȝ a sely man me by opon þe plow hongen.
> His cote was of a cloute þat cary was ycalled.
> His hod was full of holes, and his heer oute,
> Wiþ his knopped schon clouted full þykke.
> His ton toteden out as he þe londe treddede.
> His hosen ouerhongen his hokschynes on eueriche a side,

Al beslombred in fen as he þe plow folwede.
Twey myteynes, as mete, maad all of cloutes;
Þe fyngers weren forwerd, & ful of fen honged.
Þis whit waselede in þe fen almost to þe ancle,
Foure roþeren hym byforn, þat feble were worþen;
Men myȝte reken ich a ryb, so reufull þey weren.
His wijf walked him wiþ, wiþ a longe gode,
In a cutted cote cutted full heyȝe,
Wrapped in a wynwe schete to weren hire fro weders,
Barfote on þe bare ijs, þat þe blod folwede.
And at þe londes ende laye a litell crom-bolle,
And þeron lay a litell childe lapped in cloutes,
And tweyne of tweie ȝeres olde opon anoþer syde.
And alle þey songen o songe, þat sorwe was to heren;
Þey crieden alle o cry, a carefull note.
Þe sely man siȝede sore, & seide, 'Children, beþ stille!'

[And as I went along the road, weeping with sorrow, I saw a simple man near me hanging on the plough. His coat was of a cloth called shoddy. His hood was full of holes, and his hair was sticking out of it, and he had knobbly shoes very thickly patched. His toes peeped out as he trod the earth. His hose hung over his heel-sinews on every side, and were all bedabbled in mud as he followed the plough. Two mittens, to match, were all made of rags; the fingers were worn away, and hung full of mud. This creature was squelching in mud almost to the ankle, with four oxen in front of him that had grown feeble; you could have counted every rib, so hapless were they. His wife was walking with him, with a long goad, in a cutaway coat cut very short, and wrapped in a winnowing-sheet to protect her from storms, barefoot on the bare ice, so that the blood followed her. And at the end of the field lay a little scrapbowl, and in it lay a little child wrapped in rags and two of two years old nearby. And they all sang one song, so that it was misery to hear; they all cried one cry, an anguished tune. The simple man sighed sorely, and said, 'Children, be quiet!' ll. 420–42]

The terrible majesty of this, its alliterative verse so like that of *Piers Plowman* itself, and its *saeva indignatio*, must not blind us to the fact that it can hardly be by Langland himself; although in sheer shape and music it may have been easy to father it on to him, it is clear from the rest of the poem that the writer was something that Langland was not, a Wyclifite. The date, which may be fixed at just after 1393 if the persecution of Walter Brute (l. 657) is white-hot news, fits reasonably with the reshaping of *Piers Plowman* called the C-text, but is still no argument for the authorship of a man who began his great work in 1362.

What immediately follows this passage is a surprise, and what comes later perhaps an anti-climax: the simple man is resolute still, and able to show pity to others, and his first reaction to the author's staring and sighing is to offer him sustenance from his own poor store. But he soon rallies even more toughly, and launches into a sustained onslaught on everything that the friars stand for—those unforgettable babies fade into incidental stage properties; so that, strangely, a franker presentation of hardship, made vocal by one literate agitator, emerges from the song of the Yorkshire partisans of 1392 (first printed by M. H. Hewlett in *The Antiquary*, II, 1880, p. 203). John Berward, junior, of Cottingham near Hull, had his poem publicly proclaimed at Beverley on 21 July 1392, which was a Sunday, and at Hull on the following Sunday; he is neither particularly literate nor expressive, but sings with a kind of impudence the temporary success of the uprising. He records the indignation of the country, especially of the friars and other orders, that 'shrewes' (rascals) have been supported in his district, but affirms that the partisans will go on helping one another in a brotherly way 'both in wrong and right', and maintain their neighbours 'in resistance and battle'. Every man can come and go freely,

> But hething will we suffer non,
> Neither of Hobb nor of Ion,
> With what man he be.

[But we will put up with no mockery from either Bob or John, or whoever it may be. ll. 16–18]

They would be unnatural if they endured any scoundrel's mockery without paying it back double; that is their purpose—that anyone who offends any of them anywhere offends them all. A simple programme, and not surprisingly put over in homely tail-rhyme; whatever the abuses that these blunt men were suffering, their brisk anarchy has little to recommend it. Between such irresponsible violence and the reactionary timidity of Gower, it is in keeping with Langland's nature that he restlessly probes for symptoms and causes of the nation's decay, and lays bare some strange ones; for instance, he holds that it is wrong for lords and ladies to desert the hall, once so delightful a haunt of hospitality and charity, and eat in private rooms (*Piers Plowman* B. X. 94 ff.), and bewails the slovenly education that has set in:

> Gramer, the grounde of al, bigyleth now children.
> For is none of this newe clerkes, who so nymeth hede,
> That can versifye faire no formalich enditen,
> Ne nouȝt on amonge an hundreth that an auctour can construe
> Ne rede a lettre in any langage but in Latyn or in Englissh.

[Grammar, the basis of everything, now foxes children. Because there is no present-day schoolboy, as anyone can see for himself, who can compose verses nicely or write a formal letter, and not one in a hundred who can translate a classical author or read a letter of any language save Latin and English. B. XV. 365 ff.]

His list of some of the caterpillars of the commonwealth (B. II. 57–60)—twelve in four lines—is incisive and particularized: knights, clerics, jurors, summoners, sheriffs, sheriffs' clerks, beadles, bailiffs, business-brokers, purveyors, victuallers, and advocates from the Court of Arches; and this throng is far more convincing than the personified abstractions that next crowd on to his stage.

By 1399, an unknown tail-rhymer was attacking with puns and heraldry the three chief caterpillars, Shakespeare's Bushy, Bagot and Green, in a poem now editorially entitled *On King Richard's Ministers* (T. Wright, *Political Poems and Songs*, Vol. I,

London, 1859, pp. 363 ff.). It proves to be one of the cleverest secular allegories ever composed in English, its parallels neatly maintained and its thin veil of prudence easily penetrable.

> Ther is a busch that is forgrowe;
> Crop hit welle, and hold hit lowe,
>   Or elles hit wolle be wilde.
> The long gras that is so grene,
> Hit most be mowe and raken clene;
>   Forgrowen hit hath the fellde.

[There is a bush that is overgrown; crop it well, and keep it low, or else it will run wild. The long grass that is very green must be mown and raked clean; it has overgrown the field.]

Here, then, are Bushy and Green credibly depicted in a consistent landscape; the 'big bag', Bagot, of the next stanza has a broken bottom and rotten sides, so that no stitch could stay with the next to effect a patch.

> Thorw the busch a swan was sclayn.
> Of that sclawtur fewe wer fayne.
>   Alas, that hit betydde!
> Hit was a eyrer good and able,
> To his lord ryȝt profitable;
>   Hit was a gentel bryde.

[A swan was killed through the bush. Few were glad at that murder. Alas, that it ever happened! It was a good and worthy swan, very advantageous to its lord, and a noble bird.]

This reports, by means of his swan-badge, the mysterious death of the Duke of Gloucester in 1397; the topographically feasible shooting of the swan *through* a bush is especially pretty or lucky, and in the next stanza the long green grass is just as reasonably held responsible for the death of 'a strong steed'—the horse that formed the crest of the Earl of Arundel. This creature is likewise characterized as a prop of the realm; a king who owned such a steed could confidently joust on it. As for the Earl of Warwick, spared but banished, who had a bear in his armorials, he had shown favour to Sir William Bagot and was vilely rewarded for it:

> A bereward fond a rag.
> Of the rag he made a bag.
>> He dude in gode entent.
> Thorwe the bag the bereward is taken;
> Alle his beres han hym forsaken.
>> Thus is the berewarde schent.

[A bear-keeper found a rag. He made a bag out of the rag. He acted well-meaningly. The bear-keeper has been caught by means of the bag; all his bears have deserted him. In this way the bear-keeper is ruined.]

Next, the sons of these three Lords Appellant are considered:

> The swan is ded; his make is woo.
> Her eldest bryd his taken her fro
>> Into an uncod place.
> The stedes colt is ronnon away.
> An eron hath taken hym to his praye.
>> Hit is a wondur casse.

[The swan is dead; his mate is grief-stricken. Her eldest chick is taken from her into an unknown place. The steed's colt has run away. A heron has taken himself off to his prey. It is an amazing circumstance.]

These are the sons and heirs of Gloucester (imprisoned in Ireland), Arundel (safe on the Continent with his uncle, the Archbishop of Canterbury), and Gaunt; and the last is, of course, that Henry of Lancaster who would soon usurp the throne. The bear-keeper's son, we are next told, is 'tender of age, and has been put to marriage'; Richard Beauchamp, Warwick's heir, was in fact seventeen at the time and married to a Berkeley. The poet adds that he is biding his time to lead his 'bears', his father's vassals, as he pleases. Meanwhile, the heron has flown to the North, taking the steed's colt with him (all these are circumstances of 1399), and has been joined by the geese (the Percies) and the peacocks (the

Nevilles). It is the heron's intention to alight on the bush and fall on the green; 'the bag is full of rotten corn, kept so long that it is spoilt', and the peacocks, geese and other birds can be fed on it.

> The busch is bare and waxus sere;
> Hit may no lengur leves bere.
> > Now stont hit in no styde.
> Ywys I con no nodur bote
> But hewe hit downe crop and rote,
> > And to the toun hit lede.
>
> The long gras, that semeth grene,
> Hit is roton alle bydene;
> > Hit is non best mete.
> Til the roton be dynged ouȝt,
> Our lene bestes schul not rouȝt
> > Hur liflode to gete.
>
> The grete bage is so ytoron
> Hit nyl holde neyther mele ne corne;
> > Hong hit up to drye.
> Wen hit is drye, then schalt thou se
> ȝyf hit wil amended be,
> > A beger for to bye.

[The bush is bare and grows withered; it can no longer bear leaves. It cannot stand in any place now. I honestly do not know of any other remedy but to hew it down, root and branch, and cart it off to town. The long grass, which seems green, is in fact all rotten; it is not fit for any animal. Until the rotten part is flailed out, our lean animals must not root to get their sustenance. The big bag is so torn that it will hold neither meal nor corn; hang it up to dry. When it is dry, then you will see whether it can be mended well enough for a beggar to buy it.]

In this exultant mood, the poem ends with a prayer to God to grant such a sight and to let the lean animals, which have been

on the point of disaster, repose just where they please. It is noticeable that no thought is here expended on the King; the poet
obviously based all his hopes on Bolingbroke's treason, and
silently dismissed the unfortunate Richard as the creature of his
creatures.

The sequence of works on domestic history which we have
been following is crowned and concluded by the unfinished poem
of 857 alliterative long lines now called *Mum and the Sothsegger*
(and earlier *Richard the Redeless*). The same puns and heraldic
devices are the means of cloaking its more daring statements,
but the manner and metre are very different from those of the
poem that we have just considered; from its close resemblance to
Piers Plowman, and from the singular fact of its beginning with the
word 'And', it was long customary to regard it as a sequel, a
pendant added in the poet's old age when he had come back west
from London and found himself in Bristol. This is no longer
credited; the poem is in no respect a continuation of Langland's
dream-sequences, but is a piece of straightforward history and
pleading. It is given a setting at the outset of its Prologue, though
nothing is made of this beyond the credibility that it imparts:

And as I passid in my preiere, ther prestis were at messe,
In a blessid borugh that Bristow is named,
In a temple of the Trinite the toune euen amyddis,
That Cristis chirche is cleped amonge the comune peple,
Sodeynly ther sourdid selcouthe thingis.

[And as I was walking along praying, where priests were at
mass, in a blessed borough that is called Bristol, in a church
of the Trinity right in the middle of the town, called Christ
Church among the common people, suddenly some marvellous
news came out. W. W. Skeat ed., 'Richard the Redeless', in
The Vision of William concerning Piers the Plowman, Oxford,
1886 &c., I. 603 ff., ll. 1–5]

There is an unexplained oddity here; Holy Trinity, at the High
Cross of Bristol, is still 'vulgarly' Christ Church, but in this it
is joined by the diocesan cathedral at Dublin, the church now

called Christ Church Newgate (London), Christchurch Priory in Hampshire (once the Holy Trinity, and in a place called Twinham), Christchurch outside Newport (Mon.), and others. The poet's note of this is pedantic in the context, but thereafter there is no lack of incident. The news is that while Richard 'so rich and so noble' is warring in the west against 'the wild Irish' Henry has landed on the east side of England, and the people have risen with him—though their common motive is stated to be no more than 'to right his wrong'. The poet is miserable for Richard, remembering him as Prince of Wales and emphasizing, too, that he is 'our crowned King *until Christ wills it no longer*'; perhaps his presence in Bristol is not unconnected with the King's having embarked there for Ireland. Not knowing what is going to happen, and wondering whether God will give the King grace to amend and be their leader again (or otherwise cause him to hand over the rule to another), he thinks he will compose a 'writ' to persuade the King from misrule and 'refresh his mind', and then fusses and protests for over fifty lines of apology and humility, hoping that any word out of place will be corrected; this fulsome passage alone is so unlike Langland's manner that there can hardly be common authorship, and we know that for all his assurances of loyalty the poet has already heard of the fate of the three caterpillars and of Scrope, Earl of Wiltshire, and records it with relish—there is little doubt that he is totally committed to Henry's party, and though the poem pretends to advise Richard for his own good it could equally be a flattering report presented to Henry on the misdoings of Richard and his counsellors. His long-winded poem has none of the epigrammatic force of *On King Richard's Ministers*, and parts of it are turgid and obscure. The first passus is in most respects a piece of objectionable humbug; the pretence of loyalty and of wishing the King well is so thin and indefensible that it is quickly cast aside, and the fallen man is subjected to a string of insults—the epithets 'redeles' [uncounselled], 'lawless', 'wilful', 'wicked', 'cursed', the abstract nouns 'wiles', 'wrong', 'waste', 'riot', 'covetousness'. But after eight lines of this there is an attempt to substantiate these charges, by the adroit negative method of cataloguing the methods that do *not* inculcate allegiance:

fear, blows, unjust verdicts, debased coinage, plundering of subjects, the self-will and dicing debts of the sovereign, and taxes in
peacetime exacted by means of poleaxes. Against these is set one
shapely and gentle line alliterating on *l*—'Or be ledinge of lawe,
with loue well ytemprid?' [Or is it done by the guidance of the
law, well tempered with love? I. 19] With a feigned simplicity—
he is 'mad' and knows little, and has a 'dull pate'—the poet then
turns on the King's favourites 'who never knew armour or showers
of hail', who regretted their fall but never their sins (a nice show
of muscular Christianity). And then, with greater earnestness, he
pleads with Richard to understand the symbolism of his crowning:

> ȝe come to ȝoure kyngdom er ȝe ȝoureself knewe,
> Crouned with a croune that kyng vnder heuene
> Miȝte not a better haue bouȝte, as I trowe,
> So ffull was it ffilled with vertuous stones,
> With perlis of pris to punnysshe the wrongis,
> With rubies rede the riȝth for to deme . . .

[You came to your kingdom before you yourself were aware,
crowned with a crown filled so full of efficacious stones, valuable pearls to punish wrongs, and red rubies to judge the right,
that I suppose no king under heaven could have bought a better one . . . I. 32 ff.]

—and so on for a dozen richly-encrusted lines. But now the
crown and its power have been plucked away by the wretches
on whom Richard heaped titles of nobility, the 'paragals' or
younger brothers that these upstarts have become. Another
somewhat tedious passage, in which some of Richard's louts are
compared with 'Harlequin's family', ends the passus with flat
upbraiding, but it contains a promise of the harsh puns to come,
with its reference to the '*busshinge* adoun' [pushing down] of the
King's true friends and to the 'false colour' (which will be Green,
always the colour of infidelity).

Passus II is altogether more important, and its editor Skeat
starts his notes on it with the weighty reminder that its opening
passage is all about livery, that badge or uniform or even depen-
dents' allowance granted by lords to their retainers and forbidden

1 Chaucer's poem *Truth* (*see* p. 38) on left, and his description of the Parson on right

2 Tewkesbury Abbey, Glos: chantry chapel of Edward Despenser, with his figure praying in a tabernacle above (*see* p. 94).

3 Cooling Castle, Kent: scroll imitated in copper (*see* p. 82)

British Museum MS Harley 1319, fol. 44

4 Richard II captured (*see* p. 120)

5 St. Gregory's Church, Sudbury, Suffolk: the head of Archbishop Simon Sudbury (*see* p. 111)

British Museum Additional MS 42130 (Luttrell Psalter), fol. 170

6 Ploughing (*see* p. 135)

7 King's Lynn, Norfolk: Greyfriars Tower (*see* p. 109)

British Museum MS Royal 13.E.ix, fol. 287r.

8 John Ball's Letter to the Essex Peasants (*see* p. 129), beginning at the foot of the first column

9 Right wing of the Wilton Diptych: angels with White Hart Badges (*see* p. 145)

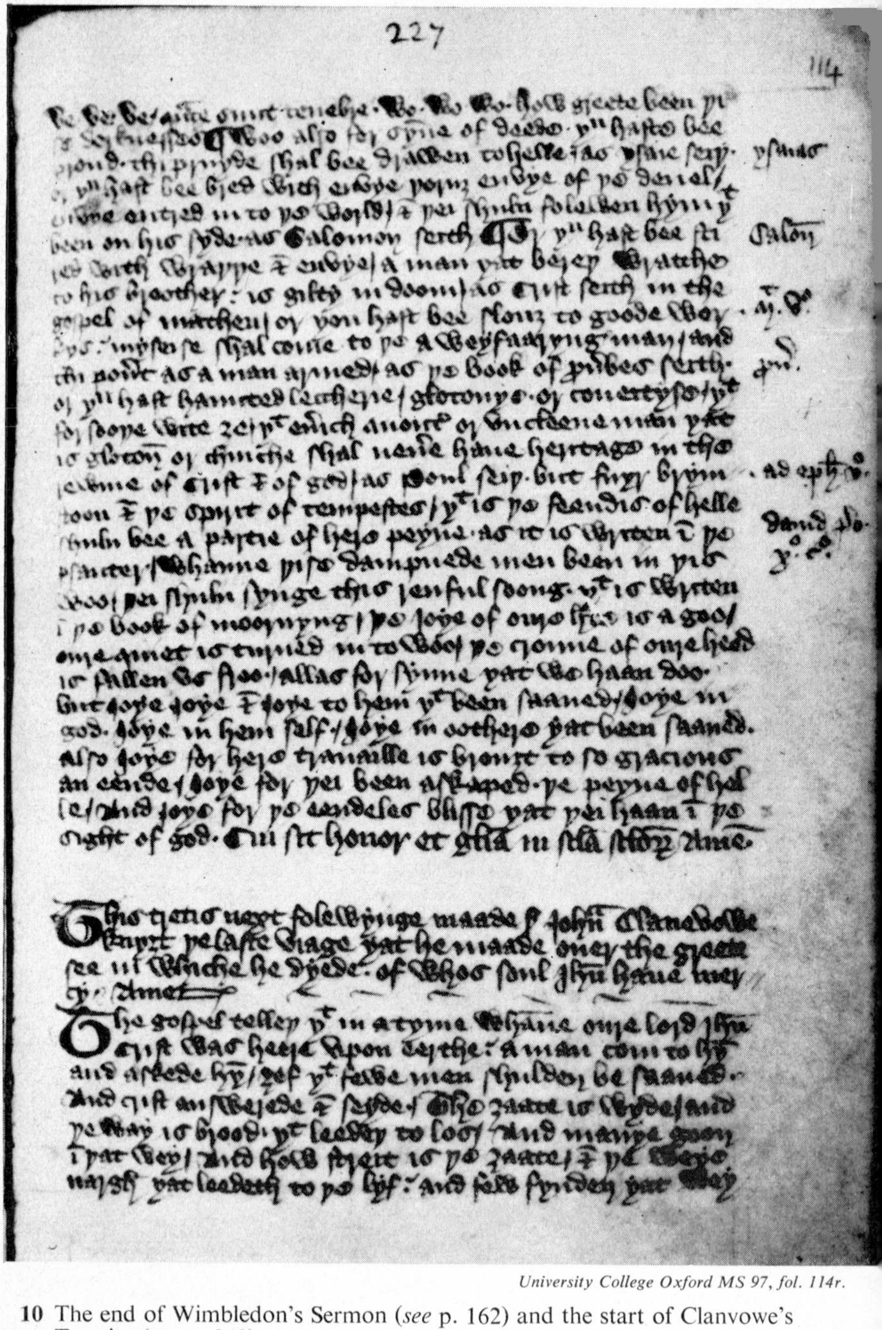
227

114

he be: be caste out into derknesse. Wo, wo, wo, how grete been þe
[illegible] derknesses. Woo also for synne of deede þou hast bee
[illegible]ond. thi pryde shal bee drawen to helle, as ysaie seiþ. ysaie
Or þou hast bee bred with envye þouȝ envye of þe devel/
deeþ entred in to þe world/ & þei shuln folewen hym þat
been on his syde, as Salomon seith. Or þou hast bee stri Salom
[illegible]ed worth wraþþe & envye/ a man þat wraþþeþ
to his brother: is gilty in doom/ as crist seith in the
gospel of matheu/ or þou hast bee slouȝ to goode wer [illegible]
kys: myschef shal come to þe as a weyfaryng man/ and
thi nede as a man armed/ as þe book of proverbes seith. pro.
Or þou hast haunted lecherie/ glotonye, or coveytyse/ þat
for soþe wite ȝe/ þat eche avoutrer or unclene man þat
is gloton or coveitous shal nevere have heritage in the
rewme of crist & of god/ as Poul seiþ. but fier brymston ad ephe.
stoon & þe spirit of tempestes/ þat is þe fendis of helle
shuln bee a partie of here peyne, as it is writen in þe David [illegible]
sautere/ whanne þise dampnede men been in þis
woo/ þei shuln synge this sorweful song, þat is writen
in þe book of mornyng/ þe joye of oure hert is agoo/
oure quer is turned in to woo/ þe crowne of oure heed
is fallen, wo is us/ allas for synne þat we haven doo.
but joye joye & joye to hem þat been saved/ joye in
god. joye in hem self/ joye in oþere þat been saved.
Also joye for here travaille is brouȝt to so gracious
an ende/ joye for þei been ascaped þe peyne of hel
le/ and joye for þe endeles blisse þat þei haven in þe
siȝt of god. Cui sit honor et gloria in secula seculorum Amen.

This tretis next folewynge maade Sr John Clanvowe
knyȝt þe laste viage þat he maade over the grete
see in whiche he dyede. of whos soul Jhesu have mer
cy. Amen.

The gospel telleþ þat in a tyme whanne oure lord Jhesu
crist was heere upon eerthe: a man com to hym
and askede hym/ ȝef þat fewe men shulden be saved.
And crist answerede & seyde/ the ȝate is wyde/ and
þe way is brood þat ledeþ to los/ and manye goon
in þat wey/ and how streit is þe ȝate/ & þe weye
narugh þat ledeth to þe lijf: and fewe fynden þat wey

University College Oxford MS 97, fol. 114r.

10 The end of Wimbledon's Sermon (*see* p. 162) and the start of Clanvowe's Treatise (*see* p. 248)

11 Twentieth-century stained glass in Westbury-on-Trym Church, Bristol (John Wyclif and John Trevisa), and in Norwich Cathedral (Dame Julian) (*see* pp. 221 ff., 18 ff., 209 ff.)

12 Exeter Cathedral: West Front carvings, executed by 1375, unrecorded in English (*see* p. 287)

13 St. Mary Redcliffe, Bristol: bay of the high vault of the North Transept (*see* p. 287)

14 St. Mary Redcliffe, Bristol: model of the above, in aisle roof-boss (*see* p. 287)

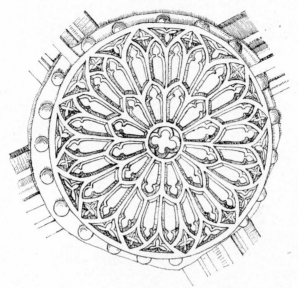

15 St. Mary Redcliffe, Bristol: design for a rose-window, in aisle roof-boss (*see* p. 287)

16 St. Mary Redcliffe, Bristol: maze, in aisle roof-boss (*see* p. 287)

17 Ashwell Church, Herts: graffito of Old St. Paul's, London, on tower wall (*see* p. 286)

18 Gloucester Cathedral: fan-vaulting in cloisters (*see* p. 28‾)

19 Old St. Paul's, London: eastern rose-window, drawn by Wenceslaus Hollar in the mid-seventeenth century (*see* p. 286)

20 Lincoln Cathedral when it had three spires (*see* p. 287)

21 Beverley Minster, Yorks: West Front (*see* p. 287)

22 Chaucer reading *Troilus and Criseyde* to the Court (*see* p. 258)

by an early statute of Henry's reign; by this he hoped to curb the extension of their powers and the maintenance of their feuds. Richard's badge was famous: the kneeling white hart, with its gold collar and chain, that figures so tenderly on the Wilton Diptych in the National Gallery. So his adherents, 'rife' throughout the country, are seen as harts, afraid of 'the eagle that brought help for us' and dashed by thoughts of the moulting season when they would lose their horns; the eagle here is a badge for Bolingbroke, and the half-year during which the herd managed to retain their horns after 'their summer was over' could feasibly extend from Richard's depriving the exiled Bolingbroke of the succession in February 1399 to his surrender to him in August of that year. But insulting a badge is insulting the bestower of it, and we cannot admire the mingled servility and insolence that the poet uses. In another long-winded passage he now stresses the ravages of these harts, with some play (though the approach to it is laboured) on their homophone *hearts*: towny people asserted that 'for one that you hit, you missed ten score homely harts/hearts'; in fact, Richard in his 'dullness' brought it about that the badges 'ruined all the broth, and upset the pot in the middle of the coals'. He has under-valued subjects who loved him loyally before this livery business started, and has supported his abettors, braggers and boasters and takers of bribes; now if only he had favoured 'the good greyhound' (who must be the Earl of Westmorland), a body of faithful re-tainers would have been assured him. It is not surprising that Richard failed the chief deer (his principal subjects), because he was never one to show compassion to the skinny 'rascal' deer whose ribs showed her lack of food; in contrast with this neglect, the eagle (Bolingbroke) protected his nestlings from the winter cold and got them ready for flight to the hill.

> Thus baterid this bred on busshes aboute,
> And gaderid gomes on grene ther as they walkyd,
> That all the schroff and schroup sondrid ffrom other;

[And so this bird battered the bushes all around, and snatched up men as they were walking on the green, so that all the scruff and scrope fell apart. II. 152–154]

K

here are Bushy and Green again, joined by Scrope—there was probably no such word as *schroup*, unless it be a variant of *scrub*, but the poet brightly insinuates that there is. With an inappropriate metaphor, we are told that the bird 'so mixed the metal with the hand-mould that they lost the dearest limbs they had'; this is Henry as the moulder of destiny, and we know that the three malefactors (as the usurper's party held them to be) were executed at Bristol. The eagle is now characterized anew as a falcon, savaging its prey, the ravenous kites, whom he plucked so fiercely as to sever their heads from their necks. 'But the bleary-eyed booby who had stolen his (Treasurer Scrope's) *bag*, where poor men's rags were very often enclosed', annoyed the eagle, who determined to have him seized; this is Bagot again, and we are told that he had led the wretched Scrope through forest and ford—before deserting him and fleeing. He was lucky; after his recapture he was publicly rebuked in Parliament, but there is no record of his judicial murder.

Passus III untidily goes back to events before the current year 1399; we have already encountered them in *On King Richard's Ministers*, and the manner of expressing them heraldically. The poet tells an old Bestiary story of how it is the nature of ageing harts to find poisonous adders and swallow them; when the venom burns them, they rush to water and drink voraciously, whereat their strength is renewed. But *these* harts have attacked the colt, the horse, the swan, and the bear (young Arundel, Arundel, Gloucester, and Warwick); and thus the rejuvenation has not come about. With some more Bestiary lore (this time of the partridge), we are shown the eagle comforting his needy nestlings; they turn from the bushes and briars (can this be Brembre again?—but he had been executed as long ago as 1388) that had hurt them, burnish their breaks and join him, babbling with their bills of how they have been beaten and vexed with twigs for twenty-two years. Their grief for the swan and the horse is compensated for when the eagle releases the bear; this is Henry's recall of Warwick from his banishment. There is even an exact reference to the unnatural behaviour of the turncoat Norfolk when as Earl Marshal he 'clothed the steed'—that is, bandaged the eyes of his own father-in-law, Arundel, for execution; but too often the poet, having found an incident which he can allegorize or elaborate, does it to death, and at this point a particularly heavy-handed passage of over 250 lines sets in, a general attack on the luxuries and corruptions of Richard's court. It is relieved by one or two happy images—'by the law of Lydford' (where they hanged and drew first, and then heard the case), 'measure a mist from morning till evening' (which is wholly Langlandian), 'every realm under the roof of the rainbow', 'to rule like bats, and rest all day', 'moppis, myrrours of synne' [fools, the mirrors of sin], and those 'chyders of Chester' [Chester wranglers], the bodyguard from the King's darling county who behaved so brutally in support of him. The unfinished fourth passus starts more precisely, with specific instances of the King's rapacity: his share in the estates of noble minors such as March and Mowbray, the custom of wool, poundage, and the fifteenth and dime (granted him by Parliament in 1398). Next, ll. 24–30 seem to refer to the tame Parliament of 1397, when Richard got his way in the matter of choosing sheriffs rather than allowing a democratic choice of them; whereafter a verbose passage of variations on this theme begins, and the poem abruptly breaks off. It is a melancholy ending to the literature of a brilliant reign.

4 : Religious Orthodoxy

For most English religious writers and their readers and audiences, the fourteenth century was, until the advent of Wyclif, an age of unswerving faith in the Roman Catholic church; what little speculation and enquiry there was, what exiguous doubt, were couched in Latin, which could accommodate niceties. The versification of scripture, often greatly amplified to the point of prolixity but sometimes illustrated and glossed with a gauche charm, was carried out in immense short-couplet poems so toneless as to suggest a lack of inspiration, though in fact proving no more than a lack of poetical ability; apocryphal stories—the Harrowing of Hell, the subsequent life of the Blessed Virgin— were similarly treated, and so were other accretions that had come to be regarded as dogma. Verse lists of things like the Seven Deadly Sins were popular, and it was no doubt a useful kind of mnemonic to have 'tables' of the Virgin's five joys and the seven sacraments and the five wits (and the Ten Commandments). Lives of saints were many, long, and incredible; excruciating tortures were recounted in detail, forming the most sensational literature of the time, but the ineffective buckets of boiling brass, the routed demons, the spiked wheels that burst asunder, and the quenched baths of fire, all necessitating a final stroke with axe or sword, are wholly monotonous and unconvincing. Most of this material is beneath the notice of our survey; it is often only marginally English literature at all, since its parent Latin or French rules its vocabulary and even takes charge of its idioms at the worst junctures. Much of it has the appearance of a set stint of versifying, and under monastic discipline may well have been so; as soon as a line, or even a whole couplet, is found to fit the not very demanding metre, it is liable to be repeated, and in the duller treatises the reader often gets that cinema feeling of 'this is where we came in'.

Yet this material was the staple of fourteenth-century readers; even granting its privileged survival—since the monastic scriptoria would produce it, the monastic libraries would shelter it, and perhaps sometimes the status of its clerical author would spread it —it becomes clear that it was written and 'published' on a huge scale. To some extent it may be fitting to call it 'popular': the first half of the century saw *The Prick of Conscience*, of all but 10,000 lines; its manuscripts exist in far greater abundance than any other Middle English work, and no amount of luck, or of the kind of privilege I have just mentioned, will account for this proliferation. Nor will its slight inherent attractiveness; its august contemporary, *Cursor Mundi*, handles its 30,000 lines more competently, but only sheer devotion will engage us with it to the end.

These mammoths survived into the second half of the century, but evolved smaller offspring; in any case, to modern readers this later period in religious literature is dominated by one poem only, Langland's alliterative *Piers Plowman*. The other great devotional poem, *Pearl* (by the *Gawain*-poet), is a highly orthodox statement of *consolatio* in deep personal crisis; by its very nature, it can hardly have been 'popular' or influential, and it survives in one meagre manuscript. Ian Bishop's *Pearl* (Oxford: Blackwell, 1969) is an excellent guide along its strange paths. By the end of this book we shall have had reason to visit Langland's idiosyncratic world quite often, though it is easy to attach too much weight to his sharp little vignettes and to forget how totally photographic—all black and white—his technique is. What is least palpable in him is the drift of his religious argument; that it riddles, and meets false informants, and reaches blank walls, and has brief revelations, is obvious, but we need a guide such as Elizabeth Salter's *Piers Plowman* (Oxford: Blackwell, 1962) to convince ourselves that it is any more than an addition to the problems it poses. The intensity of Langland's religious feeling is easily illustrated; but side by side with it, in a wholly different idiom and mood, he is anxious—with a real anxiety—to discuss one-sidedly the politics and machinery of the church he loved. This is not to speak of reform, of some stirring of the church to its very depths, but more nearly a desire to skim from its surface a scum of fairly recent formation, whose chief manifestations were the disgraceful strife between Rome and Avignon, the obtrusion by the pope of foreigners into English livings, and the extortion of annates; its chief ministers were felt to be the friars—but we shall see later that every commentator on the state of religion tends to blame the friars for every abuse. Wyclif and his immediate circle are the only writers to treat coherently the legalistic side of the church's misgovernment, and this to the detriment or ruin of their sermons; but no one speaks clearly in English of those important measures, the Statute of Provisors in 1351 and the Statute of Praemunire in 1353 and subsequently, whereby on the one hand the Pope was restricted in his providing to benefices and on the other the obtaining of papal privileges against royal rights, the appeal to papal courts in a similar flouting of royal jurisdiction, and other uses of foreign courts as a means of asserting papal supremacy, were made the subject even of confiscation and outlawry. We do Langland a great disservice if we stress the upsetting things that he says about the church (and we positively prate if we see him as an early communist, or as a Christian Hesiod in a love-hate relationship with the soil, or as a real warped underdog of the London slums, as some have perversely done); we do him a disservice, indeed, unless we see with Mrs Salter how the search for love through truth gives the poem its 'thematic as opposed to strictly narrative consistency', in which we find our end in our beginning, God or St Truth in our own hearts when the journey is over. There was, by the way, nothing eccentric in the use of a dream-framework (Chaucer was an assiduous dreamer) and nothing unorthodox; to what extent certain types of dream were a divine visitation was a matter of discussion, but on their validity and interpretation scripture held up the august examples of Joseph and Daniel and even Pilate's wife. What *is* odd about Langland's dreaming is the occasional foreknowledge of new characters met on the way, and his presence at all kinds of bypaths in the story such as the doings of Glutton in B. Passus V; but even in this respect he is sometimes very careful to dream authentically, as when in B. Passus XIII he meets 'a maistre—what man he was I neste' [somebody's with a master's degree—I didn't know what kind of man he was]—whereas the C-text, no less credibly, says that he was 'like' a friar. Within the setting of a dream one had licence to witness all kinds of unorthodox things; after all, they were not real, and one's reproduction of them carried no seal of belief or approval. The dreamer is so uninformed that he receives almost all information, misleading or salutary, with the same stolidity, but this does not mean that the reader must match him in stupidity or fail with him at the beginning of B. Passus XVII to recognize that the law given by a 'knight' on Mount Sinai means the Ten Commandments.

In a poem where so much is drab and distressful, there are still many purple passages—not contrived as such, but blazing out when the poet suddenly found a new confidence and even more when his faith exalted him—that we could use to convey his consuming interest in everything to do with religion. One of his bitterest attacks on unworthy churchmen (B. X. 292 ff.) starts in a dry and scholarly way, turns wistful, and suddenly begins to spit:

Gregorie, the grete clerke and the goed Pope,
Of religioun the reule reherseth in his *Morales*,
And seyth it in ensaumple for thei schulde do there-after:
'Whenne fissches failen the flode or the fresche water,
Thei deyen for drouthe whanne thei drie ligge.
Riȝt so,' quod Gregorie, 'religioun roileth,
Sterueth and stynketh, and steleth lordes almesses,
That oute of couent and cloystre coueyten to libbe.'
For if heuene be on this erthe, and ese to any soule,
It is in cloistere or in scole, be many skilles I fynde;
For in cloistre cometh no man to chide ne to fiȝte,
But alle is buxumnesse there and bokes to rede and to lerne.
In scole there is scorne but if a clerke wil lerne,
And grete loue and lykynge, for eche of hem loueth other.
Ac now is religioun a ryder, a rowmer bi stretes,
A leder of louedayes and a londe-bugger,
A priker on a palfray fro manere to manere,
An heep of houndes at his ers, as he a lorde were.
And but if his knaue knele that shal his cuppe brynge,

He loureth on hym and axeth hym who tauȝte hym curteisye.
Litel had lordes to done to ȝyue londe fram her heires
To religious, that haue no reuthe though it reyne on here
                                                              auteres.
In many places ther hij persones ben be hem-self at ese,
Of the pore haue thei no pite, and that is her charite;
Ac thei leten hem as lordes, her londe lith so brode.
Ac there shal come a kyng and confesse ȝow religiouses,
And bete ȝow, as the Bible telleth, for brekynge of ȝowre reule,
And amende monyales, monkes and chanouns,
And putten hem to her penaunce . . .
And barounes with erles beten hem thorough *Beatus Vir*res
                                                              techynge,
That here barnes claymen, and blame ȝow foule . . .
And thanne freres in here freitoure shal fynden a keye
Of Costantynes coffres in which is the catel
That Gregories god-children han yuel dispended.
And thanne shal the Abbot of Abyndoun and alle his issu for
                                                              euere
Haue a knokke of a kynge, and incurable the wounde.

[Gregory, great scholar and good pope, goes through the rule of the religious life in his *Moralia*, and expresses it in a parable so that they should act according to it. 'When fish lack sea or fresh water, they lie on dry land and die of drought. In just the same way,' he goes on, 'the life of religion rollicks around, dies and rots, and steals alms from noblemen, if it longs to live outside the convent and cloister.' Because if heaven is on this earth, and if there is peace for any soul, it is in the cloister or the school, as I can tell for many reasons; because no one enters the cloister to quarrel and fight, but everything is obedience there, and there are books to read and learn. No one is despised in school save the scholar who does not want to learn; and there is great love and pleasure there, because each of them loves the others. But nowadays the life of religion is a horserider, a rover along the streets, an arbiter on settlement-days, a buyer of land, a galloper on a palfrey

from manor to manor, with a pack of hounds at his backside
as if he were a lord. And unless his boy kneels when he has
to bring his cup, he scowls at him and asks him who taught
him his manners. Lords might have found something better
to do than transfer property from their heirs to religious, who
don't care if it rains on their altars. In many places where they
are vicars, cosily by themselves, they have no pity for the
poor—such is their charity. But they behave like lords, so
extensive are their domains. But a king will come and purge
you religious, and scourge you, as the Bible says, for breaking
your rule, and reform nuns, monks, and canons, and put them
to their penance . . . And barons along with earls will attack
them with the teaching of Psalm I, until their children hoot and
upbraid you violently . . . And that is when the friars will
find in their refectory a key to Constantine's coffers, in which
is the wealth that Gregory's god-children have frittered away.
And then the Abbot of Abingdon and all his issue for ever shall
get a knock from a king, and an incurable wound.]

This is a brilliant compromise between the strictest orthodoxy
and eager reform, between cloistered conservatism and a revolutionary ardour that would work through an imperfect king and
his minions; it is *not*, by the way, a prophecy of the Dissolution
of the Monasteries, and the poor Abbot of Abingdon figures
more probably for his alliteration than for the ancient status of
his house. The spirit here is insular, and amid so much that is
idiosyncratic it will be interesting to turn to the larger field of
comparative religion: the term is a little flattering, but it could be
applied to B. XV. 386 ff., where the common medieval gossip
about Mahomet is retold, very picturesquely, and then reapplied
to the state of the clergy:

For Sarasenes han somwhat semynge to owre bileue,
For thei loue and bileue in o persone almiȝty;
And we, lered and lewede, in on God bileueth.
Ac one Makometh, a man, in mysbileue
Brouȝte Sarasenes of Surre, and se in what manere:

This Makometh was a Crystene man, and for he moste nouȝte
                                                    be a pope
Into Surre he souȝte, and thorw his sotil wittes
Daunted a dowue, and day and nyȝte hir fedde.
The corne that she cropped he caste it in his ere,
And if he amonge the people preched or in places come,
Thanne wolde the coluer come to the clerkes ere,
Menynge as after meet; thus Makometh hir enchaunted,
And dide folke thanne falle on knees, for he swore in his
                                                    prechynge
That the coluer that come so come from God of heuene
As messager to Makometh, men forto teche.
And thus thorw wyles of his witte and a whyte dowue
Makometh in mysbileue men and wommen brouȝte,
That lered there and lewed ȝit lyuen on his lawes.
And sitth Owre Saueoure suffred the Sarasenes so bigiled
Thorw a Crystene clerke acursed in his soule—
Ac for drede of the deth I dar nouȝt telle treuthe,
How Englissh clerkes a coluer feden that Coueityse hatte,
And ben manered after Makometh, that no man vseth treuth.

[You see, Saracens have something resembling our faith,
because they love, and believe in, one almighty person; and
we, clergy and laity, believe in one God. But a certain man
called Mahomet led the Saracens of Syria into heresy, and
observe how he did it: This Mahomet was a Christian, and
because he couldn't be pope he made his way into Syria and
by subtle intelligence tamed a dove, and fed her day and night.
He always put in his ear the corn that was her food, and if he
preached among the people or came anywhere, then the dove
would come to this priest's ear, thinking to get food; that was
how he conjured her, and then he made the people fall on their
knees, because he swore in his sermons that the dove that
came in that way came from the God of heaven as a messenger
to Mahomet to instruct men. And thus through his cunning
wiles and a white dove Mahomet led men and women into
heresy, so that the clergy and laity there still live by his

doctrines. And since Our Saviour allowed the Saracens to be so deceived by a Christian priest damned in his soul—but not even under threat of death would I dare to tell the truth of how English priests feed a dove that is called Covetousness, and behave so like Mahomet that no one practises honesty.]

The C-text says that Mahomet was already a cardinal, and then diminishes his dignity by saying that he was like a dud coin from Luxembourg; but the story is already quaint and unsophisticated, so that its re-telling reflects more on medieval credulity than it does on Mahomet's supposed chicanery. The adherents of Islam were to medieval English Christians the objects of obloquy, fit only for slaughter; the Richard Coeur-de-Lion of legend ate Saracens' heads for pork, and it was claimed that their religion centred on idol-worship, so much so that a normal Middle English word for 'idol' was *mawmet*, and it was worshipped with marvellous anachronism by early Roman emperors.

It is clear that in passages like this *about* religion Langland's deep spirituality is hardly engaged at all. They are untranslatable (as my flat prose version makes clear) not because of any incommunicable emotion but because, as befits a dream, he is writing impressionistically, not in any logical sequence; fortunately, our purpose in reading these extensive passages is not to 'translate' them but to know what they meant, to know what they can still mean, and to miss as little of their music as possible. In these moods, admittedly, Langland is prodigal of argument and jest, of self-righteous dignity and town-bred impudence, and of ultimate seriousness, but economical in musical effects. But when he approaches the end (so he says) of his life and the climax of the poem, his love of Christ so slays any lower feelings that he rises to sublimity. The opening of Passus XVIII of the B-text recounts the Crucifixion; this is not done item by scriptural item, but by a series of little personal scenes, involving usually an action or remark, and a reciprocation, by several characters, and as bright as a little 'historiated' initial in a manuscript; nor is scripture adhered to—Faith shouting in his window, the little choristers and the strange old people with their instruments, and the enigmatic galloper on a donkey, have all the immediacy of a Stanley Spencer painting of such a subject, and the telescoping of events from Palm Sunday to Good Friday is effective but could be confusing. The dreamer is as obtuse as ever, and gets a perhaps impatient stare from Faith; but Faith's explanation of the Atonement is pretty elliptical, and it is not surprising that Langland recounts no Maundy, no Agony, no Betrayal. The dramatic nature of the little zigzagging scenes has been ascribed to Langland's having watched mystery plays, but the often clumsy itemizing of the latter is inferior and their verse cannot be uttered in the same voice as Langland's. This passage begins with five lines in which the alliteration is on the poignant, tugging, regretful letters $w \ldots w \ldots w \ldots / r \ldots r \ldots w \ldots r \ldots / y$ (spelt ʒ) $\ldots l \ldots l \ldots l \ldots / w \ldots w \ldots w \ldots w \ldots / l \ldots l \ldots l \ldots$; the l will recur when 'the Lord of life and of light then laid His eyes together', and all through the passage the tuneful scraps of Latin, the baleful repetition in adjacent lines of 'sharp thorns . . . sharp thorn', and new-made phrases like 'poison on a pole', build up to one of the greatest religious narratives in English:

Wolleward and wete-shoed went I forth after,
As a reccheles renke that of no wo reccheth,
And ʒede forth lyke a lorel al my lyf-tyme,
Tyl I wex wery of the worlde and wylned eft to slepe,
And lened me to a lenten, and longe tyme I slepte.
Reste me there, and rutte faste tyl *ramis-palmarum*.
Of gerlis and of *gloria laus* gretly me dremed,
And how *osanna* by orgonye olde folke songen,
And of Crystes passioun and penaunce the peple that ofrauʒte.
One semblable to the Samaritan and somedel to Piers the
                                          Plowman,
Barfote on an asse bakke, botelees cam prykye,
Wythoute spores other spere; spakliche he loked,
As is the kynde of a knyʒte that cometh to be dubbed,
To getem hem gylte spores or galoches ycouped.
Thanne was Faith in a fenestre, and cryde 'A! fili David!',
As doth an heraude of armes whan auntrous cometh to iustes.

Olde Iuwes of Ierusalem for ioye thei songen: *Benedictus qui*
                                        venit in nomine Domini.
Thanne I frayned at Faith what al that fare bemente,
And who sholde iouste in Iherusalem. 'Iesus,' he seyde,
'And fecche that the fende claymeth, Piers fruit the Plowman.'
'Is Piers in this place?', quod I, and he preynte on me:
'This Iesus of his gentrice wole iuste in Piers armes,
In his helme and in his haberioun, *humana natura*;
That Cryst be nouȝt biknowe here for *consummatus deus*,
In Piers paltok the Plowman this priker shal ryde,
For no dynte shal hym dere as *in deitate patris*.'
'Who shal iuste with Iesus?', quod I, 'Iuwes or scribes?'
'Nay,' quod he, 'the foule fende, and False-dome and Deth.
Deth seith he shal fordo and adown brynge
Al that lyueth or loketh in londe or in watere.
Lyf seyth that he likth, and leyth his lif to wedde
That, for al that Deth can do, within thre dayes
To walke and fecche fro the fende Piers fruite the Plowman,
And legge it there hym lyketh, and Lucifer bynde,
And forbete and adown brynge bale and deth for euere: *O*
                                        mors, ero mors tua!'
Thanne cam Pilatus with moche peple, *sedens pro tribunali*,
To se how doughtilich Deth sholde do, and deme her botheres
                                        riȝte.
The Iuwes and the iustice aȝeine Iesu thei were,
And al her courte on hym cryde '*Crucifige!*' sharpe.
Tho put hym forth a piloure bifor Pilat, and seyde,
'This Iesus of owre Iewes temple iaped and dispised,
To fordone it on a day and in thre dayes after
Edefye it eft newe (here he stant that seyde it)
And ȝit maken it as moche in al manere poyntes,
Both as longe and as large bi loft and by grounde.'
'*Crucifige!*', quod a cacchepolle, 'I warante hym a wicche!'
'*Tolle, tolle!*', quod an other, and toke of kene thornes,
And bigan of kene thorne a gerelande to make,
And sette it sore on his hed, and seyde in envye,
'Aue, rabby!', quod that ribaude, and threw redes at hym,

Nailled hym with thre nailles naked on the rode,
And poysoun on a pole thei put vp to his lippes,
And bede hym drynke his deth-yuel; his dayes were ydone.
'And ȝif that thow sotil be, help now thiseluen.
If thow be Cryst, and kynges sone, come downe of the rode;
Thanne shul we leue that Lyf the loueth, and wil nouȝt lete the
                                                                deye!'
'*Consummatum* est,' quod Cryst, and comsed forto swowe
Pitousliche and pale, as a prisoun that deyeth;
The lorde of lyf and of liȝte tho leyed his eyen togideres.
The daye for drede withdrowe, and derke bicam the sonne.
The wal wagged and clef, and al the worlde quaued.
Ded men for that dyne come out of depe graues,
And tolde whi that tempest so longe tyme dured.
'For a bitter bataille,' the ded bodye sayde;
'Lyf and Deth in this derknesse her one fordoth her other.
Shal no wiȝte wite witterly who shal haue the maystrye
Er Sondey aboute sonnerysynge,' and sank with that til erthe.
Some seyde that he was Goddes sone that so faire deyde,
And some saide he was a wicche: 'Good is that we assaye
Where he be ded or nouȝte ded, doun er he be taken.'

[I set out once again with wool next to my skin and wet feet, like a careless man who doesn't bother about hardship, and went on all through my life like a vagabond, until I grew weary of the world and longed to sleep again, and lolled around until Lent, and slept for a long time. I took my rest there, and snored hard until Palm Sunday, and had a long dream of children and of 'Glory, Laud', and how old people were singing 'Hosanna' to instruments of music, and of Christ's Passion, and of the penance which extended to the people. A man resembling the Samaritan, and something like Piers Plowman, came riding along barefoot on an ass's back, bootless, without spurs or spear; he looked lusty, as is the nature of a knight coming to be dubbed and to receive his gilt spurs or cut-away shoes. Then Faith, standing in a window, shouted 'Ah! Son of David!', as does a herald of arms when doughty knights come to the tournament. The old Jews of Jerusalem sang for joy, 'Blessed is He that cometh in the name of the Lord.' Then I asked Faith what all that stir meant, and who was going to joust in Jerusalem. 'Jesus,' he said, 'and He is going to win back what the Devil claims, Piers Plowman's fruit.' 'Is Piers in this place?' I said, and he looked hard at me: 'This Jesus, out of chivalry, is going to joust in Piers's coat of arms, his helmet and his mail, Human Nature. This horseman will ride in Piers Plowman's doublet, so that Christ be not recognized here as Almighty God. Because no stroke can hurt Him in His Father's Godhead.' 'Who is going to joust with Jesus?' I said, 'Jews or scribes?' 'Neither,' he said, '—the foul fiend, and Falsehood, and Death. Death says he is going to destroy and lay low all things that have life or sense on land or in water. Life says that he lies, and lays His own life in pledge that, for all Death can do, within three days He will come and get from the fiend Piers Plowman's fruit, carry it where he pleases, and bind Lucifer, and beat down and vanquish Sorrow and Death for ever: O Death, I will be your Death.' Then Pilate came with a great crowd, and sat in the judgment-seat, to see how valiantly Death would behave and to judge the right of the two of them. The Jews and the judge were against Jesus, and the whole of their court cried out shrilly against him, 'Crucify!' Then a robber pushed forward before Pilate and said, 'This Jesus mocked and despised our Jews' temple, saying that he would destroy it in a day and three days after rebuild it again—that's the man who said it, standing here—and further, make it as big in every kind of detail, as long and as wide, vertically and horizontally.' 'Crucify!' shouted an officer, 'I swear he's a sorcerer!' 'Take him away, take him away!' said another, and took some sharp thorns, and began to make a garland out of sharp thorn, and rammed it on His head, and said maliciously, 'Hail, Master!'—that's what that villain said, and thrust reeds at Him and nailed Him naked on the cross with three nails; they put poison on a pole up to His lips, and told him to drink His death-draught; His days were done. 'And if you are clever, help yourself now. If you are Christ, and a king's son, come down from the cross. Then we shall believe that Life loves you and won't let you die!' 'It is finished,' said Christ, and began to swoon, fearfully pale, like a dying prisoner; the Lord of life and of light then laid His eyes together. The daylight fled in fear, and the sun became dark. The wall tottered and split, and all the world quaked. At that noise, dead men came out of deep graves, and explained why that storm lasted for such a long time. 'Because of a bitter battle,' said one of the dead bodies; 'Life and Death are destroying each other in this darkness. No one will know for certain before Sunday, about daybreak, who is going to prevail'—and with these words he sank into the earth. Some said that He Who had died so nobly was God's Son, and some said He was a wizard: 'It is a good idea for us to check whether he's dead or not, before he's taken down.']

A generous fifty pages of Mrs Salter's book will help us to appreciate the extraordinary art of this poetry, which rises to its heights when the wilderness is past and discoveries have been made about the nature of love; one other scene, just 'made' for Langland's handling, may be quoted from B. XIX. 152 ff., where the eyes of two very simple and direct individuals are opened. Even here, the choice of details is capricious; we are not told that Thomas had doubted before the little demonstration to clear his doubts, and a whole anti-feminist line is devoted, at a highly devotional moment, to the idea that women can't keep secrets. But observe in these nineteen lines the brilliantly controlled elements of narrative, drama, homily, and vision, the sheer entertainment value of this old story newly thought out; there has been no space in this chapter to follow the poet's spiritual search in detail or even in outline, but enough has perhaps been said to suggest that the effort is rewarding and that the fifty-odd manuscripts surviving of it reflect how much it meant to the last medieval centuries:

Ac Marie Magdaleyne mette Hym bi the wey,
Goynge toward Galile in godhed and manhed,

And lyues and lokynge; and she aloude cryde,
In eche a compaignye there she cam, '*Christus resurgens!*'
Thus cam it out that Cryst ouercam, rekevered and lyued;
For that that wommen witeth may nouȝte wel be conseille!
Peter perceyued al this, and pursued after,
Both Iames and Iohan, Iesu for to seke,
Tadde and ten mo, with Thomas of Ynde.
And as alle thise wise wyes weren togideres,
In an hous al bishette, and her dore ybarred,
Cryst cam in—and al closed bothe dore and ȝates—
To Peter and to His aposteles, and seyde '*Pax vobis!*',
And toke Thomas by the hande and tauȝte hym to grope,
And fele with his fyngres His flesshelich herte.
Thomas touched it and with his tonge seyde,
    '*Deus meus et Dominus meus!*
Thow art my Lorde, I bileue, God, Lord Iesu!
Thow deydest and deth tholedest, and deme shalt vs alle,
And now art lyuynge and lokynge, and laste shalt euere!'

[But Mary Magdalen met Him on His way to Galilee, alive
as God and man, and she cried aloud in every group she
reached, 'Christ is risen!' That was how it became known that
Christ had conquered, recovered, and lived; because whatever
women know can't well be a secret! Peter heard all this, and
hastened after, along with James and John, looking for Jesus,
followed by Thaddeus and ten others, including Thomas of
India. And when all these wise men were together, quite shut
up in a house with their door barred, Christ came in—both
door and gates being firmly closed—to Peter and His apostles,
and said, 'Peace be unto you!', and took Thomas by the hand
and told him to touch Him and feel with his fingers the flesh
of His heart. Thomas touched it and said aloud, 'My God and
my Lord! I believe that You are my Lord and God, Lord
Jesus! You died and suffered death, and You will judge us all,
and now You are alive and have Your faculties, and You will
endure for ever!']

Sermons

All the time, despite the cruel toll of clergy taken by the Black Death, the good parsons continued their ministrations and their preaching; the pulpit remained a force, and could set a standard of English eloquence which must have played its part in the redemption of the language. Even the simplest sermons could well press into service the 'visual aids' in which medieval churches abounded: the big wall-paintings of St Christopher, of the other 'Holy Helpers', and of the Works of Mercy; the mysterious 'Christ of the Trades' and other more properly scriptural scenes; most compelling of all, the Crucifixus on the rood-screen, with His mother and St John on either side, the constant reminder for all the east-facing congregation that the true Christian desists from sin out of love, and not out of fear of hell or ambition for heaven. Some sermons gained more than a local fame, and it will be useful to consider one of these, securely dated, and another which had no vogue but of whose origin we know a little. The sermon of Thomas Wimbledon, nearly 1,200 manuscript lines, was composed in 1387 and delivered 'at two tymes' [twice, or more probably in its two parts] at St Paul's Cross in 1388; it still exists in at least fifteen manuscripts, and even found a new audience in Elizabethan times and beyond, being printed at least seventeen times by 1738. Such currency suggests real merit, and an analysis shows what care went into its composition. (I am grateful to my friend and former pupil Mr T. L. Burton for details of this sermon, and for the diplomatic transcript of the unedited MS on which my re-punctuated excerpts are based.)

Broadly, you could preach in three ways in our Middle Ages: first, by straight expounding of the scriptures, keeping to the regular order of the text, as Christ and early Fathers such as St Augustine and St Bernard had done; secondly, *per divisiones*, which was also called 'glosing', where you brought into play your logic and even your pedantry, and your skill in balancing the four levels of interpretation of Scripture—a method made fashionable by the friars and associated with the schools of the universities; thirdly, by such a goodly anecdote as the pardoner uses in *The Canterbury Tales*. Wimbledon's elaborate and highly-wrought sermon is of the second kind, with its theme or text ('Give an account of your stewardship', *St Luke* xvi. 2), its introduction, its carefully enumerated division and sub-division of the theme, and its conclusion. From the start it is clear that there is going to be a great neatness and symmetry; 'clearing the ground' in the introduction begins with a version of the Parable of the Vineyard, explains that the householder is Christ and that the hours of the day are both the scriptural epochs and the periods of man's life, and advances to show that three estates are needed for the care of that vine which is the Church: priests to cut away the void branches of sin, knights to defend the land and maintain its law, labourers to till and sweat. Before leaving this introduction Wimbledon shows how the absence of these services will destroy the vineyard, how men are interdependent, how those who slack and fail will miss the heavenly penny, how honest work will be rewarded: in fact (back to the text), 'Give an account of your stewardship'.

The division of the theme, which now starts, has a practical basis: we shall have to answer this demand, and to whichever estate we belong there will be three questions to deal with: how and why did you undertake your office, how have you discharged it and supervised those under you, and how have you lived and given example? With great skill and minuteness, these questions are searchingly applied to hypothetical members of the three estates, and we see priests who took office by pulling strings, who discharged their duties towards their flock like wolves and spent their wages on hunting and lechery, and who lived shamelessly; knights are no more kindly handled, and ordinary lay Christians (who are subjected only to the first question, with 'office' varied into 'worldly goods') are warned against practising extortion, theft, usury, and cheating. The first part of the sermon develops at this point into a discussion of Covetousness and Avarice as they apply to the three estates, and as attended by other sins in all their futility and their doomed pride of life. Now comes the second part, again in a tripartite arrangement, because the pattern is of who will call man to his first and final judgments, who will be the judge, and what rewards will be variously given. The summoners again are three: sickness, old age, death, with a brilliant double use of each, since the final judgment will have as its signs the sickness of the world (especially the cooling of man's love of God), the decrepitude of the world (witnessed by the various testimonies of those who predicted its term), and the death of the world in its end (as the Apocalypse explains). God is the Judge; this part, at least, is brief and plain. The rewards begin, in characteristic medieval manner, with the punishments—of pagans, Jews, lapsed Christians, and then the more conventional sinners; a brief triumph-song of the saved ends the whole. Any modern lover of sermons may well form the impression that this is able and salutary preaching; and it must be emphasized that the statements are not just presented in an arid and numerical way, as must appear from a summary, but with illustrative *exempla* (of Rehoboam and Susanna, Lot and Tobit, Judas and Jezebel, and many others), the powerful testimony of the authorities, picturesque *genre* scenes, and many exciting phrases. The unpublished University College, Oxford, MS 97 will afford many examples of this power and grace.

With enumeration—perhaps even with pulpit-thumping—easily goes alliteration, and it is present (in a close string of three *h*s and then two emphatic *d*s) on the very first folio: 'To spiritual vndirstoondyng þys housholdere is Oure Lord Ihesu Crist, Þat is heed of houshoold of hooly chirche & thus clepeth men in diuerse houres of þe day.' [In a spiritual sense this householder is Our Lord Jesus Christ, Who is head of the household of holy church and thus calls men at different hours of the day. fol. 101 r]. The same kind of balance is seen in 'What hath pruyde profited to vs now, or þe booke of oure richesses what hath it brouȝt to vs?' [What has pride profited us now, or what has the book of our riches brought us? fol. 107 v]—again with a thump on the closing *b*s. Or the sentiment will be enacted as it was so beautifully in the nature-poetry of *Gawain*: 'We haan been maade weery in þe wey of wykkednesse and of lost, and we han goon harde weyes . . . In oure wikkednesse we been wasted awey' [We have been made weary in the path of wickedness and of desire, and we have travelled hard paths . . . In our wickedness we have wasted away.

fol. 107 v]—where the *w* and the *l* convey regret and lassitude. Even the needful repetitions are subtly varied; yet the theme must recur in its different guises, and the recognition of its chime gives the hearer a thrill of aesthetic pleasure or of horror.

The asides (they are made to appear so, but are in fact essentials) divert the listener's mind while concentrating it, and contain lively details: 'in tilyenge of þe material vyne there been diuerse labourers, for summe kutten awey the voyde braunches, summe maaken forkes and rayles to beren vp the vyne, and summe diggen awey the oolde eerthe from the roote and leggen there fattere.' [there are different labourers for tilling the material vine, because some cut away the empty branches, some make forks and bars to support the vine, and some dig away the old earth from the root and put manure there. fol. 101 r] A sensible comment on medieval economy shows how a normal man cannot do all the processes of rearing, shearing and slaughtering, or of growing and baking: 'It is neede þat summe been acre men, & summe bakeris, & summe makeris of clooth, and summe marchauntes to fecche þat þat oo lond fauteth from a noother there it is plente.' [It is necessary for some to be husbandmen, and some bakers, and some clothmakers, and some merchants, to bring what one country lacks from another where it is plentiful. fol. 101 v] What needs a warning is written harshly, with a call on uncompromising monosyllables of Anglo-Saxon which sound very different from St Augustine's original: 'The cley of Egipt was touȝ and stynkyng and medled with bloode; þe sclattes weeren harde to been vndoon, for þei weeren baake with þe fuyr of coueityse and with þe leiȝe of lustes.' [The clay of Egypt was tough and stinking and mingled with blood; the tiles were hard to put back to their first form, because they were baked with the fire of covetousness and with the flame of desires. fol. 104 r] Indeed, the Anglo-Saxonism is everywhere striking, and there are whole sentences—even taken from the Bible—where every word is native: 'My leeste fynger is grettere þan my fadirs rygge' [My smallest finger is bigger than my father's back. fol. 105 r]; Socrates, asked 'why he leiȝede, . . . seyde, "For I see a greet þeef leede a litel þeef to hongyng" ' [why he laughed, . . . said 'Because I see a big thief leading a little thief to the gallows.' fol. 105 v] Or the appeal, even when French words are admitted, will have the same dreadful simplicity: 'Kynde maaketh noo difference bitwyn poore & riche in comyng hedir, neither in goyng hennes' [Nature makes no difference between poor and rich in coming here, or in going from here. fol. 107 v]; let the rich and poor lie a little while in their graves, and then open and look at them—and the only distinction will be that more clothes rot with the rich than with the poor. There is a grim picture of old age: 'He seeþ his heed hooren, his bak crookeþ, his breeth stynkeþ, his teeþ falleþ, hise eyen derkeþ, his visage ryueleþ, his eerys wexen heuy to heeren' [He sees his head grown grey, his back becomes crooked, his breath stinks, his teeth fall, his eyes darken, his face wrinkles, his ears grow dull at hearing. fol. 109 v), and the cumulative effect of such catalogues is very impressive, though no more memorable than the quiet touch of 'a candele newe queynt þat stynketh al þe house instede of a liȝt lanterne, . . . a smoke þat blindeth mennes eyen in place of cleer fuyr' [a candle just quenched which stinks out the whole house instead of a bright lantern, . . . a smoke that blinds men's eyes in place of a clear fire. fol. 104 v], where Wimbledon has sufficient artistry to vary his vocabulary with the English *stede* and the French *place*.

The other sermon which I want to consider is equally orthodox but on a lower intellectual plane; a friar's sermon, with an appeal to ordinary men by little stories and bright illustrations. (I am grateful to my friend and former pupil Miss Nicolette Scallon for details of this sermon, and for the diplomatic transcript of the inedited MS on which my re-punctuated excerpts are based.) It occurs solely in the manuscript we have just used for Wimbledon's more famous masterpiece, University College, Oxford, MS 97, and though it can be no more positively dated than late in the fourteenth century, its author is known, and it has a very unusual provenance for a Middle English work—Wales. John Gregory was an Austin Friar of Newport, Monmouthshire, a house now swept away (though it left its name in two streets adjoining); he uses the almost commonplace authorities of our medieval sermons —SS. Augustine, Jerome, and Bernard, numerous passages from the whole range of the Bible, and even the pagan Pliny the Elder—, but in addition he quotes the encyclopaedist Bartholomew the Englishman. Again we have the numerical balance, the development and illustration of the theme, the closing cadences of confident joy; this time the text quickly lends itself to material illustration, since it is 'By His own blood he entered in', and Gregory at once adduces the three-fold parallels of the dry tree made fruitful by blood, sick bodies healed by it, and walls strengthened by its being mixed with the mortar. Even the tree can signify man; did not St Mark write 'I saw men walking like trees'? And a man grows dry when he sins, whereat the 'humour' of grace is withdrawn from him; but the roots can be watered by the hot blood of Christ if we meditate devoutly, and then the tree will bear good fruit. An absurd story follows, and a piece of homoeopathy:

> We redyn of Constantyne þe Emperour, whan he was meselle hit was conselde hym þat he shulde haue a bathe of childes blode to hele hym of his sekenesse. Þere is a certeyn sekenesse which is ycleped þe sengles, and hit is a perelous sekenesse; but þe best medicyne þerto is for to take þe blode of a nother whiche þat hath yhade þe same sekenesse, and anoynt hym with hys blode, and þus he may be helyd.

> [We read of the Emperor Constantine that when he was a leper it was advised him that he should have a bath of child's blood to heal himself of his sickness. There is a certain sickness which is called shingles, and it is a dangerous sickness; but the best remedy for it is to take the blood of another who has had the same sickness, and anoint him with his blood, and thus he can be cured. fol. 162 v]

The proper adornments of persuasive prose are rarer here than in Wimbledon's work, but there are some scraps of alliteration such as 'Oure deth He deynge destrued' [He, dying, destroyed our death; fol. 163 r], where the effect may have been suggested partly by the *mortem . . . moriendo* of the Latin original. Too slavish translation of the many sources is responsible for some wrenched syntax, as when 'The furst mescheue was from þe syȝt of God a shameful outputtynge, the secunde vnabelyd to alle meritory dedys worchynge.' [The first disaster was a shameful expulsion from the sight of God, the second prevented the doing of all meritorious deeds. fol. 163 v] The repeated figure of blood seems to obsess Gregory, but when he reaches a new subject he can write with greater gusto. Pliny, he tells us,

> telleth of two propretes of þe Elephant. Þe furst proprete is þis, þat þe Elephant is wonder colde of kynde, & because þerof he nys nouȝt herty to fiȝt in baytale (a mere bad spelling for *batayle*), but be sight of blode he is made herty. Þe secunde proprete is this; amonge alle þe vnresonable bestes þat þer beth he is most of wytte and of knowynge & beste wele ben ytaght to worsshipp a kynge. Gastely be þis Elephant is vnderstond man, whiche þat be reson shulde worsship a kynge; þis kynge is kynge of alle kynges and lord of alle lordes.

> [tells of two characteristics of the Elephant. The first characteristic is this, that the Elephant is marvellously cold by nature, and because of this he is not eager to fight in battle, but is made eager by the sight of blood. The second characteristic is this; among all the unreasoning animals that there are, he is the greatest in understanding and knowledge, and a beast that can easily be taught to honour a king. Spiritually by this Elephant is understood man, who should by reason honour a king; this king is King of all kings and Lord of all lords. fol. 165 v]

The impact of these pieces of natural history on a lay audience must have been strong and memorable, and not surprisingly Gregory follows up this easy success with some loud pleading to them to shun the fires of hell. But he soon returns to the Elephant, since in I Maccabees vi. 34 'the king's servants showed the elephants the blood of the grape and of the blackberry to urge them on into the battle.' Some of the conceits are stranger even than all this: just as Joseph's father loved him and gave him a multi-coloured coat down to his heels, even so God loved man, His youngest child, so much that He gave him a similar all-embracing coat—the passion of Christ; it was white, blue, red, and black—white for His virginity and His virgin mother, blue for His beating and scourging, red with His own blood, black with His congealed and cooled blood—, and it was down to the heels because no part of His body escaped injury. The oddest and most protracted of the illustrations is the story of the lord (God) who had the loveliest possible daughter (man's soul), and loved her beyond every earthly thing, but a certain person (the devil) came and wooed her, and she went away with him for a long time (Adam's five thousand years out of Paradise). But a certain mediator (Christ) who loved the girl and her father reconciled them, and the daughter was received back and married (by baptism in the font) to the worthy knight who had interceded. At her wedding she received royal gifts; her father gave her a coat down to her heels (Christ's passion) suitably inscribed; and four inscribed rings (the two wounds in Christ's hands, and the two in His feet), and her husband gave her an inscribed seal (the wound in His side). With a final touch of that over-exactness, that too neat double meaning, which now makes its strongest appeal to the intellect only, Gregory points out that the wound in Christ's heart was shaped like a bishop's seal; when it was opened, Hell's gates closed and the gates of paradise were flung wide, which is why St Bernard says 'The blood of Christ is the key of paradise.'

Religious Lyrics

There survive from the latter half of the fourteenth century a fair body of religious lyrics, almost none of them ascribable to a named poet, but often so grouped in metre and manner as to suggest common authorship or a 'school' of writers; the manner, for instance, of the hermit Richard Rolle, who died in 1349, was much imitated. The grievous casualty rate in so many classes of Middle English literature may suggest that we have lost much in this field, too; but the occurrence of some of the twenty-eight lyrics of MS Bodley Vernon Eng. Poet. a. 1 variously in its 'echo' MS British Museum Additional 22283 (Simeon) and in the Garrett MS at Princeton, MS Bodley Ashmole 343, MS British Museum Cotton Caligula A. ii, MS British Museum Sloane 2593, MS Trinity College Cambridge 1450, MS Balliol College Oxford 354, MS Advocates Library Edinburgh 19. 3. 1, and MS National

Library of Wales Peniarth 395 (Art 4), seems to require a wholly different interpretation, as if these minor collections had little to draw on save the more important Vernon series, and as if the age was making do with comparatively few vernacular English lyrics to help with its devotions. It was also an age of anthologists, when a pious eclectic, with no thought of his own repute, would gather the best of other men's flowers that he could cull; thus of the six groups distinguished by Carleton Brown in his beautiful *Religious Lyrics of the XIVth Century* (Oxford, 1924; revised by G. V. Smithers, 1957) two are the collections of John Sheppey, Bishop of Rochester from 1353 to 1360, and the Franciscan friar John Grimestone, active in 1372.

In general, the poets use various arrangements of three-stress and four-stress lines, sometimes in artful rhyme-schemes that lead to curious statements or droll words; alliteration is very common, especially in the Rolle-type verses and (oddly for a Southern provenance) the Vernon series. The least interesting and personal, though not necessarily the least dexterous, are the mere paraphrases of hymns or of parts of the liturgy; the *Veni Creator*, the *Ave Maris Stella*, the *Jesu Dulcis Memoria*, are little less singable in these translations than their originals. Very proper, too, but dry or devoid of all feeling save wrath, are those *memento mori* lyrics which had always been popular; they often took as their butt the lovely (and perhaps culpably proud) lady in her chamber in her tower, and went beyond speculation to certainty as to what would become of her golden hair and her white throat, one day that to her would be no day. The most savage in our period is general:

> Wrecche mon, wy artou proud,
>   Þat art of herth imaked?
> Hydyr ne browtestou no schroud,
>   Bot pore þou come & naked.
> Wen þi soule is faren out,
>   Þi body with erthe yraked,
> Þat body þat was so ronk and loud
>   Of alle men is ihated.

[Wretched man, why are you proud, you who are made of

earth? You brought no garment here, but came poor and naked. When your soul has gone out, and your body is covered over with earth, that body that was so confident and loud-mouthed is hated by all men. Brown No. 133]

There is more consideration in the warning poem (Brown No. 101) that urges men who are 'merriest at their meal', with plenty of food and drink, and honour and high standards of courtesy, to 'think of yesterday'; it goes on too long, it shows off its knowledge of Solomon and Socrates, and it over-alliterates, but this last trick has its own disagreeable strength in phrases like 'our carrions couched under clay'. The same power and realism—surely in part attributable to seeing the disasters of the age side by side with its pomp—is concentrated into the eight lines of No. 53 in Brown's collection (the scribe thrice writes *yogh* for *thorn*):

> Kyndeli is now mi coming
> > into ʒis werld wiht teres and cry.
> Litel and pouere is myn hauing,
> > briʒel and sone ifalle from hi.
> Scharp and strong is mi deying;
> > I ne woth whider schal I.
> Fowl and stinkande is mi roting;
> > on me, Ihesu, ʒow haue mercy!

[My coming into this world now with tears and crying is according to the course of nature. My possessing is little and poor, brittle, and soon fallen from on high. My dying is sharp and strong; I do not know whither I must go. My rotting is foul and stinking; Jesus, have mercy on me!]

Or with great elaboration, in matching stanzas, some moral attitude will be defended; the second-rate feature of these lyrics, as Christian literature, is their advocacy of a kind of insurance (I suppose I should really say 'assurance'; they all mention the death that awaits the unwary). These, again, are the typical product of an age of the more peremptory natural phenomena. One in the Vernon MS (Brown No. 118) says that the best thing to do is just 'suffer'; don't be too 'nice' (that is, fussy or squeamish), but remember what Socrates said about the glass pot's daring to come up against a cauldron—Chaucer, too, adapted this Aesop's fable (for such it is) in *Truth*, another poem of endurance and compromise. The Vernon poet's idea of *Truth* (Brown No. 108) is pedestrian, though with a glance at the decay of this sovereign abstraction in the realm where he was 'at one time . . . a lord', as Spain and Brittany will bear record; we should hunt falsehood as a cat does mice. Four other Vernon poems are little more than homely advice, though made to look polished by means of their involved stanzas: that on *Charity* (Brown No. 109) seeks to deal with its subject in 112 lines without a single mention of Christ apart from an oath by His rood; another (Brown No. 116) urges man not to procrastinate, but this involves devout prayers to Christ and to 'Mary mother, maiden mild', and Christian teaching that 'If you brag of your bright bezants, behold how bare you were born', which has the right thump of emphasis; one, of which the refrain is 'make amends' (Brown No. 117), starts like a secular narrative lyric with the poet alone in the wood and the birds singing, but he is led on to remember that everyone must have a grave 'When top and toe together is knit', that no one knows the time that his 'last bower must be a bier', and that one's destination is quite unknown, with the added criticism that a deadly sinner will grasp a friar to confess to, being ashamed to keep to the parish priest; the fourth begs us 'always try to say the best' (Brown No. 115), for the love of Mary, 'Christ's dame', and of Him 'Who died on tree'. However often these slow lyrics make mention of the Persons of the Trinity, they seem content to repeat the platitudes of man's instinctive schemes for survival—dull poems for humble men; but one of the more elaborate in the Vernon series (Brown No. 110), strangely over-alliterated and with the exacting rhyme-scheme *abababbcbc*, maintains that 'From women comes this world's weal' by repeated praise of Mary and hasty dismissal of what women did to Adam, Samson, and Solomon.

The most moving lyrics are those in which the love of Christ for man is central; these are wholly orthodox, though their biblical simplicity is such that no good Wyclifite would have found fault with them. Sometimes nothing is presented but Our Lord's love-song (in this delicate example the effect is certainly not attained by dainty French words, since there is only one, *peace*; the scribe spells badly, putting *th* for ȝ and even for ȝt):

> Loue me brouthte,
> & loue me wrouthte,
>> Man, to be þi fere.
> Loue me fedde,
> & loue me ledde,
>> & loue me lettet here.
>
> Loue me slou,
> & loue me drou,
>> & loue me leyde on bere.
> Loue is my pes;
> For loue I ches
>> Man to byȝen dere.
>
> Ne dred þe nouth;
> I haue þe south
>> Boþen day & nith.
> To hauen þe
> Wel is me;
>> I haue þe wonnen in fith.

[Love brought me, and love wrought me, man, to be your mate. Love fed me, and love led me, and love abandoned me here. Love slew me, and love drew me, and love laid me on the bier. Love is my peace; for love I chose to buy man dearly. Do not be afraid at all; I have sought you both day and night. I am glad to have you; I have won you in fight. Brown No. 66]

By comparison with this love,

> Al oþer loue is lych þe mone,
>> Þat wext and wanet as flour in plein;

[All other love is like the moon, that waxes and wanes as a flower in the meadow. Brown No. 49]

and the thought of Christ's grief for man's ingratitude elicits a reciprocal feeling of grief when eye to eye with Him:

Luueli ter of loueli eyჳe, qui dostu me so wo?
Sorful ter of sorful eyჳe, þu brekst myn herte a-to.

[Lovely tear of lovely eye, why do you grieve me so much?
Sorrowful tear of sorrowful eye, you break my heart in two.
Brown No. 69, refrain]

From the cross, Christ comforts His mother, or has a dialogue
with man, or pleads with him so as to dissuade him from sin or
indifference. One of the colloquies (Brown No. 67) simply makes
Christ complain of His torment, on which His mother comments
inconsolably, after which He commits her to John and explains
the Atonement; in one tiny lyric (Brown No. 60) she asks to be
crucified with Him. The plea to man may have a theological twist,
such as asking for a full confession:

I am Iesu, þat cum to fith
    Withouten seld & spere;
Elles were þi det idith
    ჳif mi fithting ne were.
Siþen I am comen & haue þe broth
    A blisful bote of bale,
Vndo þin herte; tel me þi þouth,
    Þi sennes grete an smale.

[I am Jesus, Who comes to fight without shield or spear; your
death would have been appointed if it had not been for my
fighting. Since I have come and brought you a joyful remedy
for sorrow, unlock your heart; tell me what is in your mind,
your sins big and little. Brown No. 63]

This has the heartening image of Christ as a champion, and one
of the lyrics that Bishop Sheppey gathered lets Him speak in the
same stirring way after man has bewailed His sufferings and His
humiliation; the startling 'change of key' in the middle, accompanied by a complete change in the metre, leads on to a triumphant
four-level allegory of Christ not at all resembling the contorted
figure on the usual medieval crucifix:

I sayh Hym wiþ ffless al bisprad;
  He cam vram est.
I sayh Hym wiþ blod al byssad;
  He cam vram west.
I sayh þet manye He wiþ Hym brouȝte;
  He cam vram souȝ.
I sayh þet þe world of Hym ne rouȝte;
  He cam vram norþ.

'I come vram þe wedlok as a svete spouse,
  Þet habbe my wif wiþ me innome.
I come vram viȝt a staleworþe knyȝt,
  Þet myne vo habbe ouercome.
I come vram þe chepyng as a riche chapman,
  Þet mankynde habbe ibouȝt.
I come vram an uncouþe londe as a sely pylegrym,
  Þet ferr habbe isouȝt.'

[I saw Him with His flesh all covered; He came from the east.
I saw Him with His blood all shed; He came from the west.
I saw that He brought many with Him; He came from the
south. I saw that the world did not care about Him; He came
from the north. 'I come from the marriage as a sweet husband,
and have brought my wife with me. I come from the fight as a
stalwart knight, and have overcome my enemy. I come from
the market as a rich merchant, and have redeemed mankind.
I come from a strange land as a blessed pilgrim, and have
sought far.' Brown No. 36]

This lyric is so extraordinary, so close in its first part to folk-song
or counting-song, that it is disappointing to find that in its manuscript it is associated with both a Latin original and an English
analogue; but then, it is disappointing to find how many religious
lyrics are not original, and the feeling grows that these are not
the deeply-felt hymns of a Charles Wesley or a dying Lyte, or the
splendid decisions of the early Greek and Latin Fathers, but set
exercises, copies, formulae. Almost, we might say, the better
formulated and metred, the less lyrical.

So that it is with more confidence that we turn to a remarkably ill-framed but direct appeal of Christ to man, with its sharply exciting parallels between the divine sacrifice and the human response to it; many adjustments would be necessary before it fitted into any metrical pattern—for instance, the fifth line might have its *sharpe þornes* varied to *þornes kene*, with the same sense and a better rhyme—, but it is possible that the poem is a hybrid, with its last two stanzas, in rather conventional tail-rhyme, from elsewhere:

> Ihesus doþ Him bymene
>   And spekeþ to synful mon:
> 'Þi garland is of grene,
>   Of floures many on;
> Myn of sharpe þornes—
>   Myn hewe it makeþ won.
>
> Þyn hondes streite gloued,
>   White & clene kept;
> Myne wiþ nailes þorled
>   On rode, & eke my feet.
>
> Acros þou berest þyn armes,
>   Whan þou dancest narewe—
> To me hastou non awe,
>   But to worldes glorie;
>   Myne for þe on rode
>   Wiþ þe Iewes wode
> Wiþ grete ropis todraw.
>
> Opyne þou hast þi syde,
> Spaiers longe & wide,
> For ueyn glorie & pride,
>   And þi longe knyf astrout—
>   Þou ert of þe gai route;
> Myn wiþ spere sharpe
> Ystongen to þe herte,
> My body wiþ scourges smerte
>   Biswongen al aboute.

Al þat Y þolede on rode for þe
  To me was shame & sorwe;
Wel litel þou louest me,
And lasse þou þenkest on me,
  An euene & eke amorwe.

Swete broþer, wel myȝt þou se
Þes peynes stronge in rode tre
Haue Y þoled for loue of þe;
Þei þat haue wrouȝt it me
  Mai synge welawo.
Be þou kynde pur charite.
Let þi synne & loue þou me.
Heuene blisse Y shal ȝeue þe,
  Þat lastep ay & oo.'

[Jesus complains, and speaks to sinful man: 'Your garland is green, with many flowers; mine is of sharp thorns—it makes my complexion pale. Your hands are neatly gloved, white and kept clean; mine are pierced with nails on the cross, and so are my feet. You hold your arms outstretched, when you dance closely—you have no reverence for me, but only for the glory of the world; mine for you are stretched out with thick ropes on the cross by the mad Jews. You wear your sides open, with long, wide slits, for vain glory and pride, and your long knife sticking out—you keep gay company; mine are stabbed to the heart by a sharp spear, and my body is beaten all over by painful scourges. All that I suffered on the cross for you was shame and sorrow to me; you love me very little, and think of me less, in the evening and also in the morning. Sweet brother, you can surely see that I have suffered these violent pains on the cross-tree for love of you; those who have done it to me may sing "alas!". For charity's sake be kind. Give up your sin and love me. I shall give you the joy of Heaven, which lasts for ever and always.' Brown No. 126]

This does not read easily, as if the poet were confused by emotion;

M

and the rhymes are even worse than they look—in the first stanza *mon* and *won* have a short vowel, *on* a long one. But the comparison in so few words of the world of pretty flowers, dainty hands, dancing, fantastic clothes, and daggers, with death on the cross is momentous. Alas, it is not of the poet's devising, and R. T. Davies (in his *Middle English Lyrics*, Evanston, 1964) quotes analogues in an 11th-century Pseudo-Augustine, the 13th-century *Legenda Aurea*, and our own John Myrc's *Festial* of before 1415.

The question *Is it nothing to you, all ye that pass by?* (*Lamentations* i. 12) forms the substance of some packed little lyrics. Two in a clearly Northern dialect are of the type associated with the tradition of Richard Rolle, and it is not surprising to find his 'erotic mysticism' expressed in terms of man as Christ's sweetheart:

> Lo, lemman swete, now may þou se
> Þat I haue lost my lyf for þe.
> What myght I do þe mare?
> Forþi I pray þe speciali
> Þat þou forsake ill company,
> Þat woundes me so sare.
>
> And take myne armes pryuely,
> & do þam in þi tresory,
> In what stede sa þou dwelles;
> And, swete lemman, forget þow noght
> Þat I þi lufe sa dere haue boght,
> And I aske þe noght elles.

[Look, sweet lover, now you can see that I have lost my life for you. What more could I have done for you? Therefore I beg you particularly to give up bad company, which wounds me so sorely. And take my arms secretly and put them in your treasury in whatever place you live; and, sweet lover, do not forget that I have bought your love so dearly, and I ask you for nothing else. Brown No. 78]

This, of course, is in tail-rhyme, but it is carefully handled; the three real examples of enjambement (ll. 1–2, 4–5, 10–11) give

suppleness and pace, and a delicate pattern of alliteration
(*l l s s l l m m*) emerges from the first triplet and then fades away,
as if enticing the passer-by to listen; further, whereas the *b* rhymes
are feminine, the *a* and *c* rhymes are all masculine, so that each
of the triplets ends with a lilt. The other Northern piece (Brown
No. 46) shows less skill but equal feeling, with crude alliteration:

> . . . think opon my payns strang,
> And styll als stane þou stand.
> Bihald þiself þe soth, & se
> How I am hynged here on þis tre;

[. . . think of my severe pains, and stand as still as a stone.
Observe the truth for yourself, and see how I am hanged here
on this tree]

but the spirit goes out of it at the end, when the 'clever' French
words *alleggance* (relief) and *affyance* [trust] occupy and clot their
couplet. One of the lyrics in Friar John Grimestone's commonplace book (Brown No. 74) is arresting in its simplicity, its un-
demanding rhyme-scheme (only alternate lines rhyme), and its
native vocabulary (only the stem of *pasen* is from French):

> 3e þat pasen be þe wey3e,
> Abidet a litel stounde.
> Beholdet, al mi felowes,
> 3ef ani me like is founde.
> To þe tre with nailes þre
> Wol fast I hange bounde,
> With a spere al þoru mi side
> To min herte is mad a wounde.

[You who pass by the way, wait a little moment. See, all my
fellow-men, whether anyone is found like me. I hang bound
to the tree very firmly with three nails, and a wound is made
to my heart with a spear right through my side.]

An elaborate type of lyric (for instance, Brown No. 55) lists
the Hours of the Cross and provides a quatrain of meditation
on each, the whole forming a prayer as well as a narrative; but

Sheppey's collection has the cross honoured, not blamed, in a tiny lyric too tender for epigram:

> Steddefast crosse, inmong alle oþer
>   Þow art a tre mykel of prise;
> In brawnche and flore swylk anoþer
>   I ne wot non in wode no rys.
> Swete be þe nalys, and swete be þe tre,
> And sweter be þe birdyn þat hangis vppon the!

[Steadfast cross, among all others you are a tree of great value; I know of no such other one, for branch and flower, in wood or thicket. May the nails be sweet, and the tree, and sweeter the burden that hangs upon you! Brown No. 40]

This looks back to the Anglo-Saxon *Dream of the Rood*, where the cross maintained a dignified pride in the part it had taken in the Atonement.

As might be expected, the lyrics of the Nativity are pretty and personal, but less gripping. Friar Grimestone seems to have had a liking for them, and an especial cultus of the Christ Child. He even imagines Him shivering with cold in the manger; His mother, in humble tail-rhyme and tearful apology, suggests a practical solution:

> 'Ihesu, suete sone dere,
> In porful bed þu list now here,
>   & þat me greuet sore;
> For þi credel is als a bere,
> Ox & asse ben þi fere—
>   Wepen may I þerfore.
>
> Ihesu, suete, be nout wroth:
> I have neiþer clut ne cloth
>   Þe inne for to folde.
> I ne haue but a clut of a lappe;
> Þerfore ley þi feet to my pappe,
>   & kep þe fro þe colde.'

['Jesus, dear, sweet son, you are lying here now in a poor bed,
and that grieves me sorely; because your cradle is like a byre,
and ox and ass are your companions—and that must make
me weep. Sweet Jesus, do not be angry: I have neither rag nor
cloth to fold you in. I have only a ragged fold of garment;
so put your feet on my breast, and keep yourself from the cold.'
Brown No. 75]

Man's apology has to be profounder, and the penitent in another
Grimestone lyric (Brown No. 59), whereas he calls Jesus 'little
child', 'little creature', 'little baron', 'little king', is sensible of his
own weight of sin and even takes Adam's sin upon himself, saying
that he took 'an apple in a pitiful hurry' and that this fall is
causing the Child to weep; another stanza skilfully varies this
idea—how God had forbidden the apple of that tree, and he had
thus earned damnation, if it had not been for the Child's weeping.
This treatment of the theme at first seems more apt than that in
the two dramatic lyrics in the same manuscript where the poet
has night-visions of the Incarnation; in one (Brown No. 56), he
lay on Christmas night in his unhappiness and saw a maiden
rocking a child—it is the pious application of the secular (and
normally amorous) *chanson d'aventure*, with its setting of time
and place and its male and female principals; yet, however studied
is the dialogue between mother and Son that follows, it is extremely
good theology, though some curiously unscriptural things happen.
The Child feels that His mother is wronging Him by not singing,
and points out that every efficient mother is accustomed to sing
her child to sleep. But what can she sing? She knows nothing of
Him except Gabriel's greeting (though she then goes on to give
a fair account, even if not a song, of the events leading up to the
Nativity). The Child then gives her more material for her song—
His Circumcision, Epiphany, and Presentation, His teaching in
the Temple, His parting from her when He is thirty, His Baptism
by John, His Temptation, His disciples, the people's wish to make
Him king. Obtusely, she interrupts—she looks forward to *that* day;
but He silences her, reveals His true mission and His Crucifixion,
and reconciles her to what they must both suffer. Stranger, though

no less medieval, is the vision (Brown No. 58) of a poet lying one night and gazing at a 'strand' (it must be a stretch of country); he sees a gentle-looking girl holding a Child, and speculates curiously that 'She would have done mankind an injustice unless she had been a virgin.' Now Joseph takes up the tale, and explains the mystery of the Incarnation—old Joseph, shown in medieval plays as an old man grumbling at being cuckolded, until an angel firmly tells him the facts, but here already informed and very dignified:

> Be hire sat a sergant
>   Þat sadli seide his sawe;
> He sempte be is semblant
>   A man of þe elde lawe.

> His her was hor on heuede;
>   His ble began to glide.
> He herde wel wat I seyde,
>   & bad me faire abide.

> 'Þu wondrest,' he seyde, 'skilfuli
>   On þing þu hast beholde,
> & I dede so treuli
>   Til tales weren me tolde.'

[By her was sitting a dignitary who was talking gravely; he seemed from his appearance to be a man of the Old Testament. The hair of his head was grey; his colour was starting to fade. He heard clearly what I said, and asked me politely to wait. 'You are wondering', he said, 'and with good reason, about the things you have seen, and so did I, certainly, until information was given me.']

He gives the poet a simple narrative of his first doubt and puzzlement, and then of his absolute trust that a virgin birth was likelier than Mary's deception of him; and he emphasizes with strange pride the heavenly nature of his wife's Child. 'But', says the poet, and takes the point further; this Child that he saw is God 'and man', and the lyric ends with his thanks to Joseph and a prayer to Christ.

There are many love-poems, and those to Mary can easily borrow from, and contribute to, the purely secular poems of love for some peerless girl. To modern taste, those that stress her physical beauty—even her slimness—seem to be meddling with inessentials, but it was surely felt that the finest and purest woman that Earth had known would also be dowered with the greatest beauty; on a different plane, young Havelock, *de jure* King of Denmark and soon to be *de facto* King of England as well, was patently the handsomest, strongest, nicest, most popular, and most gallant man in England, kindest to children and most thoughtful to the old, even when in the drab rags of a fisherboy and a scullion. Goodness shone through beauty of this kind, and evil had a correspondingly ugly face. But we now prefer those lyrics in which her part in the redemption of mankind is stressed; there was a plentiful Latin literature on this subject, and even the most English-looking lyrics, as simple as little descriptive pendants to pictures, may be found to have an older Latin hymn behind them. Bishop Sheppey records one such:

> Lefdy blisful, of muchel miȝt,
> Heyere þanne þe sterres liȝt,
> Hym Þe þe made wumman best
> Þou ȝoue Hym souken of þi brest.
> Þet þet Eue vs hadde bynome
> Þow hast iȝolde þorw þy Sone.
> Þow art in heuene an hole imad
> Þorw which þe senful þorwgeþ glad.
> Þow art þe kynges ȝate idyȝt;
> Briȝtore þow art þan eny liȝt.
> Lif þorw Marye vs is iwrouȝt;
> Alle ben glade þet Crist haþ ibouȝt.

[Joyful lady, of great efficacy, higher than the light of the stars, you gave Him Who made you the best of women your breast to suck. What Eve had deprived us of, you have repaid through your Son. You are an entry made in Heaven through which the sinful man gladly goes. You are set up as the king's gate; you are brighter than any light. Life is made for us through Mary; all whom Christ has redeemed are glad. Brown No. 38]

One of the Vernon poems (Brown No. 111) lets the poet languish in a love of very secular sound—'Love has brought me into miseries'—, yet he hopes desperately for a sight of her in heaven; by a curious conceit, he lets other men observe the privilege of not loving, but reserves to himself the superior rite of love for the Virgin:

> Hose lust not loue, let hym beleue,
>   For I wol holde þat I haue hiht;
> Þat lust schal no mon from me reue
>   Þat I nul loue my ladi briht.

[Whoever does not desire to love, let him desist, because I am going to hold to what I have promised; no man shall deprive me of that desire and prevent me from loving my radiant lady.]

But many humbler people must have been content to murmur repeatedly the gawky little versions of the *Ave Maria* such as

> Heil, Marie, ful of wynne.
> Þe Holy Gost is þe wiþinne.
> Blesced be þou ouer alle wymmen,
> And þe fruit of þin wombe. Amen.

[Hail, Mary, full of joy. The Holy Ghost is within you. Blessed may you be beyond all women, and the fruit of your womb. Amen. H. A. Person, *Cambridge Middle English Lyrics*, Seattle, 1953, No. 11]

The sophisticated would extend the concept of love to the Church and its ministers; one lyric in the Vernon MS (Brown No. 114) runs to sixty-four lines on this subject, with a hinted background of those who already 'work against' the Church. 'Priests were at our beginning', and God gave them power to direct us and to

sing: 'There is no dignity so great'; they preside at our baptism
and our burial, and no one else can 'make God's body'—not even
a king or emperor, even the one who wears the fleurdelys. The
priest's august status, his absolutely essential part in every man's
life and dying, and the honour due to him, only just leave room
for a hasty prayer to Jesus; but whether those who 'work against'
the Church are heretics or friars is not made clear! Another poem
on love, which pretends to examine the subject exhaustively,
succeeds in its ninety-six lines only in making little jabs at it, with
much vagueness and repetition, and much declaration of ecstasy
without illuminating the steps by which it is attained; K. Sisam
(in *Fourteenth Century Verse & Prose*, Oxford, 1921 and subsequently, pp. 37–40) tentatively leaves it in the Rolle canon, though
it may equally be by a follower. It tries very hard (as if it indeed
were an imitation of another's fires), but its ardour does not seem
to me infectious; its artifice and strain are seen in the opening
stanza:

> Luf es lyf þat lastes ay, þar it in Criste es feste.
> For wele ne wa it chaunge may, als wryten has men wyseste.
> Þe nyght it tournes intil þe day, þi trauel intyll reste.
> If þou wil luf þus as I say, þou may be wyth þe beste.

> [Love is life that lasts for ever, provided it is fixed in Christ.
> It cannot change for weal or woe, as the wisest men have writ-
> ten. It turns the night into day, and your toil into rest. If you
> are willing to love in the way I have said, you can be with the
> elect.]

The unrelenting rhyme-scheme, with internal rhymes, of *abababab*
is the first unnecessary discipline, on which is imposed a wayward
alliteration—three *l*s in the first half-line, four *w*s in the second
line, then silence on that score; not surprisingly, *wyseste* has to be
forced into rhyme by an arbitrary accent on its final syllables, and
the second line has an un-English inversion of *may chaunge* and a
gross disarray of *wyseste men has wryten* for the rhyme's sake.
Religious ecstasy is an imperative and private thing, and the
attempt to box it in a pedantic and public metre is a failure from
the start.

Left to themselves, the musing minds of the half-century produced some desultory lyrics, pardonably shapeless, and hoped that they would do good to others; one (Brown No. 91) asks Jesus to *write* the details of His Passion in his penitent mind, and with much trochaic emphasis anticipates something of the more robust Victorian hymnology:

> In myn hert ay mot hit be—
> Þat hard knotty rode tree. . . .

[May it always be in my heart—that hard, knotty cross-tree.]

> Ihesu, make me glad to be
> Sympil & pouer for loue of þe . . .

[Jesus, make me glad to be simple and poor for love of You.]

It is not surprising that the scribe put this heading to the poem: 'In seiynge of þis orisoun stynteth & bydeth at euery cros & þynketh whate ye haue seide. For a more deuout prayere fond I neuer of the Passioun, whoso wolde deuoutly say hitte.' [As you say this devotion stop and wait at every cross and think what you have been saying. Because I never found a more devout prayer of the Passion, whoever would say it devoutly.] An inferior but earnest piece (in Person, op cit., No. 7) tunelessly specifies Christ's wounds as remedies against the Sins, with the nails in His right and left hands as inducements to the Virtues of almsgiving and forgiveness. A more forced simplicity is seen in some clever stanzas (Brown No. 97) where a minstrel, altogether too precocious in his wording, bows out to a more genuine balladry audience of 'bernes, buirdus, bolde and blyþe' [men and ladies, bold and cheerful], thanking them a thousand times and taking his leave against his will. Sometimes the individuality is seen chiefly in the fictional setting adopted; here again, the secular *chanson d'aventure* background of the wildwood, the place for amorous mischief, the haunt of Robin Goodfellow and the dangerous incubus, was pressed innocently into service. One of the Vernon poets (Brown No. 107) was wandering westwards by the skirts of a forest, when he saw a man settling down under a bough and beginning a desperate plea to God for mercy; another of them (Brown No. 95) starts magnificently:

> Bi west, vnder a wylde wode-syde,
>   In a launde þer I was lente,
> Wlanke deor on grounde gunne glyde,
>   And lyouns raumping vppon bente,
> Beores, wolues, wiþ mouþes wyde;
>   Þe smale beestes þei al torente.
> Þer haukes vnto heore pray þei hyde,
>   Of whuche to on I tok good tente—
>   A merlyon a brid had hente,
>   And in hire foot heo gan hit bringe;
>   Hit couþe not speke, but þus hit mente,
>   How merci passeþ alle þinge.

[To the west, by the side of a wild wood, in a glade where I was reclining, proud creatures were moving over the ground, lions were rearing up on the grass, and there were bears and wolves with wide mouths; they were tearing the little animals quite to pieces. Hawks were hurrying to their prey there, and I paid great attention to one of them—a merlin that had caught a bird and was bringing it in her claw; it could not speak, but what it was trying to express was that mercy surpasses all things.]

There is a strange resemblance here to the stanza of *Pearl*; the tight rhyme-scheme (*ababababbcbc*), the alliteration (though far less consistently, and less heavily, than in *Pearl*), the linking of stanzas on a 'refrain' line (and thus the linking of them throughout on the same *c*-rhyme), and even the odd resemblance of phrase ('Þouȝ we plese þe not to pay', l. 186; 'plesaunte to prynces paye', *Pearl*, l. 1); and the introduction of Christ's Passion, a versification of the Seven Works of Mercy, and the plea not to dismember Christ's Body by oaths on it, gives the material the same careful didacticism as in the greater poem. The setting in yet another of the Vernon series (Brown No. 96) is exceptional in being a church, where the poet was kneeling 'the other morning';

he enjoyed the service, and so stayed on all the longer, until a priest brought out a book with musical notation in it, and soon found what to sing: *Deo gratias*. All the choristers took it up, in such lovely music that the poet (incredibly ignorant of the meaning) approached a silk-clad priest for a translation; the priest leaned over a lectern to tell him, so that by the time he left the church he had picked up the phrase and was praying not to forget it.

I have left until last a lyric in the Vernon MS (Brown No. 106) not at all in keeping with the heavy theology of most of the contents, and indeed out of step with almost every other lyric of its age in its daring and restless speculation. Its refrain is 'Þis world fareþ as a fantasy' [This world proceeds, or behaves, like an illusion], which was trite enough; behind this truism the poet erects a series of dangerous questions as if scripture and dogma had supplied none of the answers. Yet his basis is certain portions of *Ecclesiastes*, which may give some cover to his saucy rationalism. The opening lines have a fluttering impatience in them, conveyed by the repeated alliteration on the swift *w*, the cutting *f*, and the lifting *h*:

> I wolde witen of sum wys wiht
> > Witterly what þis world were.
> Hit fareþ as a foules fliht;
> > Now is hit henne, now is hit here.

[I should like to know from some wise person what this world is for certain. It proceeds like the flight of a bird; now it is away, now it is here.]

And we may not be wrong in seeing scorn in that first line, which perhaps writes off the wisdom of the sages, who must stop short at their own mortality. The inexorable way of Nature is stressed:

> Þe sonnes cours, we may wel kenne,
> > Aryseþ est and geþ doun west.
> Þe ryuers into þe see þei renne,
> > And hit is neuer þe more almest.
> Wyndes rosscheþ her and henne;
> > In snouȝ and reyn is non arest.

[The sun's course, as we can well know, rises in the east and goes down in the west. The rivers run into the sea, and it hardly seems to get any bigger. Winds rush up and away; there is no cessation of snow and hail.]

Only God knows when all this will cease; the earth is now dewy, now dry. But man 'goes away like a guest' (or, rather, 'like a visitor', as R. T. Davies nicely puts it).

In a stanza that bristles with long and learned words ending in -*ation*, the poet achieves the extra force of deriding those clever people who 'for all their preparations' are (with a harsh fall to Anglo-Saxon monosyllables) 'forgotten as clean as a bone', and reverts in the next stanza to the epigrammatic simplicity that needs no scholarship to colour it:

> Whuch is mon, ho wot, and what,
>   Wheþer þat he be ouȝt or nouȝt?
> Of erþe & eyr groweþ vp a gnat,
>   And so doþ mon, whon al his souht;
> Þauȝ mon be waxen gret and fat,
>   Mon melteþ awey so deþ a mouht.
> Monnes miht nis worþ a mat,
>   But nuyȝeþ himself and turneþ to nouȝt.

[Who knows what man is like or what he is, and whether he is anything or nothing? A gnat grows up out of earth and air, and so does man, when all is said and done; although a man has grown big and fat, he melts away like a moth. Man's strength is not worth a straw pallet, but he only hurts himself and turns to nothing.]

The mysterious *mat* is probably the humble (and sometimes verminous) woven straw sleeping-mat of the type that the decaying corpse of Bishop Bush is shown lying on in Bristol Cathedral, his episcopal trappings mockingly stacked with him. We soon reach the fireworks of rhetoric again, after a hasty and surely heretical question, 'Who knows anything by any experience save speculation?', and the long words in the *b*-rhymes add their sly power to the opening chiasmus:

> Dyeþ mon, and beestes dye,
>   And al is on ocasion;
> And alle o deþ bos boþe drye,
>   And han on incarnacion.
> Saue þat men beoþ more sleyȝe,
>   Al is o comparison.
> Ho wot ȝif monnes soule styȝe
>   And bestes soules synkeþ doun?
> Who knoweþ beestes entencioun,
>   On heor creatour how þei crie,
> Saue only God þat knoweþ heore soun?
>   For þis world fareþ as a fantasye.

[Man dies, and animals die, and it is all the same happening; and all of both of them must suffer the same death, and have the same birth. Except that men are cleverer, it is all of a likeness. Who knows if man's soul rises and the souls of animals sink down? Who knows the motive of animals, and how they cry to their Creator, save only God, That knows Their voice? Because this world behaves like an illusion.]

The poet has grown reckless; no Christian could accept that the death of a baptized and repentant human was quite the *same* as that of an animal, however humane the sentiment might seem, and the Vernon MS is too orthodox a neighbour for such an enquiry. Yet against the background of an age somewhat callous towards beasts, the picture of their crying to their Creator is deeply moving and even sublime. Now emboldened, the poet turns at once to the jarring of sects:

> Vche secte hopeþ to be saue
>   Baldely bi heore bileeue;
> And vchon vppon God heo craue—
>   Whi schulde God with hem Him greue?
> Vchon trouweþ þat oþer raue,
>   But alle heo cheoseþ God for cheue,
> And hope in God vchone þei haue
>   And bi heore wit heore worching preue.

[Each sect hopes confidently to be saved by their belief; and each one prays to God—why should God trouble Himself with them? Each one is sure that the next is mad, but they all choose God as Lord, and each of them has hope in God and justifies his actions by his understanding.]

This is characterized as stumbling, and the impairing of one's wit; people variously believe in this person or that thing, 'like children learning to spell'. But the poet is soon off to another climax—the attack on clever arguments, on searching the unsearchable, on defining the indefinable; it might almost be an attack on the too great precision of Transubstantiation, but is just as likely to be a mockery of the Schoolmen, the friars especially, and their proud certainty on piffling points:

> Wharto wilne we forte knowe
>   Þe poyntes of Godes priuete?
> More þen Him lustes forte schowe
>   We schulde not knowe in no degre,
> And idel bostis forte blowe
>   A Mayster of Diuinite.
> Þenk we lyue in eorþe her lowe,
>   And God an heiȝ in mageste.
> Of material mortualite
>   Medle we & of no more maistrie.
> Þe more we trace þe Trinite,
>   Þe more we falle in fantasye.

[Why do we want to know the details of God's secrets? We should not in any respect know more than it pleases Him to show, for a Master of Divinity to utter empty boasts. Consider that we live here below on earth, and God on high in majesty. Let us concern ourselves with material mortality and with nothing more important. The more we explore the Trinity, the more we fall into illusion.]

The contempt for the world has rarely been upheld with more eloquence; the futility of sectarianism was part of it, but now the plea is almost for innocence and ignorance, fortified by that love of God which dominates the next stanza; it is pointed out that, in any case, He can turn species 'upside-down', having made all species out of nothing. And

> Whon al vr bokes ben forþ brouht,
>   And al vr craft of clergye,
> And al vr wittes ben þorw-out souȝt,
>   ȝit we fareþ as a fantasye.

[When all our books are brought out, and all our professional scholarship, and when all our findings are completely investigated, we still behave like an illusion.]

The conclusion is more pedestrian, though it has some happy commonsense in its injunction 'let us make merry, and kill worry, and worship God while we are here, spend our fortune and save little, and cheer one another up, and remember how we came here quite naked—our departure is a matter of doubt'; there is a final analogy, of man seen as a huge and rooted tree, which neither diminishes the earth nor increases it 'a pound':

> Þus waxeþ & wanieþ mon, hors, & hounde,
>   From nouȝt to nouȝt þus henne we hiȝe;
> And her we stunteþ but a stounde,
>   For þis world is but fantasye.

[Thus man, horse and dog wax and wane, and thus from nothing we hasten away to nothing; and we stop here for only a season, because this world is only an illusion.]

The last two stanzas have this subtle change in their refrain: the world is not just *like* an illusion—it *is* one.

I suppose this is the most breathtaking lyric in all Middle English, and proof that the unsatisfied minds of Roger Bacon and William of Ockham and other seekers had left at least one highly articulate follower. Not that it has any lightness or economy of wording; it is in the slow-moving *Pearl* stanza, which asks for encrusted ornament and receives some here, even in the poet's most desperately sincere moments. In the following century, six of its lines (ll. 97–102) find an echo:

But leue we vre disputisoun,
   And leeue on Him Þat al haþ wrouȝt.
We mowe not preue bi no resoun
   How He was born Þat al vs bouȝt;
But hol in vre entencioun,
   Worschipe we Him in herte & þouȝt.

[But let us leave our disputation and believe in Him Who has made everything. We cannot prove by any reasoning how He Who bought us all was born; but united in our purpose, let us worship Him in heart and mind.]

This idea (obscurantist at worst, but eminently reasonable) was picked up by Reginald Peacock, fifteenth-century Bishop of Chichester and suspect heretic, and had currency in his quatrain which acquired several forms but of which the rough Englishing would be:

Wits wonder that reason not tell can
How a virgin is a mother and God is man.
Leave your reason; believe in a wonder.
Because faith is above, and reason is under.

But the general picture that emerges from the other lyrics is of steady and yet studious acceptance, and there is little doubt that the great luminaries among the orthodox religious writers of the time are, apart from Langland and the writer of *Pearl*, the lyrists and the prose mystics.

The Monks

A study of the state of the religious houses at the time will obviously help us to assess the religious endeavour, here linked with the composition or copying of writings in the three tongues; but the mere figures, suggesting lost impetus, will be dangerous evidence, and it must be remembered that the Black Death had tragically cut down the numbers of religious, and that the country was already thickly studded with their houses before 1350. Some clear facts, however, emerge. First, the total number of new

N

foundations for monks, canons regular, friars, and their women counterparts, was only about twenty from 1350 onwards. Secondly, the 'alien' priories—houses that were dependencies of foundations abroad—were remarkably bullied into being wound up or accepting a kind of naturalization: they had to become 'denizen', a process that was a reflection of the new nationalism of England, but in the event some seventy were confiscated and finally suppressed between 1350 and 1414. So far, the picture suggests decay, but the next reign would soon show, in its splendid royal foundation of Syon Abbey for the new Bridgettine order, that the patronage of the mightiest was still active; further, about seventy hospitals—all, of course, religious houses—were founded in our half-century, and newcomers called Bonshommes received their handsome church at Edington, Wilts., after 1352. But the most striking manifestation of religious and even mystical fervour was the great group of new houses of the Carthusians; this most strict, austere, and incorruptible order imposed solitude on its members and induced the contemplative spirit that expressed itself in some remarkable writings, and there is no doubt that the wealth of English mysticism at the time is connected with the feelings that led to the founding and difficult recruiting of the Charterhouses at Axholme, Lincs. (1397–98), Coventry (1381), Hull (1377), London (1371), and Mount Grace, Yorks. (1398). Small—a mere dozen solitaries at a time—and never elaborate, these houses must have exercised a great influence on the devotional literature of the period.

Contemporary comment on the monks is, apart from some fulmination by Wyclif and his school, non-committal and not very interesting. The one clear picture is, not surprisingly, Chaucer's in the Prologue of *The Canterbury Tales*; his monk has qualities good and less good as a man, but few qualifications for his calling, yet his rank in life is such that he is described next after the knight and his 'staff' and the prioress and hers. Despite an appearance of hearty approval, Chaucer lets us see him as fat, foppish, and footloose; most of the lines are taken up with praise of his prowess at hunting, his horses and hounds, his liking for roast swan, his gold pin with a love-knot on it, his wide interpretation of the monastic rule, his contempt of study in the cloister, and his full-blooded physique, but no evidence is given for the two hasty statements that he was 'fit to be an abbot' and 'a fine prelate'. Yet when the cavalcade has moved off towards Canterbury, and the dramatic principle of the *Tales* begins to operate, the monk is seen in a new dimension; he is the first after the knight to be asked for a tale, but the miller interrupts and disturbs the sequence. When Chaucer's own two strange tales are over, Rochester has been reached, and the host is full of jocose self-pity over his domineering wife, so that in quite reckless rudeness he turns on the monk, and asks (without bothering to get an answer) whether he's Dom John or Dom Thomas or Dom Alban, and what his house is. The last of these names is rare, and *Dom* indicates a Benedictine, so that a hint of his being from the great Benedictine abbey of St Albans is possible. The host then sniggers into an embarrassing attack on clerical celibacy, in which the monk is addressed as if he were simply a good specimen of breeding stock; but he takes it all patiently, and without comment on it promises to tell several tales, beginning with some of the hundred tragedies that he has in his cell. His choice of this theme suggests a depth not hinted at before, and he is careful to explain that a tragedy is a tale, taken from 'old books', of one who, from great prosperity and high rank, fell to a wretched ending; with no concession to humour or to optimism, he works through seventeen brief life-stories of this type, until the knight—who has probably seen enough of reverses and their horrors from Alexandria, Prussia, Granada, and Turkey, to the other fields where he has fought his fifteen mortal battles—interrupts him, as gentleman to gentleman, and begs for something more cheerful. The host, heartily in agreement, cannot resist some more rudeness; calling the monk 'Dom Piers', he asks him for a different story—only the monk's bridle-bells have kept him awake during the telling. But the worldly monk will not narrate for amusement; with quiet gravity, he claims that he has told, and that another must now tell. Indirectly, in fact, though Chaucer makes nothing extra of it, the monk has been insulted already when one 'Dom John', an 'outrider' like him, has been made the seducer in *The Shipman's Tale*, a point oafishly taken up by the host afterwards; and the prioress's aside in her tale, that the abbot 'was a holy man, as monks are— or else ought to be', may have been loaded against him, too.

The Friars

The friars, to use a modern phrase, 'didn't have a good press'. The first flush of evangelical fervour on their arrival in England— the Dominicans in 1221, the Franciscans in 1224, the rest later— was long over, their poverty and simplicity had yielded to huge airy churches, and commentators had grown monotonously hostile. Three of the greatest writers of the age—Chaucer, Langland, and Wyclif—are unanimous in condemning them, but the little critics are just as lively. There is Lollard reasoning in the complaint thrust into the mouth of a friar on the flyleaf of St John's College, Cambridge, MS 195 (printed by H. A. Person, *Cambridge Middle English Lyrics*, Seattle, 1953, pp. 42–3, and by R. H. Robbins, *Historical Poems of the XIVth and XVth Centuries*, New York, 1959, pp. 166–7):

> Allas, what schul we freris do,
>   Now lewed men kun holy writ?
> Alle abowte wherre I go
>   Þei aposen me of it.
>
> Þen wondriþ me þat it is so
>   How lewed men kan alle wite.
> Sertenly we be vn-do
>   But if we mo amende it.
>
> I trowe þe deuel browȝt it aboute
>   To write þe gospel in Englishe,
> ffor lewed men ben now so stowt
>   þat þei ȝeuen vs neyþer fleche ne fishe.
>
> When I come in-to a schope
>   For to say *In principio*,
> Þei bidine me, 'Goo forþ, lewed poppe!',
>   & worche & win my siluer so.

If Y sae hit longoþ not
   ffor prestis to worche where þei go,
Þei leggen for hem holi writ,
   And sein þat Seint Polle did soo.

Þan þei loken on my nabete,
   & sein forsoþe, withoutton oþes,
'Wheþer it be russet, black, or white,
   It is worþe alle oure werynge cloþes.' . . .

[Alas, what must we friars do, now that laymen understand
holy scripture? Everywhere I go, they examine me on the
subject. Then I marvel how it is that laymen can know everything. We'll surely be done for unless we can put it right. I
reckon the devil brought about the writing of the gospel
in English; because now laymen are so independent that they
give us neither meat nor fish. When I enter a shop to say *In
principio*, they tell me, 'Get out, ignorant pup', and tell me to
work, and earn my money like that. If I say it isn't fitting for
priests to work their way, they quote holy scripture for themselves, and say that St Paul did. Then they look at my habit
and declare without swearing, 'Whether it's grey, black, or
white, it's worth all our everyday clothes.']

Wyclif would have endorsed the exposure of this transparent
friar, who fears the open scriptures, who shivers at the thought
of working, and who finds himself dealing with realists whose
austerity forbids them the easy oaths and blasphemies of the day.
His complaint is ostensibly in answer to a surly attack (Person,
op. cit., pp. 41–2; Robbins, op. cit., p. 166) written on the same
flyleaf:

Þou þat sellest þe worde of God,
Be þou berfot, be þou schod,
   Cum neuere here.
In principio erat verbum
Is þe worde of God alle & sum
   Þat þou sellest, lewed frere.

Hit is cursed symonie

> Eþer to selle or to bye
> Ony gostly þinge . . .

[You who sell the word of God, whether you are discalced or
shod, stay away from here. *In principio erat verbum* is the
word of God entirely, and you're selling it, you ignorant friar.
It is cursed simony either to sell or buy any spiritual thing.]

But even an ostensibly orthodox moralist, who introduces his
carol (R. L. Greene, *A Selection of English Carols*, Oxford, 1962,
No. 73) with an appeal to Christ's sacrifice, closes it with
the need for shrift, and occupies it chiefly with references to the
more awful natural phenomena of the age, still gloatingly manages
to get in a dig at the Whitefriars, as we saw earlier.

Now there was a smart acrostic joke that you could use against
the friars; Wyclif put it over in Latin, but it was exploited far
more amusingly in an impudent and long-winded poem of *c.* 1382
(Robbins, op. cit., pp. 157–62) that gives exhaustive eye-witness
evidence, by a renegade friar who escaped just before he was
professed, for their greed and lechery. By putting in order the
initial letters of *Carmelite, Austin, Iacobin* (Jacobin or Dominican),
and *Minorite* (Franciscan), you got the name *CAIM*, the normal
Middle English spelling of the first murderer; which of course
proved to the critics' satisfaction that he had founded the lot.
To reach this climax, the poem starts as if gently, with a stanza
of undeviating praise for their study and devotions; then to their
meagre fare—but the poet notices what fat bottoms they have,
and how each one makes a horseload when he packs himself off.
And what a pity it is that they have to wander, despite their
education, from place to place seeking sustenance!—yet how odd
that they sell mercery just like pedlars. Then the fury begins to
mount: if you have womenfolk, keep the friar out, and his trinkets
of purses, pins, knives, belts, gloves; he can seduce a wife with a
pound of soap, and wheedle some new clothes as well. Beneficed
clergy can't keep up with them, because they have so profitable a
line of singing private masses; in fact, the only thing to do with
them is to disband them, as the king did with the irreligious and
sensual Templars.

Another poem of about 1382, in the same MS (Robbins, op. cit., pp. 163–4), attacks them specifically for their visual representation of scriptural scenes; the early editors' assumption that friars' religious plays are being criticized now seems less likely than a gibe at their wall-paintings, since the subjects they depict are said to be: God, hung on high on a green tree among bright leaves and blossoms; God on the cross high up in the sky, with wings fastened on Him as if He were going to fly; somebody in a grey gown coming out of the sky and looking like a hog-herd hurrying to town; a friar bleeding from his side and with wide wounds in hands and feet (this will be St Francis receiving the stigmata), while a pope holds the cupping-dish; and a fiery cart (presumably Elijah's) with a greyfriar in it. Friars are 'hauteyn' [haughty] now, after their initial humility, and instead of praising St Paul they lie by the name of St Francis. They eke out their 'visual aids' by trotting out bits of scholarship—when they don't even know their Creed! They deserve to be destroyed; only the fire is lacking, and it is a nice coincidence that one of them is shown in his fiery cart—the poet hopes to see them burning. Their advocacy of poverty is a pretence; they scour the town for good food, they live in big and beautiful houses, and for sixpence they will absolve you from patricide and incest. The only positive praise in this savage piece, with its swinging refrain of 'With an O and an I', is given to 'Armachan'—Richard Fitzralph, Archbishop of Armagh (†1360), the inveterate enemy of friars.

The acknowledged Lollard attack on them is heavy and unrelenting, and will be considered when we reach Wyclif; but Chaucer can be relied on to be subtler. The friar of his *Canterbury Tales* is described next after the monk in the Prologue, and in a smilingly hostile vein; the very first epithet applied to him is 'wanton', and the picture is carefully built up of a lisping, eye-rolling, plausible, fastidious sybarite, getting a shoeless widow's last farthing off her with his pretty *In principio*, haunting the taverns and rich houses, selling his absolutions, and shunning lepers and beggars of the kind that his order had once relieved. Chaucer, ascribing to him a brighter tongue than anyone in the 'four orders' (there were more than four, so perhaps Chaucer had Abel's brother in mind, too), scatters suspicious trifles about his dealings with women—paying for young ones' marriages, welcomed by 'worthy women of the town', giving pretty wives knives and pins out of his tippet, acquainted with all the barmaids, useful on love-days; we know that these last were settlement-days, when a clerical arbiter would be welcome, but in a two-level description of this sort the overtones may sound louder than the music. That this 'worthy limiter' Hubert was more 'virtuous' than any other man anywhere is so patently incredible that Chaucer isn't afraid to state it; in the case of the monk, we know the worst in the Prologue, and his quite likeable character will thereafter mature, but for the friar the worst is to come.

The tales are half over before he reappears, and then he briefly and jovially interrupts the woman from Bath's prologue with the protest that it is a 'long preamble'; his natural enemy the summoner has been waiting for such an opportunity, and rebukes him for meddling, whereat the friar promises a risible tale or two about summoners, and gets the return threat of two or three tales about frairs before the party reaches Sittingbourne. The woman is quick with her revenge on him: her story opens with the picture of Britain in King Arthur's days, filled with fairies and with the dance of the elf-queen in every meadow; but that was hundreds of years ago, and now there are no elves to be seen. What has made them go?—

> For now the grete charitee and prayeres
> Of limitours and othere holy freres,
> That serchen every lond and every streem
> As thikke as motes in the sonne-beem,
> Blessinge halles, chambres, kichenes, boures,
> Citees, burghes, castels, hye toures,
> Thropes, bernes, shipnes, dayeryes,
> This maketh that ther been no fayeryes.
> For ther as wont to walken was an elf,
> Ther walketh now the limitour himself
> In undermeles and in morweninges,
> And seyth his matins and his holy thinges
> As he goth in his limitacioun.
> Wommen may go saufly up and doun

In every bush, or under every tree:
There is noon other incubus but he,
And he ne wol doon hem but dishonour.

[Because now the great charity and prayers of limiters and other holy friars, who haunt every piece of land and every stream as thick as motes in the sunbeam, blessing halls, rooms, kitchens, bed-chambers, cities, boroughs, castles, lofty towers, hamlets, barns, sheds, and dairies, causes there to be no fairies. For where the elf was accustomed to walk there now walks the limiter himself in afternoons and mornings, and says his matins and his holy bits as he goes his bounds. Women may safely go up and down through every bush, or under every tree; there is no other incubus but he, and he will do them nothing but dishonour.]

This brilliant mixture of idyll and venom, conveyed in an assured heroic couplet that sometimes admits a 'headless' one-syllable foot to begin the line (*Bléssinge—, Cítees—, Thrópes—, Wómmen—*), presents the typical friar as the only incubus lying in wait for foolish women in the wildwood, and silences Hubert till her tale is done; then, still called 'worthy' and 'noble', he gives the woman some affected praise and at once promises a nasty tale about a summoner (at whom he has been glaring all the time). The host says he should be courteous in view of his status, and let the summoner be; but the latter isn't worried—he'll have his own back afterwards. . . . It is hard to say who wins the exchange; the friar's tale of the heartless summoner seized by the fiend is morally sound and crisply told, and is literally damning, but the summoner's of the humiliated friar, though unsavoury and eventually tedious, has a meticulous study of the friar's methods and especially of how he gets his feet under welcoming tables. Despite the friar's protest, the summoner shows him going from house to house with scrip and staff, begging meal, cheese, malt, wheat, rye, cakes, halfpennies or mass-pennies, brawn, bacon, beef, even a piece of blanket; meanwhile his companion writes on ivory tablets with a stylus the names of all the donors, for future prayers, and immediately erases them before proceeding to the next establishment! But to any decent-minded Briton of the twentieth century what happens next is a far more telling instance of the friar's perfidy; he enters a familiar house,

> And fro the bench he droof awey the cat

[And he drove away the cat from the bench]

before sitting down—do we need to hear more?

Yet Chaucer's piecemeal essay on friars is a mere sketch compared with Langland's treatment of them, which runs inexorably through the Prologue and the twenty Passus of *Piers Plowman*. It is made more persuasive by his praise of St Francis (B. IV. 121), and of St Paul the Hermit for founding the Austin Friars (B. XV. 284); friars *could* be equal to the Twelve Apostles, if they lived virtuously and humbly as Dominic and Francis bade them (B. XV. 409–15), and Repentance can even tell us how he would behave in an honourable and charitable friary, taking no tainted money even for vestments or the church fabric (B. V. 268–9); and they are still not beyond reformation—

> And thanne freres in here freitoure shal fynden a keye
> Of Costantynes coffres in which is the catel
> That Gregories god-children han yuel dispended:

[That is when the friars will find in their refectory a key to Constantine's coffers, in which is the wealth that Gregory's god-children have frittered away. B. X 323–25]

that is, the original endowments of the church will pass to them from the hands of the English monks, and they can stop their begging.

For the rest, Langland makes them sound as wrong as can be. The old accusations are trotted out, especially that they take over the spiritualities of parishes from the incumbents by their indulgent shriving (B. XX. 282–91), and develop effective flattery for gentlemen and insidious small-talk for ladies, until the priests, getting no profits from confessions, denounce the friars from their pulpits, and are slanged in return (B. V. 136–45). The poet is sometimes outrageously unfair, as when he says of Our Lord's Nativity

If any frere were founde there ich ȝif the fyue shillynges.

[I bet you five shillings there wasn't a friar found there.
B. XII. 146]

Even his attack on bishops *in partibus infidelium*, who never
visited their high-sounding sees long in Moslem hands, could
be represented in another way; a number of these prelates were
friars (such as the Dominican Thomas Waleys, Bishop of Lyco-
stomium in 1353; the Franciscan Thomas Botyler, Bishop 'Basi-
liensis' in 1394; and the Carmelite John Leicester, Bishop of
Smyrna in 1398; and all working in England), but their elevation
to episcopal rank at least suggests a combination of some of the
qualities of energy, fluency, efficiency, and even goodness. There
was no chance of Christian armies effectively reaching these parts
now, much less missionaries, and the retention of the titles was
pathetic but not culpable. And at home talented friars were occupy-
ing sees equally with secular and regular clergy: Thomas Rushook,
Provincial of the Dominicans, was consecrated to Llandaff in
1383 and translated to Chichester in 1385; William Bottisham,
another Blackfriar, held Bethlehem *in partibus* in 1385, Llandaff in
1386, and Rochester in 1389 (but Llandaff was a poverty-stricken
see, which perhaps sheds light on the impatience of these friars
with it); above all, the Austin friar Robert Waldby, D.D., was
Archbishop of Dublin in 1390 and even Primate at York by 1397.
Obviously, not all friars were the pert layabouts that our poets
were suggesting.

Five extended pictures of friars in *Piers Plowman* are of particular interest. When we are meeting society in the Field Full of
Folk of the Prologue, it is with a sense of climax that we reach the
notorious four orders:

> I fonde there freris, alle the foure ordres,
> Preched the peple for profit of hemseluen,
> Glosed the gospel as hem good lyked,
> For coueitise of copes construed it as thei wolde.
> Many of this maistris freris mowe clothen hem at lykyng,
> For here money and marchandise marchen togideres.

[I could see friars there, all four orders of them, and they were preaching to the people for their own gain, interpreting the gospel just as they pleased, and put their own meaning on it in their greed for rich garments. Many of these friars who have masters' degrees can wear just what they want to, because their profit and their trade go hand in hand. B. Prologue, 58–63]

That they devoted this not entirely to their own persons and pleasures, but often to their churches, is borne out by the lively picture of the friar hearing the confession of the wicked Lady Mede; she gives him a nice gold coin to be her beadsman and her agent, and after promptly absolving her he wheedles her as follows:

'We han a wyndowe a wirchyng wil sitten vs ful heigh.
Woldestow glase that gable and graue thereinne thi name,
Siker sholde thi soule be heuene to haue.'

['We're having a window made, and it's going to cost us a lot. If you would pay for the glazing of the whole gable and have your name engraved in the glass, your soul would be sure of having heaven.' B. III. 48–50]

Mede, after a pretty little plea for the absolution of all lustful lords and ladies, makes him an offer in return:

'And I shal keure ȝowre kirke, ȝowre cloystre do maken,
Wowes do whiten, and wyndowes glasen,
Do peynten and purtraye, and paye for the makynge,
Than eury segge shal seyn I am sustre of ȝowre hous'.

['And I shall roof your church, and have your cloister built, your walls whitewashed and your windows glazed, have paintings and statues done, and pay for the work, so that every-one will say I'm a lay-sister of your house.' B. III. 60–3]

Wasted loveliness, however sincerely it was sometimes applied! Nothing remains on the soil of England of the great friary churches, save a couple of towers such as those at Lynn and the Yorkshire Richmond, the now secularized Blackfriars at Norwich, and some re-used fragments; the greatest architectural loss in the

Second World War was perhaps the vast Decorated church of the Austin Friars in London, which was completely wiped out.

The dreamer himself is made the means of refuting the friars at the start of Passus VIII. Wandering around in his search for Do-well, he meets a pair of them:

> . . . it bifel on a Fryday two freres I mette,
> Maistres of the menoures, men of grete witte.
> I hailsed hem hendely, as I hadde lerned,
> And preyed hem par charitee, ar thei passed forther,
> If thei knewe any contre or costes, as thei went,
> Where that Do-well dwelleth. 'Doth me to wytene.'
> For thei ben men on this molde that moste wyde walken,
> And knowen contrees and courtes, and many kynnes places,
> Bothe pryncees paleyses and pore mennes cotes,
> And Do-wel and Do-yuel where thei dwelle bothe.
> 'Amonge vs,' quod the menours, 'that man is dwellynge,
> And euere hath, as I hope, and euere shal here-after.'
> '*Contra*,' quod I as a clerk, and comsede to dispuite.

[One Friday it happened that I met two friars, Fransciscans and Masters of Divinity, men of great understanding. I addressed them politely, as I had been taught, and asked them for the love of God not to go on until they had told me if they knew of any country or regions anywhere on their travels where Do-well lives. '*Do* tell me.' Because they go further afoot than anyone on earth, and they know various countries and courts, and many kinds of places from princes' palaces to poor men's cottages, and where Do-well and Do-evil both live. 'That man lives with us,' said those minorites; 'he always has, I believe, and he always will.' 'I dispute that,' I said, as they do in the Schools, and began to argue. B. VIII. 8–20]

Not that his argument is subtle; he says that Do-well and Do-evil cannot live together, and therefore Do-well cannot always domesticate with the friars. The friars take this mildly, and he is soon excusing himself for a further act of obtuseness.

The friar with an academic degree sitting at Conscience's hospitable board in Passus XIII is more of a caricature than the rest. He stuffs himself on dainties of a sloppy and pappy kind, while the better characters use their jaws on hard and simple tack of an improving nature and even with improving titles; he washes down his soups and minces with' draughts of wine, and follows them with puddings and tripe and boar's-flesh and eggs fried in fat. The dreamer is cross, because only four days ago the great hypocrite was preaching at St Paul's about that Apostle's mortifications; though the personified abstractions who are his companions try to restrain him, he offers some pertinent rudeness, but the doctor, rose-red and bloated now, produces a few choice remarks of the most superficial theology, insults Patience as a typical lying pilgrim, and yet gets a nice goodbye from Conscience.

Even the melancholy ending in the house called Unity is occasioned by Conscience's conditional acceptance of friars, provided they give up logic for Christian love, renounce temporal things as did Francis and Dominic, and go without wages; Envy instead induces them to go off to the university and study logic, law, contemplation, Plato, Seneca, and arguments in favour of communism, but one of them is soon back. His name is Friar Flatterer, alias Slinker-into-Houses (*Penetrans-domos*), and his soft absolution lulls Contrition first, and then the rest of the inhabitants, into an indifference to their sin, so that the house is weakened against the assaults of Antichrist. By the company they keep throughout the poem, the whole function of the friars within the church is undermined: Envy's garment has foresleeves made out of a friar's habit (B. V. 81), Falsehood flees to the friars (B. II. 210) and Liar is rescued by them (B. II. 229), one of the disreputable witnesses at Mede's wedding is a pardoner of the Pauline Order or 'Crutched Friars' (B. II. 108), and Sloth gets a mention at the friars' mass by having brought them a letter of fraternity (C. VIII. 27). Since pestilence time the friars have gone in for clever theological quibbles which they show off at St Paul's Cross to attract the proud and spite the clergy (B. X. 71–3); their preaching on the Trinity is full of stuff beyond the layman's reach, insoluble and fallacious (B. XV. 68–9 and C. XVII. 231), and they avoid preaching on the Ten Commandments and the Seven Deadly Sins, which would expose their own vanity and intellectual pride (B. XV. 72 ff.). The dreamer's own experience is that Fortune bore him company until old age seized him, and then she turned against him; he was further reduced by the onset of poverty, and then the friars avoided him, too—apparently because he decided to be buried at his own parish church and not at their friary (B. XI. 59–64).

This has been a melancholy section. The great age of English mendicants—of Roger Bacon and William of Ockham—may have been over, but it is hard to believe in Langland's total good faith. Our reading of Wyclif—a writer of a quite different religious temper from Langland—will, however, tend to confirm it.

The Solitaries

The unorganized solitaries—hermits with their lonely jobs and anchorites in the elected silence of their sealed cells—continued undiminished; Rotha Mary Clay's *The Hermits and Anchorites of England* (1914), and her voluminous notes towards a projected second edition, list about 180 sites where they were working and praying between 1350 and 1400. Only a third of these were occupied by true recluses—anchorites or ancresses—, and the spiritually simpler hermits in general had secular duties such as the maintenance of bridges, causeys, ferries, or highways; eight in marshy Cambridgeshire were making themselves useful in these ways. We must have lost all trace of many unobtrusive sites and their humble occupants; but, however thick they already were on the ground, at least five new hermitages were set up—one for a bridge and causey at Chester, others with the Black Prince's favour at Bodmin, the Bishop of Durham's at Eighton (County Durham), and Lord Berkeley's at Redcliffe (Bristol), and one at King's Lynn. In the Farne Islands, off the Northumberland coast, John Whiterig in 1363 offered himself with another man for the occupation of austere and lonely quarters that had a venerable history of eremitical life; his colleague looked after the buildings, the boat, and the fishing, but Whiterig, who had been novice master at Durham, devoted himself to contemplation, and his *Meditations* are in Durham Dean and Chapter MS B. iv. 34; he died in his hermitage in 1371.

Needless to say, the true recluses, freed from all secular duties and worldly sights, had always been enabled to make great gifts to the church of intense spirituality, which the most inspired of them put into writing. Seen in one way, their lives were monotonous: 'that is why an anker is called an anker, and anchored under the church like an anchor under the ship's board to hold the ship so that waves and storms don't overturn it', as the unknown writer of *Ancrene Wisse* had said long before; but then the infinitude of their greatest visions, the studied rhythms and repetitiveness of their daily lives, and the echoes of the liturgy, occasioned a prose in which cadences and alliterations and even rhymes sweep us upwards in the path of their dead ecstasy. Seven anchorites and ancresses are recorded in our period as moving into newly-appointed cells: one at Ainderby Steeple (Yorks) because in her old one she couldn't watch the sacraments at the altar, others on the special petitions of Queen Isabella and of the Earl of Warwick; at Holy Trinity, Dartford (Kent), the Bishop of Rochester in 1395 refounded and rebuilt the ankerhouse to accommodate Edward Aleyn, a parishioner eager to become a contemplative.

I am not merely trying to refute Langland's angry summary of hermits in *Piers Plowman* (B. Prologue 53–7):

> Heremites on an heep with hoked staues
> Wenten to Walsyngham, and here wenches after;
> Grete lobyes and longe, that loth were to swynke,
> Clotheden hem in copis to ben knowen fram othere,
> And shopen hem heremites, here ese to haue.

[Hermits with crooked sticks went crowding to Walsingham, and their women behind them; big tall lubbers, who didn't want to work, clothed themselves in cowls so as to be distinguished from other men, and dressed like hermits so as to get an easy life.]

Piers Plowman contains an even harsher account than this (C. x. 140 ff.) of the life of a hermit, who is seen sprawled in front of his evening fire, roasting himself and basting his back, draining the pot, and so to bed; his day starts when he feels inclined, and his morning walk directs him to the various attractions of bacon, cash, boiled meat, bread, or a lump of cheese, all at the expense of someone else's toil. Such hermits never marry their wenches, and their bastards are natural beggars; in fact, they break limbs, or even the backs, of these poor children, and use them to elicit alms. After following various trades and occupations, they set up as hermits on main roads, or in towns near the pubs, and beg in the churches. Whence the pretended confusion over whether Lollards were essentially 'mumblers' or 'babblers' from a Dutch word, or 'lollers-around' from an English one, or even (if you wanted to be fanciful) 'sowers of tares' from Latin *lolium*; there is no ambiguity really, though Langland in this context seems to foment it by lumping heretics with spurious hermits. But he had praised the solitaries of fixed abode in l. 28 of his poem, and even as he writes this tart passage he admits that there had been good solitaries, in woods among bears and lions, living on their scholarship and the labour of their hands, and even supplied with food by the birds; however much of nostalgic charm there may be in this little picture, its spirit is borne out by the surviving documents far more convincingly than is Langland's venom: true, the reformer Swinderby—deemed heretical in the 1380s—had been a hermit at a chapel of St John Baptist in woods near Leicester, but the only scandal recorded concerns Henry Hermyte of South Stoneham (Hants.), suspected in 1383 as a highwayman and harbourer of felons yet possibly nicknamed only.

Above them all tower two great figures in the history of English devotional writing: Dame Julian of Norwich and Walter Hilton; I am tempted to add the unknown author of *The Cloud of Unknowing* (readily available in the Penguin translation by Clifton Wolters, 1961), but for all the lively and deeply personal details of his splendid treatise he cannot be assigned to any certain status in the religious life. It would of course be quite wrong to see these three elect figures as accurately reflecting the religious thought of their time and country, but their mere occurrence, along with the fumbling Margery Kempe, proves how satisfactory, to the point of supernatural vision, an unquestioning orthodoxy could still be to some rare spirits. Dame Julian was in her thirty-first year when

o

she had her revelations of divine love on 8 May 1373; as ancress at the church of St Julian, in Conisford, Norwich, she achieved great repute, utter spiritual calm and optimism, and an old age far beyond the normal medieval span. The scribe of the Amherst MS in the British Museum prefaces her book with his own wonder at her piety and longevity:

> Here es a vision schewed be the goodenes of God to a deuoute woman, and hir name es Julian, that is recluse atte Norwyche and ʒitt ys on lyfe Anno Domini millesimo CCCC xiij°; in the whilke visyon er fulle many comfortabylle wordes and gretly styrrande to alle thaye that desyres to be Crystes looverse.
>
> [Here is a vision shown by the goodness of God to a devout woman whose name is Julian and who is a recluse at Norwich and still alive in the year of Our Lord 1413; in which vision are very many cheering and deeply moving words for all those who want to be Christ's lovers.]

She lives for many visitors to old English churches in her words, so often exhibited in porches, assuring us that God wants us to be familiar with him but reminding us not to take that familiarity so far as to forget courtesy; she still imparts the serenity of God's promise to her that 'all shall be well, and all shall be well, and all manner of things shall be well'; she still startles with a little cluster of words such as 'God never *began* to love mankind', and makes what she arrived at by so hard a way seem easy and obvious: 'He did not say, "You will not be tempested; you will not be travailed; you will not be distressed". But he *did* say, "You will not be overcome." '

Dame Julian—'first English woman of letters', though not of course as a professional writer—lives on despite the destruction of her cell at the Reformation and of St Julian's in the Second World War; an old man living by the ruins in 1943 told me there, tremulously and with no regard for the dedication of the church, 'I don't know who she was, but she certainly looked after her flock', since the bomb had thereby missed the crowded air-raid shelters. On 8 May 1953 a restored and rebuilt chapel and shrine on the site, with the stump of the round tower, were dedicated by the Bishop of Norwich in thanksgiving for her life and work, and put under the care of the sisters of the Anglican Community of All Hallows. It is interesting that the most attractive book on her was the work of a nonconformist minister: P. Franklin Chambers, *Juliana of Norwich* (London, 1955). Walter Hilton, enclosed at Thurgarton (Notts.) about 1375, later an Augustinian Canon at the Priory there, later still perhaps a Carthusian monk, and dead by 1395, has necessarily been less 'popular'; *The Ladder of Perfection* (readily available in the Penguin translation by Leo Sherley-Price, 1957) is far more speculative, more bitter against heresy, than Dame Julian's personal record needed to be, and a kind of coldness may appear to the superficial reader. Yet its style is entrancingly metaphorical; Hilton's exaltation, and the imaginative leaps of his mind, make natural the linking of metaphors mild or violent—the roots and streams and cloak and shadow of sin, the fastening with the nails of Christ's love, the tight-drawn knot of love, the needle-sharp pricking of the heart, the grinding in humility's mortar, the foot of true desire treading its patrimony in heaven, and hundreds more. His loathing of heretics, and his crazy statement that the unbaptized baby is an image of the fiend and brand of hell, are repellent; but in general he illustrates the clemency, the understanding of ordinary men, the pastoral endeavour, and the prolific vernacular writings, that distinguish the Augustinians, and it is refreshing to see him putting formal prayers and physical privations a poor second. Don't just slack, he warns us, and think that you're contemplating; even a spirituality that ignores practical jobs and soaks itself in prayer is 'tending God's head and neglecting His feet'.

Other works that have found their way into the Hiltonian canon are slighter. Expositions of the Psalms *Qui Habitat* and *Bonum Est* (Björn Wallner, *An Exposition of Qui Habitat and Bonum Est in English*, Lund, 1954) are markedly less Christocentric, but the similes are lively: the righteous man's refuge in God is 'As a mon, in sauyng of his bodi for drede of stormes, fleoþ to house & holdeþ him þer-inne þat he perissche not' [as a man, in saving his body for fear of storms, flees to a house and keeps himself inside so as not to perish]; Our Lord's shoulders are 'As þe hen kepeþ hire briddes vnder schadewyng of hire whinges from takyng of þe kuite' [as the hen protects her chicks under the shadow of her wings against capture by the kite]; worldlings leagued for wickedness 'cleuen alle to-geder as burres don' [all cleave together as do burrs], but will eventually hate one another and 'gnawen to-geder as felle houndes' [snap at one another like savage hounds]. But here the metaphors are duller (save for the stinking glue of fleshly love that binds such people), as if the writer were imitating Hilton's method without being able to meditate so consistently in terms of imagery. A genuine Hiltonic piece, albeit a translation, *Eight Chapters on Perfection*, is even slighter, with a few unexcited metaphors rising to 'a place and a priuy chaumbir to þi Lord Iesu Crist þi spouse in þi soule' [a place and private chamber in your soul for the Lord Jesus Christ, your spouse], and again a stronger vein of simile: bringing things to mind in Jesus's presence is compared, in lovely simplicity, with taking a thing out of a dark place to know what it is. And, despite a too great silkiness of style, there is one ringing sentence of native alliteration: 'it is wondur stif, streyt and strong, as a þing þat myȝte not be stirid ne chaungid' [it is surprisingly stiff, strait and strong, as a thing that could not be stirred or changed]. A very attractive little edition, with pictures of specimen pages of all eight MSS, is by Fumio Kuriyagawa, *Walter Hilton's Eight Chapters on Perfection* (Tokyo, 1967).

Margery Kempe

On a lower plane than the true mystics stands Margery Kempe, *née* Brunham, of King's Lynn; unfortunately for our present purpose, thirty-eight years of her long *floruit* lie in the next century, but she was born about 1373, grew up in Lynn during considerable terms of mayoralty on her father's part, and about 1393 married John Kempe, recently admitted into the liberty of the town. For her garrulous spiritual diary she had one poor qualification, illiteracy, but long-suffering amanuenses have left us the first real autobiography in our language; over 250 pages of frank and often neurotic self-examination; dialogues with God, and authentic bickerings with her detractors; parish squabbles, and hardy journeys to Norway and Santiago and Jerusalem; visions obscene and incandescently divine. For a time, her parish priest at St Margaret's in Lynn was William Sawtre the Lollard, whose recantation in St James's churchyard she may have witnessed on 25 May 1399, and who was the first heretic to be burnt at the stake; her own heightened orthodoxy was later questioned, and she was even accused of being the daughter of the heresiarch Cobham, but none of the learned prelates who questioned her could honestly ascribe heresy to her. The hostility of the Archbishop of York towards her in 1417 may go back to the 1399 proscription in England of the sect of Flagellants, who, dressed in white from top to toe, went around scourging themselves; she, with little tact, was wearing all white clothes, which with her prostrations, tears and screams earned her his sharp question 'Why gost þu in white? Art þu a mayden?' ['Why do you go about in white? Are you a virgin?']. The most Wyclifite things that she did were to quote Scripture and to give informal sermons; otherwise she was deeply committed to the usual religious practices and superstitions of her era.

Whatever value we may now place on her mystical experiences—finding them, at worst, self-induced or grossly exaggerated or bookishly derived from real women contemplatives—her diary is a valuable mirror of the social life and human relationships of the time, and still another contribution to our remarkably full record of Lynn dialect. The fourteenth-century period of her life is covered, in lively detail but with haphazard chronology, when she recounts her marriage (S. B. Meech and H. E. Allen, *The Book of Margery Kempe*, Early English Text Society No. 212, London, 1940, pp. 6–11):

Whan þis creatur was xx ʒer of age or sumdele mor, sche was maryed to a worschepful burgeys and was wyth chylde wyth-in schort tyme, as kynde wolde. And, aftyr þat sche had conceyued, sche was labowrd wyth gret accessys tyl þe chyld was born, & þan, what for labowr sche had in chyldyng & for

sekenesse goyng beforn, sche dyspered of hyr lyfe, wenyng
sche mygth not leuyn. And þan sche sent for hyr gostly fadyr,
for sche had a thyng in conscyens whech sche had neuyr
schewyd be-forn þat tyme in alle hyr lyfe. For sche was euyr
lettyd be hyr enmy þe Deuel euyr-mor seyng to hyr whyl sche
was in good heele hir nedyd no confessyon but don penawns
be hir-self a-loone, & all schuld be forȝouyn, for God is
mercyful j-now. And þerfor þis creatur oftyn-tymes dede greet
penawns in fastyng bred & watyr & oþer dedys of almes wyth
devowt preyers, saf sche wold not schewyn it in confessyon.
And, whan sche was any tym seke or dysesyd, þe Deuyl
seyd in her mende þat sche schuld be dampnyd, for sche was
not schreuyn of þat defawt. . . . &, whan sche cam to þe poynt
for to seyn þat þing whech sche had so long conselyd, hir
confessowr was a lytyl to hastye & gan scharply to vndyr-
nemyn hir er þan sche had fully seyd hir entent, & so sche
wold no mor seyn for nowt he mygth do. And a-noon, for
dreed sche had of dampnacyon on þe to syde & hys scharp
repreuyng on þat oþer syde, þis creatur went owt of hir mende
& was wondyrlye vexid & labowryd wyth spyritys half ȝer
viij wekys & odde days. And in þis tyme sche sey, as hir thowt,
deuelys opyn her mowthys al inflaumyd wyth brennyng lowys of
fyr as þei schuld a swalwyd hyr in, sum-tyme rampyng at hyr,
sum-tyme thretyng her, sum-tym pullyng hyr & halyng hir
boþe nygth & day duryng þe forseyd tyme. And also þe deuelys cryed up-on hir wyth greet thretyngys & bodyn hir sche
schuld forsake hir Crystendam, hir feyth, and denyin hir God,
Hys Modyr, & alle þe seyntys in Heuyn, hyr goode werkys &
alle good vertues, hir fadyr, hyr modyr, & alle hire frendys.
And so sche dede. Sche slawndred hir husbond, hir frendys,
and her owyn self; sche spak many a repreuows worde and
many a schrewyd worde; sche knew no vertu ne goodnesse;
sche desyryd all wykkydnesse; lych as þe spyrytys temptyd
hir to sey & do, so sche seyd & dede. Sche wold a fordon
hir-self many a tym at her steryngys & a ben damnyd wyth
hem in helle, & in-to wytnesse þerof sche bot hir owen hand so
vyolently þat it was seen al hir lyfe aftyr. And also sche roof hir

skyn on hir body a-ȝen hir hert wyth hir nayles spetowsly, for sche had noon oþer instrumentys, & wers sche wold a don saf sche was bowndyn & kept wyth strength boþe day & nygth þat sche mygth not haue hir wylle.

[When this creature was twenty years old, or somewhat more, she married a respectable burgess and was with child in a short time, as nature demanded. And after she had conceived she suffered from severe attacks of illness until the child was born, and then, what with the labour she had in childbirth and the preceding sickness, she despaired of her life and thought that she could not live. And then she sent for her spiritual father, because she had something on her conscience that she had never revealed before that time in all her life. For she was always prevented by her enemy the Devil's evermore saying to her, while she was in good health, that she needed no confession except to do penance by herself alone, and all would be forgiven, because God is very merciful. And therefore this creature often did great penance by fasting on bread and water, and other acts of alms-giving, with devout prayers, except that she would not reveal it in confession. And when she was at any time sick or disturbed the Devil said in her mind that she would be damned, because she was not absolved from that sin. . . . And when she came to the point of saying that thing which she had so long concealed, her confessor was a little too hasty and began to reprove her sharply before she had fully said what she intended, and so she would not say any more despite all his efforts. And at once, because of the dread she had of damnation on the one hand and his sharp reproof on the other, this creature went out of her mind and was marvellously troubled and tormented by spirits for half a year, eight weeks, and a few days. And during this time she saw, so it seemed to her, devils opening their mouths all inflamed with burning flames of fire as though they would have swallowed her in, sometimes ramping at her, sometimes threatening her, sometimes pulling and dragging her, both night and day during the above-mentioned time. And also the

devils shouted at her with great threats and ordered her to
forsake her Christianity, her faith, and deny her God, His
mother, and all the saints in heaven, her good deeds and all
good virtues, her father, her mother, and all her friends. And so
she did. She slandered her husband, her friends, and her own
self; she spoke many reproving and churlish words; she knew
no virtue or goodness; she desired every wickedness; just as the
spirits tempted her to say and do, so she said and did. She
would have destroyed herself many times at their promptings
and been damned with them in hell, and in token of it she bit
her own hand so violently that it could be seen all her life
afterwards. And also she tore her skin on her body opposite
her heart spitefully with her nails, because she had no other
instruments, and she would have done worse except that she
was bound and restrained forcibly both day and night so that
she could not have her will.]

But one day, when her keepers were absent, Jesus appeared to
her, sitting on her bed in a purple silk mantle, and spoke words
of gentle reproach to her; she saw how

þe eyr openyd as brygth as ony levyn, & He stey up in-to þe
eyr, not rygth hastyli & qwykly, but fayr & esly, þat sche
mygth wel be-holdyn hym in þe eyr tyl it was closyd a-geyn.
And a-noon þe creature was stabelyd in hir wyttys & in hir
reson as wel as euyr sche was be-forn, and preyd hir husbond
as so soon as he cam to hir þat sche mygth haue þe keys of
þe botery to takyn hir mete & drynke as sche had don be-
forn.

[the air opened as bright as any lightning, and He ascended
up into the air, not very hastily and quickly, but nicely and
gently, so that she could easily see Him in the air until it had
closed again. And at once the creature was made as stable in
her faculties and in her reason as she had ever been before, and
begged her husband as soon as he came to her that she might
have the keys of the buttery to get her food and drink as she
had done before.]

Her maidservants and keepers advised him against this, saying

that she would only give everything away; but with his usual
tenderness and compassion he complied with her wishes, and
after taking sustenance she recognized her friends, household,
and visitors. With this came a new dependence on God and a
longing to be His servant.

Neuyr-þe-lesse, sche wold not leeuyn hir pride ne hir pompows
aray þat sche had vsyd be-for-tym, neiþyr for hyr husbond
ne for noon oþer mannys cownsel. And ʒet sche wyst ful wel
þat men seyden hir ful mech velany, for sche weryd gold pypys
on hir hevyd, & hir hodys wyth þe typettys were daggyd. Hir
clokys also wer daggyd & leyd wyth dyuers colowrs be-twen
þe daggys þat it schuld be þe mor staryng to mennys sygth and
hir-self þe mor ben worshepd. And, whan hir husbond wold
speke to hir for to leuyn hir pride, sche answeryd schrewydly &
schortly & seyd þat sche was comyn of worthy kenred—hym
semyd neuyr for to a weddyd hir, for hir fadyr was sum-tyme
meyr of þe town N. and sythyn he was alderman of þe hey
Gylde of þe Trinyte in N. And þerfor sche wold sauyn þe
worschyp of hir kynred what-so-euyr ony man seyd. Sche had
ful greet envye at hir neybowrs þat þei schuld ben arayd so
wel as sche. Alle hir desyr was for to be worshepd of þe pepul.
Sche wold not be war be onys chastysyng ne be content wyth
þe goodys þat God had sent hire, as hir husbond was, but
euyr desyryd mor & mor. And than, for pure coveytyse & for
to maynten hir pride, sche gan to brewyn & was on of þe
grettest brewers in þe town N. a iij ʒer or iiij tyl sche lost mech
good, for sche had neuyr vre þerto. For, thow sche had neuyr
so good seruawntys & cunnyng in brewyng, ʒet it wold neuyr
preuyn wyth hem. For, whan þe ale was as fayr standyng vndyr
berm as any man mygth se, sodenly þe berm wold fallyn down
þat alle þe ale was lost euery brewyng aftyr oþer, þat hir
seruawntys weryn a-schamyd & wold not dwellyn wyth hir.

[Nevertheless, she would not desist from her pride or her
showy attire that she had affected hitherto, either for her
husband or for any other man's advice. And yet she knew that

people were saying a great deal of evil about her, because she wore gold piping on her head and her hoods with their tippets were scalloped. Her cloaks, also, were slashed and backed with various colours between the slashes so as to make it the more conspicuous to men's sight and make her be more respected. And when her husband tried to speak to her to make her give up her pride, she answered churlishly and rudely and said that she had come of an important family—he had never been fit to marry her, because her father was formerly mayor of the town of N and was afterwards alderman of the worshipful Guild of the Trinity in N. And therefore she would preserve the honour of her family, whatever any man said. She was very envious indeed that her neighbours should be dressed as well as she. Her whole desire was to be respected by people. She would not take warning from having been once chastised or be content with the good that God had sent her, as her husband was, but always wanted more and more. And then, for mere covetousness and so as to maintain her pride, she began to brew and was one of the chief brewers in the town of N for three or four years until she lost a lot of money, because she had never had any experience at it. For though she had servants who were ever so good, and smart at brewing, yet things never turned out right with them. For when the ale was standing as nicely under barm as any man could see, suddenly the barm would fall down, so that all the ale was lost in every brewing, one after another, so that her servants were ashamed and would not stay with her.]

Seeing this as another punishment from God, she apologized to her husband for rejecting his advice and promised to amend her pride.

But ȝet sche left not þe world al hol, for now sche be-thowt hir of a newe huswyfre: sche had an horsmille. Sche gat hire tweyn good hors & a man to gryndyn mennys corne & þus sche trostyd to getyn hir leuyng. Þis provysion duryd not longe, for in schort tyme aftyr on Corpus Cristi Evyn fel þis merueyl. Thys man, beyng in good heele of body & hys tweyn

hors craske & lykand þat wel haddyn drawyn in þe mylle be-
for-tyme, as now he toke on of his hors & put hym in þe mylle
as he had don be-for, & þis hors wold drawe no drawt in þe
mylle for no-þing þe man mygth do, þe man was sory & asayd
wyth al hys wyttys how he schuld don þis hors drawyn. Sum-
tyme he led hym be þe heed, sum-tyme he beet hym, & sum-
tyme he chershyd hym, and alle avayled not, for he wold raþer
gon bakward þan forward. Þan þis man sett a scharp peyr
sporys on hys helys & rood on þe hors bak for to don hym
drawyn, & it was neuyr þe bettyr. Whan þis man saw it wold be
in no wey, þan he sett up þis hors a-geyn in þe stabyl and ȝafe
hym mete, & he ete weel & freschly. And sythen he toke þe
oþer hors & put hym in þe mylle. And lech as hys felaw dede
so dede he, for he wold not drawe for any-thing þat þe man
mygth do. And þan þis man forsoke hys seruyse & wold no
lengar abyden wyth þe fornseyd creatur.

[But still she did not abandon the world entirely, because she
now thought of a new domestic occupation: she had a horse-
mill. She got herself two good horses and a man, to grind
people's corn, and thus she trusted to earn her living. This
arrangement did not last long, because a little while afterwards
the following miracle occurred on the eve of Corpus Christi.
This man, whose bodily health was good and whose two
horses were lusty and in good condition and had pulled well
in the mill before that time, when he took one of his horses and
put him in the mill as he had done before, and this horse would
not pull at all in the mill for anything that the man might do,
the man was worried and tried with all his wits to make this
horse pull. Now he led him by the head, now he beat him, and
now he patted him, and it was all no use, because he would
sooner go backwards than forwards. Then this man put a sharp
pair of spurs on his heels and rode on the horse's back to make
him pull, and it was none the better. When this man saw that
it was not to be by any means, he put this horse back in the
stable and gave him food, and he ate well and eagerly. And
then he took the other horse and put him in the mill. And he

behaved as his companion had, because he would not pull for anything that the man might do. And then this man gave up his job and would not stay any longer with the above-mentioned creature.]

The town was full of rumours that she was cursed, or the victim of God's vengeance; but wise men saw it as Christ's calling her from the pride and vanity of this wretched world, and it is clear that she dates her conversion from this crisis.

On a nygth, as þis creatur lay in hir bedde wyth hir husbond, sche herd a sownd of melodye so swet & delectable, hir þowt, as sche had been in Paradyse. And þerwyth sche styrt owt of hir bedde & seyd, 'Alas, þat euyr I dede synne! It is ful mery in Hevyn.' Thys melody was so swete þat it passyd alle þe melodye þat euyr mygth be herd in þis world wyth-owtyn ony comparyson, & caused þis creatur whan sche herd ony myrth or melodye aftyrward for to haue ful plentyuows & habund-awnt teerys of hy deuocyon wyth greet sobbyngys & syhyngys aftyr þe blysse of Heuen, not dredyng þe schamys & þe spytys of þe wretchyd world.

[One night, as this creature lay in her bed with her husband, she heard a sound of melody as sweet and delightful, it seemed to her, as if she were in Paradise. And at that she started out of her bed and said 'Alas, that I ever sinned! It is very pleasant in Heaven.' This melody was so sweet that it surpassed all the melody that could ever be heard in this world, without any comparison, and caused this creature, when she heard any mirth or melody afterwards, to have very plentiful and abundant tears of high devotion, with great sobbings and sighings for the joy of Heaven, not fearing the shames and spites of the wretched world.]

The strange set purpose of Margery Kempe's life, and with it her alarming energy and persuasive power, were to come after 1400, but already we can sense these better qualities behind the hysteria and gush of this description of the years that formed her.

5: Religious Heterodoxy

Clerical Heterodoxy: The Wyclifites

WE must now turn from orthodoxy, in which our mystics and lyrists were the only great luminaries, to heterodoxy, which was centred on John Wyclif and his following. His writings, with other 'Wyclifite' tracts stirred in, will be found in:

T. Arnold, *Select English Works of John Wyclif*, 3 vols. (Oxford, 1869–1871);

F. D. Matthew, *The English Works of Wyclif Hitherto Unprinted*, Early English Text Society No. 74 (London, 1880);
and a very attractive anthology, with Introduction and apparatus, H. E. Winn, *Wyclif: Select English Writings* (Oxford, 1929). 'The Morning Star of the Reformation' was a Yorkshireman (his surname is a village on the Tees), but his influential use of the East Midland dialect, equally with Chaucer, helped to confirm it as our standard; that he was 'Father of English Prose' is more doubtful than his other title, but his aggressiveness in using English where Latin had sufficed made him one of the saviours of our language. He went up to Oxford before the Black Death, was Master of Balliol College by 1360, and after the prescribed years of meticulous study and teaching obtained his doctorate in 1372, with a mind highly trained in theology, philosophy, and other academic disciplines. Even when he left to become a country rector he had to absent himself from time to time to continue his studies, and in the year of his doctorate became, as it were, a civil servant and a trusted officer of the Crown; so far, he sounds the typical scholar, pluralist, and political churchman, but his administrative activities were directed at the cleansing of the Church and the weakening of the Pope, and he had soon worked out his profound and elaborate ideas on 'Dominion'—the interrelation of Church, State, and God—which dwell in his Latin

treatises and cannot be coherently studied in English. His trust in political institutions as a safeguard against ecclesiastical tyranny was rather indiscreetly expressed in his adherence to the imperfect John of Gaunt; but for a time the young king and Joan, 'Fair Maid of Kent' and the king's mother, were behind him, too, and always the secular clergy at Oxford championed him. While he fulminated against the Pope and against the abuses in the Church he was safe and even popular, despite the efforts of bishops and subtle friars to destroy him, but his denial of Transubstantiation left him an alarmingly lonely figure, and he retired to his rectory of Lutterworth to continue his campaign, composing tracts of mounting fury, and sending out his Poor Priests. He was lucky; despite a vast output of 'heretical' writings, he remained unmolested and escaped the fire, dying in 1384 after a couple of years of paralysis. His lieutenants at Oxford served him variously: Philip Repingdon after 1382 was forced into a recantation and did very well out of it, becoming Bishop of Lincoln and actually a Cardinal! Nicholas Hereford, after a similar condemnation, wrote the lively *Lincolniensis* and had manful adventures in a Roman prison, in the English missionary field, in an English prison from which he escaped, in more preaching and tract-writing in the West Country, and finally in the Archbishop of Canterbury's torture-chambers at Saltwood; whereafter he turned, or was turned, and became as fierce an anti-Lollard as anyone. John Purvey (Winn, op. cit., pp. 147–149) remained faithful, staying with his master at Lutterworth, revising Hereford's wretched *Early Version* of the Bible into the far more idiomatic *Later Version*, and pouring out tracts that included even a proposal to turn the Church's wealth over to founding fifteen universities and a hundred almshouses. By 1400 he, too, had found his way to Saltwood, and a recantation at St Paul's Cross was wrung or won from him the year after; he resigned the living with which he was paid for this, and by 1405 was active again, but nothing more is known of him for certain.

These were the great clerical Lollards, the doomed reformers who by 1395 included no noted scholar save Purvey. Their chief literary activity was the translation and spread of the English Bible, and doughty Protestants may well see the turncoat Hereford as no great loss to the cause, since his version (C. Lindberg, *MS. Bodley* 959, Stockholm, 1959 etc.) is just an insensitive word-for-word glossing of each Latin word, often in a totally Latin order, into English. We can only wince at what he does to *Genesis* I. 1–4: 'In þe first made God of nouȝt heuen and erþ. Þe erþ forsoþe was veyn withinne and void, and derknesseȝ weren vp on þe face of þe see. And þe spirite of God was yborn vp on þe waters. And God seid, "Be made liȝt", and made is liȝt'; or the 23rd Psalm: 'Þe lord gouerneþ me and no thing to me shal lacken: in þe place of lesewe wher He me ful sette. Ouer water of ful-filling He broȝte out me; my soule He conuertide'; or *Ecclesiastes* XII. 1: 'Haue mynde of þi Creatour in þe daiys of þi ȝouþe, and er tyme come of tormenting and neȝen þe ȝeeris of þe whiche þou seye "Þei plesen not to me".' [In the first made God of nothing heaven and earth. The earth forsooth was empty within and void, and darknesses were upon the face of the sea. And the spirit of God was borne upon the waters. And God said, 'Be made light', and made is light./The lord governs me and nothing to me shall lack, in the place of pasture where He me quite set. Over water of fulfilling He brought out me; my soul He converted./Have mind of thy Creator in the days of thy youth, and before time comes of tormenting and approach the years of the which thou sayest, 'They please not to me'.]

The stalwart John Purvey had no use for such pinchbeck stuff. In a deservedly famous prologue (Winn, *op. cit.*, pp. 26–9) to his revised version of the Scriptures, he says that laymen are crying out for it despite opposition, and that he and his helpers have collected old Bibles and glosses, and commentaries such as Nicholas de Lyra's, and have consulted old grammarians and divines over difficult points and used clever men to correct the final translation. Next, his statement on the method of translation is one of the most important documents in the early history of linguistic study: 'First it is to knowe that the best translating is out of Latyn into English to translate aftir the sentence, and not oneli aftir the wordis, so that the sentence be as opin either openere in English as in Latyn, and go not fer fro the lettre; and if the lettre mai not be suid in the translating, let the sentence evere be hool and open, for the wordis owen to serve to the entent and sentence, and ellis the wordis ben superflu either false. In translating into English, manie resolucions moun make the sentence open, as an ablative case absolute may be resolvid into these thre wordis, with covenable verbe, *the while, for, if,* as gramariens seyn. As thus, *the maistir redinge, I stonde* may be resolvid thus: *While the maistir redith, I stonde* either *If the maistir redith* either *For the maistir,* etc. And sumtyme it wolde acorde wel with the sentence to be resolvid into *whanne* either into *aftirward.* Thus, *Whanne the maister red, I stood* either *After the maistir red, I stood.* And sumtyme it may wel be resolvid into a verbe of the same tens, as othere ben in the same resoun, and into this word *et,* that is, *and* in English. And thus, *Arescentibus hominibus prae timore,* that is, *And men shulen wexe drie for drede.* Also, a participle of a present tens either preterit, of active vois either passif, may be resolvid into a verbe of the same tens and a coniunccioun copulatif. As thus, *dicens,* that is, *seiynge,* mai be resolvid thus, *and seith* either *that seith.* And this wole in manie places make the sentence open, where to Englisshe it aftir the word wolde be derk and douteful.' He points out that he has had trouble with incorrect Latin Bibles, but that St Jerome and others have been his authorities for the original Hebrew meaning. 'Lord God! Sithen at the bigynnyng of feith so manie men translatiden into Latyn, and to greet profyt of Latyn men, lat oo symple creature of God translate into English for profyt of English men; for if worldli clerkis loken wel here croniclis and bokis, thei shulden fynde that Bede translatide the Bible and expounide it myche in Saxon, that was English either comoun langage of this lond in his tyme. And not oneli Bede, but also King Alured, that foundide Oxenford, translatide in hise laste daies the bigynning of the Sauter into Saxon, and wolde more if he hadde lyved longere. Also Frenshemen, Beemers and Britons han the Bible, and othere bokis of devocioun and exposicioun, translatid in here modir langage. Whi shulden not Englishmen have the same in here modir langage I can no wite, nobut for falsenesse and necgligence of clerkis, either for oure puple is not worthi to have so greet grace and ȝifte of God, in peyne of here olde synnes. But in translating of wordes equivok, that is, that

hath manie significacions undur oo lettre, mai liʒtli be peril. . . .
Therefore a translatour hath greet nede to studie wel the sentence
both bifore and aftir, and loke that suche equivok wordis acorde
with the sentence. And he hath nede to lyve a clene lif, and be ful
devout in preiers, and have not his wit ocupied about worldli
thingis, that the Holi Spiryt, autour of wisdom and kunnyng and
truthe, dresse him in his werk and suffre him not for to erre. Also
this word *ex* signifieth sumtyme *of*, and sumtyme it signifieth *bi*,
as Jerom seith. And this word *enim* signifieth comynly *forsothe*
and, as Jerom seith, it signifieth cause, thus, *forwhi*. And this word
secundum is taken for *aftir*, as manie men seyn, and comynli; but
it signifieth wel *bi* eithir *up*; thus *bi ʒoure word* either *up ʒoure
word*. Manie such adverbis, coniuncciouns and preposiciouns ben
set ofte oon for another, and at fre chois of autouris sumtyme;
and now tho shulen be taken as it acordith best to the sentence.
By this maner, with good lyvyng and greet travel, men moun come
to trewe and cleer translating, and a trewe undurstonding of Holi
Writ, seme it neuere so hard at the bigynnyng. God graunte to us
alle grace to kunne wel and kepe wel Holi Writ, and suffre
ioiefulli sum peyne for it at the laste. Amen.' [First it must be
realized that the best translation out of Latin into English is to
translate according to the sense, and not only according to the
words, so that the sense is as plain in English as in Latin, or
plainer, and does not stray far from the letter; and if the letter
cannot be followed in the translation, let the sense always be
complete and plain, because the words ought to serve for the meaning and sense, and otherwise the words are superfluous or false.
In translating into English, many resolutions can make the sense
plain; for instance, an ablative absolute case can be resolved into
these three words—with suitable verbs—. 'the while', 'for', 'if',
as grammarians say. For example, 'the master reading, I stand'
may be resolved like this: 'While the master reads, I stand' or
'If the master reads' or 'Because the master reads', etc. And
sometimes it would suit well with the sense for it to be resolved
into 'when' or into 'after'. So, 'When the master was reading, I
was standing' or 'After the master had read, I stood'. And sometimes it can well be resolved into a verb of the same tense, as

P

others are in the same sequence, and into the word 'et', that is, 'and' in English. And so, 'Arescentibus hominibus prae timore', that is, 'And men shall grow dry for fear'. In the same way, a participle of present or preterite tense, of active or passive voice, may be resolved into a verb of the same tense and a copulative conjunction. And so, 'dicens', that is, 'saying', may be resolved like this, 'and says' or 'who says'. And this will in many places make the sense plain, whereas to English it according to the word would be dark and ambiguous./Lord God! Since at the beginning of faith so many men translated into Latin, and to the great benefit of Latin men, let one simple creature of God translate into English for the benefit of Englishmen; for if worldly scholars examined their chronicles and books well, they would find that Bede translated the Bible and expounded it greatly in Saxon, which was the English or normal language of this land in his time. And not only Bede, but also King Alfred, who founded Oxford, translated the beginning of the Psalter into Saxon in his last days, and would have done more if he had lived longer. Also, Frenchmen, Bohemians and Welshmen have the Bible and other books of devotion and exposition, translated into their mother tongue. Why Englishmen should not have the same in their mother tongue I cannot imagine, unless it is through the falseness and negligence of scholars, or because our people are not worthy to have so great a grace and gift of God, as a penalty for their old sins. But in translating equivocal words, that is, those that have many meanings under one spelling, there may easily be danger. . . . Therefore a translator has great need to study well the sense both preceding and following, and see to it that such equivocal words agree with the sense. And he has need to live a pure life, and be very devout in prayers, and not have his understanding occupied with worldly things, so that the Holy Spirit, the author of wisdom and knowledge and truth, may direct him in his work and not allow him to err. Likewise, the word 'ex' sometimes signifies 'of', and sometimes signifies 'by', as Jerome says. And the word 'enim' usually signifies 'indeed' and, as Jerome says, it signifies cause, that is, 'because'. And the word 'secundum' is taken as 'according to', as many men say, and normally; but it certainly signifies 'by' or 'upon'; so, 'by your word' or 'upon your word'. Many such adverbs, conjunctions and prepositions are often put for one another, and sometimes at the free choice of authors; and now they must be taken as suits best with the sense. By this means, with a good life and hard work, men may come to an accurate and clear translation, and an accurate understanding of Holy Scripture, however hard it may seem at the beginning. May God grant to all of us grace to know and keep Holy Scripture well, and joyfully endure some pain for it at the last. Amen.]

Wyclif himself, in Chapter XV of his *De Officio Pastorali* (Winn, op cit., pp. 19–20; and K. Sisam, *Fourteenth Century Verse and Prose*, Oxford, 1921 etc., pp. 117–19), states with equal force the case for vernacular scriptures, but plays down the problems involved. As we would expect, he sees the friars in the van of opposition to the translation, with their belief that it is heresy to put God's law into English. This law, he says, must come to us in God's words, comprehensibly in our own tongue; the Apostles were given 'wit' on 'Wit' Sunday so that they could teach different peoples in different tongues. (This philological blunder, and Wyclif's tedious over-use of 'wit' in various senses, underlines his indifference to those 'equivok' words that had troubled Purvey.) St Jerome translated the Scriptures into Latin so that they might spread thence into other languages; why should the process not continue? France, despite opposition, has vernacular scriptures, and English lords can own copies, 'so it were not aȝenus resoun þat þey hadden þe same sentense in Engliȝsch; for þus Goddis lawe wolde be betere knowun, and more trowid, for onehed of wit, and more acord be betwixe reumes.' [so it would not be unreasonable for them to have the same matter in English; because in that way God's law would be better known, and more believed, because of uniformity of interpretation, and there would be more agreement between realms.] The phrase 'onehed of wit' illustrates the sometimes excessive economy and Anglo-Saxonism of Wyclif's sharper phrasing; English was not yet a satisfactory vehicle for all branches of recondite argument, and words like *one-hood* have, in fact, even now not displaced their Romance rivals save on the lips of people who like calling an omnibus a 'folk-wain'. Why, he

goes on to ask, do friars teach the Lord's Prayer in English, and
not the whole of the Gospels of which it forms part? To be saved,
we must follow Christ's teaching and his life; to hinder knowledge
of the Gospel is to hinder men from reaching heaven. There may
be faults due to incorrect translating—and there may have been
many when the Hebrew was put into Greek and the Greek into Latin:
'But lyve men good lif, and studie many persones Goddis lawe,
and whanne chaungying of wit is foundun, amende þey it as
resoun wole.' [But let men live a good life, and let many people
study God's law, and when a change of meaning is discovered,
let them emend it as reason demands.] The lack of scholasticism
in this bright demand for a good life followed by enlightenment is
typical of Wyclif, and after a further attack on the friars he ends
the passage with the resounding cry, 'God move lordis and
bischops to stonde for knowing of His lawe!' [May God move
lords and bishops to stand for the knowledge of His law!]

The pungency and irony of Wyclif's freer style is seen in Nicholas
Hereford before torture broke him, and contrasts strangely with
the clotted English of his Bible version. In *Seven Deadly Sins* he
shows himself an uncompromising pacifist: 'Jesus Christ, duke of
oure batel, taught us lawe of pacience, and not to fight bodily.'
(Arnold, op. cit., III. 138) [Jesus Christ, leader of our battle,
taught us the law of patience and taught us not to fight with our
bodies.] And in his *Lincolniensis* (Winn, op. cit., pp. 38–40; it
looks back and praises Grosseteste, Bishop of Lincoln) a fine
gruffness come out in alliteration such as 'þe reume of Englonde
schal scharply be punyschid for prisonynge of pore prestis [the
realm of England shall be severely punished for the imprisonment
of poor priests]; in the delicate understatement of his summary
of the religious orders, 'hit is likely þat al þis private religioun
makes not such a legioun of seyntes in Heven' [it is likely that all
this private religion does not make such a legion of saints in
Heaven]; and in the deliberately ugly image by which he shows the
reproved friar growing angry, 'as a horce unrubbed, þat haves
a sore back, wynses when he is oght touched or rubbed on his
rugge.' [as an unrubbed horse, that has a sore back, winces when
he is in any way touched or rubbed on his back.] It is possible to

see the beginnings of modern English humour here and throughout the Wyclifite canon; not only its roughness, but the reticent wit of that second sarcasm. Similarly, the real beginnings of continuous English prose are to be found in the works of the school, and especially of Wyclif, in his logical and delicate use of anticipatory and recapitulatory 'particles'—*For, and thus, And so, And if you say, I well know*—by which the sense of a sentence is linked backwards and forwards to that of its neighbours with a resulting strength akin to that of the Greek particle system. None of his followers surpassed him in his control of the logical flow of argument; his late and mature work, *The Chirche and hir Membris*, which it would be unfair to quote piecemeal (Winn, op. cit., pp. 118–39), is the consummation of his views, his style, and his mastery of one-sided discussion (with hypothetical objectors interrupting and put to silence), and in one of its climaxes it bears out my praise of his dry and modern wit: the friars are exalting themselves above Christ in their attempt to make a new world—'But þes Goddis varien.' [But these Gods vary.]

Clerical Heterodoxy: Wyclif

Some fifteen English works can safely be attributed to Wyclif; one of these items, the body of nearly three hundred sermons, hugely outweighs all the others. Little of the whole corpus was first composed in English, and the powerful treatise *Of Feyned Contemplatif Lif* is the only one of these 'original' works to have great merit; yet it would be wrong to dismiss the rest as mere translations—their dependence is on Latin works by Wyclif himself, and the method of translating is variously close and loose, sometimes little more than a digest. The sermons, especially, are briefer and more 'popular' in their English form, and show how the depths and the niceties of theology could be conveyed more comfortably in Latin. It would be unfair to judge Wyclif's religious and political thought on his English writings; what he had to say systematically was best said in the traditional tongue of medieval scholarship.

The sermons can well be examined with three objectives: to hear them *qua* sermons, to recognize the first murmurs of our

English Bible in the versions which Wyclif prefaced or inserted as his texts, and to reel at the startling polemic which occupies so much of them. As sermons they will disappoint or even disgust many, because of their way of turning from their ostensible subject to yet another attack on friars or popes, indulgences or pilgrimages; yet the plea behind all this is often desperately tender. Further, it is made clear that each sermon is capable of ramification along more purely evangelical lines; it is not just for straight pulpit delivery, but a source-book and, in its many attacks on the opponents within the church, a justification of its own existence as a vernacular sermon. That for the first Sunday after Trinity ends with hints on how to expand and develop the material given (T. Arnold, *Select English Works of John Wyclif*, Oxford, 1869–1871, I. 3); another gravely gives the five duties of preachers as healing the bodily or spiritually sick, raising the dead (that is, the dead through sin), healing the leprous (that is, heretics), casting out fiends, and 'þankful traveilinge' [gratuitous hard work]—they should avoid simony, and not sell their preaching or their other duties (ibid., I. 281–282). The exegesis is sound when it is devotional; and, throughout, the stock sermon technique obtains of raising objections and then providing the answer to them.

Their loveliest feature, however, is their translation from Holy Scripture. This so far outdoes the slavish and uncouth *Early Version* by Hereford, and so far antedates the *Later Version* by Purvey, that we are left regretting that Wyclif did not turn his energies from vituperation to a complete translation of the Bible. It is delightful to read the best of these Gospel or Epistle passages, rendered *ad hoc* by Wyclif for each sermon, and then to find their echoes in Tyndale, Coverdale, the Authorized Version, and the rest. The plainer narratives are matched by a style of great simplicity and charm:

> Crist stood by þe river of Genazereþ, and fisheris comen doun to waishe þerynne þer nettes. And Crist wente up into a boot þat was Symonis, and preiede him to move it a litel fro þe lond, and he sate and tauȝte the peple out of the boot. And whanne Crist ceesside to speke, he seide to Symoun,

'Lede þe boot into þe hey see, and late out your nettis to takyng of fishe.' And Simoun answerynge seid to him, 'Comandour, al þe nyȝt traveilinge token we nouȝt; but in þi word shal Y lose þe nett.' And whan þei hadden done þis, þei token a plenteuouse multitude of fishe, and þer nett was broken. But þei bekeneden to þer felowis þat weren in þe toþer boot, to come and helpe hem; and þei comen and filliden boþ botes of fishe, so þat wel nyȝ were þei boþe dreynt. And whanne Petre hadde seen þis wounder, he fell doun to Jesus knee, and seide, 'Lord, go fro me, for Y am a synnful man.'

[Christ stood by the river of Gennesaret, and fishermen came down to wash their nets in it. And Christ went up into a boat that was Simon's, and asked him to move it a little from the land, and he sat and taught the people out of the boat. And when Christ ceased to speak, he said to Simon, 'Lead the boat into the open sea, and let out your nets for the taking of fish.' And Simon in answer said to him, 'Commander, toiling all the night we took nothing; but at Thy word I shall loose the net.' And when they had done this, they took a plentiful crowd of fish, and their net was broken. But they beckoned to their fellows who were in the other boat, to come and help them; and they came and filled both boats with fish, so that they were both almost sunk. And when Peter had seen this marvel, he fell down at Jesus's knee, and said, 'Lord, go from me, for I am a sinful man.' ibid., I. 12–13]

This story has the advantage of being reproduced entire in a block; some, however, are presented sentence by sentence and punctuated with profuse commentary, and some are eked out with explanatory phrases of Wyclif's own which can sound irritatingly like notes. He does not risk presenting the needful Epistle in continuous passages, but glosses lengthily each difficult sentence after another; even the subtlest Gospels, on the other hand, could be left to speak more for themselves, and the spiritual deeps of Christ's teaching subsist in a style that is both touching and powerful. Here, for instance, is the penitent Magdalen:

O Farisey preiede Jesus to ete wiþ him, and Crist entride into þe Phariseis hous, and sat doun to þe mete. And lo, a synful womman þat was in þe citee, whanne she knewe þat Jesus restid in þe Phariseis hous, she brouȝte a box of oynement, and stood bihynde biside þe feet of þe Lord Jesus, and bigan wiþ teeris to waishe his feet, and wipte hem wiþ þe heeris of her heed, and kisside his feet, and anoyntide hem wiþ þe oynement. And þe Pharisey þat clepide Crist, seynge þis dede of þis womman, seide wiþinne to himsilf, 'He þis, ȝif he were a prophete, certis he shulde wite who and which is þe womman þat touchiþ him, for she is a synful womman.' And Jesus answeride, and seide to þis Pharisey, 'Symount, Y have sumwhat to seie to þee.' And Symount seide, 'Maistir, seie.' And Jesus answeride, and seide, 'Þer weren two dettouris to an usurer; oon ouȝte fyve hundrede pens, and anoþer fifty. And whanne þei hadden not for to paie, he forȝaf hem boþe. Who þerfore loveþ him more?' And Symount answeride, and seide, 'Y gesse, þat he to whom he ȝaf more.' And Jesus seide to him, 'Þou hast jugid riȝtly.' And Crist, turned to þe womman, seide to Symount, 'Seest þou þis womman? I have entrid in to þin hous; þou ȝavest noo water to my feet, but she þis haþ waished my feet wiþ teeris, and haþ wipt hem wiþ heeris of her heed. A cos þou ȝavest me not, but she þis, fro Y was entrid, cesside not to kisse my feet. Wiþ oile þou anoyntidist not myn heed, but she þis anoyntide my feet wiþ oynement. Þerfore Y seie to þee, many synnes ben forȝovun her, for she haþ myche loved; for to whom is lesse forȝovun, he loveþ lesse, as þou hast seid.' And Jesus seide to hir, 'Þi synnes ben forȝovun þee.' And summe þat saten togidere at þe mete bigunnen to seie wiþinne hem silf, 'Who is he þis þat þus forȝyveþ synnes?' And Jesus seide to þis womman, 'Þi bileve haþ maad þee saaf; go þou in pees.'

[A Pharisee invited Jesus to eat with him, and Christ entered into the Pharisee's house, and sat down to the meal. And behold, a sinful woman who was in the city, when she knew that Jesus was resting in the Pharisee's house, brought a box of ointment, and stood behind near the feet of the Lord Jesus

and began to wash His feet with tears, and wiped them with
the hairs of her head, and kissed His feet, and anointed them
with the ointment. And the Pharisee who had invited Christ,
seeing this deed of this woman, said inwardly to himself, 'He
here, if He were a prophet, should certainly know who and
what the woman is who is touching Him, because she is a sinful woman.' And Jesus answered, and said to this Pharisee,
'Simon, I have something to say to you.' And Simon said,
'Master, say.' And Jesus answered, and said, 'There were two
debtors to a usurer; one owed five hundred pence, and the
other fifty. And when they had no means to pay, he forgave
them both. Who therefore loves him more?' And Simon
answered, and said, 'I suppose, that one to whom he gave
more.' And Jesus said to him, 'You have judged rightly.'
And Christ, having turned to the woman, said to Simon,
'Do you see this woman? I have entered into your house;
you gave no water for my feet, but she here has washed my
feet with tears, and has wiped them with hairs of her head.
You gave me no kiss, but she here, from the time that I had
entered, did not cease to kiss my feet. You did not anoint my
head with oil, but she here anointed my feet with ointment.
Therefore I say to you, many sins are forgiven her, because
she has loved much; because he to whom less is forgiven loves
less, as you have said.' And Jesus said to her, 'Your sins are
forgiven you.' And some that were sitting together at the meal
began to say within themselves, 'Who is he who is thus forgiv-
ing sins?' And Jesus said to this woman, 'Your belief has made
you saved; go in peace.' ibid., II. 205–206]

But it is in their highly topical and earnest polemic that Wyclif's
sermons are of greatest service to the historian. The state of
religion as he saw it, and the reforms that he suggested, are
presented cumulatively and even repetitively, with techniques
sometimes effective and sometimes invalidated by breathless anger.
There is fine scorn, biting alliteration, harsh wit, eminent period
sentences of Latinate form, skilful juxtaposition of shapely long
Romance words and the brief realism of Anglo-Saxon, and

always a sustained supernatural charade in which the four 'new sects' put on various guises. The 'sects' are prelates, monks, canons regular, and (newest and worst) friars; these last were in fact not so very new—they had started in the 1220s—but for them the real venom is kept. Eventually the allegorical equivalence of these four 'sects' with Scribes, Pharisees, Sadducees, even (ibid., II. 36) Essenes, must be taken for granted; on other levels, friars are false prophets, ravening wolves (ibid., I. 139), tares—'For many wete someres ben comen to þe Chirche' [for many wet summers have come to the Church, ibid., I. 96], and 'stynkinge ordres' [stinking orders, ibid., I. 67]. The 'sects' are without mercy or charity; they infringe the sixteen conditions of charity; the realm would profit financially by their suppression; they are full of pride, covetousness, and sensuality; even if God gave them to the Church, He gave them in His wrath; they hear, and do not do, the Word; St James the Less does not know them in his Epistle on pure religion, and Augustinians in no way resemble St Augustine of Hippo; men think them limbs of the fiend; they hate the elect of God; 'alle moten lyve on þe peple' [they all have to live on the people]; they are the thirteenth sin of the flesh; and, in fact, we should help friars to leave their sinful courses, by withholding our alms from them (ibid., II. 257–64, 266–68, 269, 287–88, 298, 299, 301, 260; I. 44, 173, 226; II. 349, 353). In a clever comparison of the friars with St John the Baptist, Wyclif calls them cowards for clinging to cities and the 'castelis' that they build, and thus avoiding the desert; the Baptist's converts acknowledged their sins, not by muttering them as is now the practice; he had neither coat nor breeches, ate off the land, and was houseless, whereas they live in luxury (ibid., II. 3).

It is obvious that these are strange sermons indeed. Yet they are not all invective, and many points of doctrine and of humanitarian endeavour are examined; never coolly, but with uncomprising honesty. In each particular, Wyclif's views are revolutionary, and his treatment of war is typical of this: those who go to war cannot with justice say the Lord's Prayer. 'And herfore þe seven axingis þat Crist techiþ in þe Pater noster meneþ . . . algatis to axe in charite, and þerfore men þat lyven in werre ben unable to

have þer axinge; but þei axen þer owne dampnynge in þe fifte
peticioun, for þer þei axen þat God forȝyve hem þer dettis þat þei
owen to Hym, riȝt as þei forȝyven men þat ben dettours unto hem.'
[And for this reason the seven askings that Christ teaches in the
Lord's Prayer mean . . . at all events to ask in charity, and therefore men that live in war are unable to have what they ask; but
they ask for their own damnation in the fifth petition, because
there they ask that God may forgive them their debts that they
owe to Him, even as they forgive men that are debtors to them.
ibid., I. 148] But what was the situation in which the divided
Church now found herself?—the Pope offering indulgences to
those who would fight against the antipope (a subject extensively
treated in a sermon on Martyrs, ibid., I. 209–212), and Bishop
Despenser of Norwich leading his beastly and futile 'crusade' of
1383 against Flanders: 'now men seyen þat þei shulden, bi lore
of þer feiþ, werre upon Cristen men, and turnen hem to þe Pope,
and slee þer persones, þer wyves, and þer children, and reve hem
þer goodis, and þus chastise hem. But certis þis came nevere of
chastyment of Crist, siþ Crist seiþ He cam not to lese lyves but
save hem. And herfore þis is chastyment of þe felle fend, and
nevere chastyment of Crist, þat uside pacience and myraclis.'
[now men say that they should, by the teaching of their faith, war
upon Christian men, and win them over to the Pope, and kill their
persons, their wives, and their children, and rob them of their
goods, and thus punish them. But certainly this kind of punishment never came from Christ, since Christ says He came not to
destroy lives but save them. And for this reason this is a punishment from the dreadful fiend, and never a punishment from
Christ, who used patience and miracles. ibid., I. 115] Yet 'blynde
heretikes wanten witt as ydiotis, whan þei seien þat Petre synnede
not in smytynge of Malcus ere, but ȝaf ensaumple to preestis to
fiȝt' [blind heretics lack understanding, like idiots, when they say
that Peter did not sin in striking off Malchus's ear, but set an
example to priests to fight. ibid., I. 123]—though Christ prevented
him from fighting further. 'Lord, where þis Pope Urbane hadde
Goddis charite dwelling in him, whan he stirede men to fiȝte and
slee many þousaund men, to venge him on þe toþer Pope and of

men þat holden wiþ him?' [Lord, did this Pope Urban have God's charity dwelling in him, when he incited men to fight and kill many thousand men, to avenge himself on the other Pope and on men who belong to his side? ibid., II. 319] The friars, says Wyclif, preach to a bellicose text—that the English must get in first with their attacks on their enemies in other countries, for fear *they* do the same and sin be increased on both sides; a hideous doctrine of sinning so as to do good (ibid., II. 41).

This new pacifism may have been distasteful to readers who still enjoyed the memory of Crécy and Poitiers and to the old soldiers who must have figured among the 1381 malcontents; the attack on superstitious practices may have charmed a wider audience, and it certainly had the merit of novelty. Wyclif will not tolerate apocryphal yarns about saints, of which he quotes an excellent instance: when 'Jesus toke a litil child' [Jesus took a little child] Petrus Comestor and Nicholas de Lyra asserted that it grew up to be St Marcialis, apostle of the Limoges district, but Wyclif neither knows nor cares. 'Rekke we not who þis man was, ne trowe we not to mennis talis þat þis was Marcial, or Joon, or anoþer apostle; for ȝif Crist wolde þat we couden þis, He wolde have tolde þis in His gospel.' [Let us not care who this man was, or believe men's tales that this was Marcial, or John, or another apostle; because if Christ wanted us to know this, He would have told us this in His gospel. ibid., I. 399]

Then there are those perennial topics, the endowment of churches and the celibacy of the clergy; priests, he says, 'ben dowid and wyflees aȝens Goddis autorite; for Crist forfendid dowyng boþe in Him and in Hise apostlis, and approvede wedding in apostlis and many oþer.' [are endowed and wifeless against God's authority; because Christ forbade endowment both in Himself and in His apostles, and approved of marriage for apostles and many others.] In fact, celibacy is just one of the devil's wiles to tempt pastors to sin; in apostolic days 'men hadden comounly wyves and children, as preestis han wers now, for þei han out of wedloke.' [men normally had wives and children, just as priests have worse now, because they have them out of wedlock. ibid., I. 364, 59] As for endowments, it is argued 'þat it falliþ not to Cristis

viker ne to preestis of holy Chirche to have rentis here in erþe.
But Jesus shulde be her rente, as He seiþ ofte in the olde lawe;
and þer bodily sustynaunce þei shulden have of Goddis parte,
as of dymes and offryngis and oþer almes taken in mesure.' [that
it is not right for Christ's vicar or for priests of holy Church to
have incomes here on earth. But Jesus should be their income, as
He often says in the Old Testament; and they should derive their
bodily sustenance from God's share, such as tithes and offerings
and other alms taken in moderation.] Therefore lords should rescue
priests from the heresy of endowment, and restore them to due
meekness and poverty, by withdrawing such financial support
(ibid., I. 147, 199).

The pious custom of pilgrimage is now a source of danger;
when Joseph and Mary missed Jesus after their pilgrimage to
Jerusalem, it was because they had travelled separately, in the
segregated groups, each supposing the child to be with the other,
but now pilgrimages are a means to compass lechery (ibid., I. 83).
Nor should it be necessary to go to Rome to obtain dispensation
from vows; 'if a man avowe a þinge, and he wite after þat it were
betere to leve it, þanne he shal leve it, and have sorewe of his foly
biheste, but him nediþ not to go to Rome to perfourme þis medeful
dede.' [If a man vows something, and realises afterwards that it
would be better to leave it, then he must leave it, and regret his
stupid promise, but he need not go to Rome to perform this
rewarding action. ibid., I. 81] Again, too many saints are being
canonized by Rome—and through money or influence; thus too
many saints'-days are being held, with a proliferation of feasts
and images and ceremonies, to the harm of true religion. Fasting
can be silly; it is in itself no more salutary than eating, since over-
indulgence in both can impair a man's ability to serve God. The
cloistered religious are merely denying light to their brethren;
their enclosure in high houses, founded by men, is irrelevant to
Christ's law (ibid., I. 329–330; II. 39; I. 272).

Now much of this criticism is recklessly destructive, and there
are moments when Wyclif almost slangily dismisses the abuse of
the moment: he has just been deploring the accretion of new
ceremonies in the Church, and its excessive government by prelates,

when he leaves his Latin original to say jocosely, 'Þe frogge seide to þe harwe, "Cursid be so many lordis." Now Cristene men ben chullid, now wiþ popis, and now wiþ bishopis, now wiþ cardinalis of popis, now wiþ prelatis under bishopis, and now þei clouten þer shone wiþ censuris; as who shulde chulle a foot-balle.' [The frog said to the harrow, 'Cursed be so many lords.' Now Christian men are pushed around, now by popes, and now by bishops, now by popes' cardinals, now by prelates under bishops, and now they cobble their shoes with censures; it is like someone pushing a football around. ibid., II. 239–280] On the subject of indulgences, whether granted by popes or prelates (ibid., I. 189, 237), Wyclif grows angry often and wildly, as he does with every other transaction involving the sale of spiritualities: priests selling grace; the taints of usury within the Church; gifts and privileges from the Pope; letters of fraternity admitting civilians to the mendicants' third order (and useful only for covering mustard pots, he adds); and the Pope's bestowal of bishoprics and benefices, 'for moneie or for preier of princis', on 'many men þat ben unable to bere haly water in chirchis' [for money or at the entreaty of princes/ many men who are unable to carry holy water in churches, ibid., I. 10; II. 252, 297; I. 67, 381, 304]—too incompetent, that is, even to be the acolyte with the aspersorium. The Vicars of Christ impose harsh penances on men, which can be bought off very expensively with money; and did not a Pope mulct the realm of England of 900 marks a year in King John's time (ibid., II. 61)? In fact, the whole Church is full of simony; its priests sell doves in the Temple when they peddle the sacraments that belong to the Holy Spirit (ibid., II. 89). By the buying and selling of pardons, sin is concealed, when all the time none can forgive offences against God save God alone; men even think that they can buy absolution for after Doomsday, and documents promise their ascent to heaven as soon as they die (ibid., I. 35, 47, 60). Thus priestly absolution, and all its costly trappings, have no efficacy; with it goes auricular confession, the newly-adopted 'rownyng shrifte' [whispering shrift], which has good elements and some scriptural authority, but which is dangerous and—if the sinner genuinely gives up his sin— unnecessary (ibid., II. 206).

Then on to the two points of order and of doctrine which made Wyclif so likely a candidate for the fire. First, the Pope is Antichrist, sacrificing the lives of many for his own foul life, introducing new laws for his own gain, ill-elected, no more impeccable than Peter, failing to preach, making exaggerated claims for his keys, grabbing first-fruits, and wasting money on the advancement of cardinals; why should the Pope be called 'most holy father'?—or the bishop 'most reverend?' The Pope and his court think that they are floating in Peter's boat, and cannot sink; but the whole hierarchy are corrupt and peccant, prelates have empty scabbards or leaden swords to assail the enemies of the Church, 'feiþ and good religioun stondiþ in seculer men' [faith and good religion depend on the laity], and the purging of the sanctuary must begin with its priests. Thus from Antichrist down to his friars nothing but uprooting will serve; the four 'sects' are opposed to unity, priests enter holy orders for the sake of their ten marks a year, monastic rule is obviously inferior to Christ's obedience, the Christian duty of 'snybbing' [reproof] is impaired by the existence of monastic orders, and we have no martyrs now (ibid., I. 138, 304, 225; II. 412–16; I. 241, 248; II. 229; I. 375, 40; II. 368, 28; I. 25; II. 358; I. 291, 84; II. 76; I. 233). This faulty family of God is best summed up in the friars, who, following neither Christ nor the Baptist, beg so as to build fine houses, and thus sell their services indirectly and bargain about the value of their sermons; their preaching is not on the Gospel but on dreams and fables. Thus 'in a passage late to Flandris þe freres prechiden a lady dreem, and bi a feyned soilyng þei spuyliden þe peple.' [in an expedition recently to Flanders the friars preached a lady's dream, and by a pretended absolution destroyed the people. ibid., I. 73, 58, 200, 282; II. 166] Canon law and civil law are too highly regarded, by comparison with God's law; surely God's realm is within *us*, the limbs of Christ's Church, and not within the Pope alone (ibid., I. 227; II. 36).

In any case, we have now not one supreme pontiff, but two; the Great Schism is raging. To heal this rift only the weapons of the spirit should be used; Christ had foretold it on the Mount of Olives—these were the 'opynyons of batels' [rumours of wars] of which He spoke, and Wyclif is scandalized that Christian men should be called on to take arms in these rival causes, when the obvious solution is for the two popes to go humbly to the Emperor, and renounce their secular lordships, and live a poor life as Peter and Paul did. Since no man can love God unless he loves his brother, the behaviour of the two popes shows that they are the fiend's children (ibid., I. 246, 229, 243–44; II. 314–16). The authority even of an unchallenged pope is questionable: 'And þus seien sum men þat þe bishop of Rome, þat þei clepen heed of þe Chirche, and þerto Pope, and Cristis viker, doiþ more harme to þe Chirche of Crist þan doiþ viker of Thomas in Inde, or viker of Poul in Grees, or þe Soudan of Babilon. For þe rote of which he came—þat is, dowynge of þe Chirche and heyng of þe Emperoure—is not ful holy ground, but envenymed wiþ synne.' [And thus some people say that the bishop of Rome, whom they call head of the Church, and Pope as well, and Christ's vicar, does more harm to the Church of Christ than does Thomas's vicar in India, or Paul's vicar in Greece, or the Sultan of Babylon. Because the root from which he came—that is, endowment of the Church and advancement by the Emperor—is not very holy ground, but poisoned with sin. ibid., I. 152–153] With mounting sarcasm, Wyclif in two sermons exposes the Pope for what he is by relating one of his recent actions:

Þe Pope . . . made now late a praier þat he clepiþ 'Domine Jesu Christe', and he grauntide to þis praier, at þe bidding of þe Kyng of Fraunce, to ech man þat is contrit, for oo seiyng of his preier, two þousand ȝeer of indulgencis fro þe peyne of purgatorie. And so men neden not to go to Rome to gete hem plein indulgence, siþ a man mai gete here indulgence for many þousand ȝeer after domesday, siþ he may geten in half a day an hundrid þousend ȝeer and more.

[the Pope . . . just recently composed a prayer which he calls 'Lord Jesus Christ', and he granted to this prayer, at the request of the King of France, to every man who is contrite, for one saying of this prayer, two thousand years of indulgences from the pain of purgatory. And so men need not go to Rome to get themselves plenary indulgence, since a man can get indulgence here for many thousand years after doomsday, since he can get in half a day a hundred thousand years and more. ibid., II. 302, with another account at I. 137]

But it was on a vital point of Christian doctrine that Wyclif was most revolutionary, and his carefully formulated views on it were the hinge of his career; when he denied the real presence of Christ at the Eucharist the 'moderates' took fright, John of Gaunt began to drop his dangerous company, and he was left alone with his closest Oxford adherents and the anonymous body of ordinary people whom they converted. Not that his views in this were violently anti-sacramental: his belief was not in the orthodox Transubstantiation, but in something near to Consubstantiation, a Lutheran idea and one which does not deny Our Lord's definition, 'This is My Body'. He maintained that whereas the substance or 'subject' of the bread remained after consecration, so did its qualities or 'accidents', and that the sacramental Body of Christ was also now present. What he rejected was the heresy of accidents without subject, the idea that the substance ceased. As a philosopher and a precise scholar, he must have felt pressed for a precise formulation; but in his later years he seems to have reached the wholesome view that trying to pinpoint these mysteries was trying to define what is clearly indefinable to mortal man. (Yet in other respects he was a realist, holding that the divine mysteries are for investigation.) In various sermons he admits that after consecration the bread is not principally bread; it is bread naturally, but God's body in figure, sacramentally; whereas the friars preach that it is 'an accident wiþouten ony suget' [an accident without any substance], and men who say they eat Christ bodily, parting each of His members—neck, back, head, foot—, are coarse heretics. He says that, according to the friars, the court upholds their false doctrine (ibid, I. 125, 133, 213; II. 169; I. 247); and this was probably the case, so that Wyclif's eclipse as a servant of the crown was inevitable. Lest I have given the impression that Wyclif's treatment even of the Eucharist was mainly polemical, I must emphasize that his principal passages

Q

on it are lofty and earnest, compellingly good sermons with their backs turned on the enemies of commonwealth and Church. In the Ferial Sermon on the Saturday Gospel for the fifth week in Lent (ibid., II. 110–113) he gives a searching exposition of bodily and spiritual food, with the grave qualification that Christ's words in the sixth chapter of St John's Gospel can be referred in only a limited sense to the Holy Sacrament.

On other points of pure doctrine he was much less upsetting. He held that nice doubts originating in speculation should be referred 'to þe scole of Oxenforde' [to the school of Oxford, ibid., I. 93], his own university, and shared with earlier homilists a belief in the four senses of Holy Scripture, those four levels of understanding—literal, allegorical, tropological, anagogical—to which (along with the prophesying of the New Testament throughout the Old) all canonical Scripture was subjected (ibid., I. 30). He maintained a deep devotion to the Blessed Virgin, but without using the medieval excesses of mariolatry that turned her into a kind of heavenly receptionist, sole mediator between man and her Son; she receives unwavering praise in the sermons for understanding and keeping God's word, and his belief in her protection of the Church comes out in phrases such as 'And Marie helpe þe Chirche þat it be so' [And may Mary help the Church for this to happen. ibid., I. 146]. On one highly controversial point of theology, Wyclif writes with accuracy and obvious interest: the double procession of the Holy Spirit, whereby He proceeds from the Father *and the Son*—that *Filioque* clause which had helped to split Eastern and Western Christianity. He says that Christ taught thus, and adds the analogy of wine's coming from earth and water; all that the Father had was the Son's, and this must include the Spirit. But the Latins, he feels, have sinned somewhat in imposing this dogma, when more vital points—such as papal authority and auricular confession—need to be settled; and the Greeks are in the wrong, but simply through misinterpreting (ibid., I. 135, 146, 152). He makes the Christian duty of love shine over all these controversies, and it is disappointing when the Epistle sermon for the first Sunday after Trinity, with its early declaration, 'In þis þing apperide Goddis charite in us, þat he sente his oon born sone in to þe world, and made him man, þat we lyve bi his sone' [In this thing appeared God's love to us, that He sent His only-born Son into the world, and made Him man, so that we should live by His Son. ibid., II. 313], lapses into another onslaught against friars. Christ 'lediþ þe daunce of love' [leads the dance of love], but in another context He 'was porest man of alle whan He chese to be bischope' [was the poorest man of all when He chose to be bishop.] (*þe Chirche and hir Membris; þe Seven Werkys of Mercy Bodily.*)

On the mechanics of reform—the Poor Priests and the English Bible—the sermons are not very vocal; but of course the Priests were the recipients of the sermons, and the Bible was their chief equipment, so that a knowledge of both is assumed throughout. We are given a picture of the Priests assailed by the friars and other enemies, and forbidden to preach by bullying English bishops; poor men and feeble, for whom the stones will cry out if they are silenced, but who may protect themselves by sticking close to the Gospels (ibid., I. 176, 63; II. 50, 173). He makes the plea for the vernacular in Christian teaching both methodically and emotion-ally: thus 'bi autorite of þe lawe of God men schulden speke her wordis as Goddis lawe spekiþ . . . and algatis beware þat þe puple undirstonde wel' [by authority of the law of God men should speak their words as God's law speaks . . . and by every means see to it that the people understand properly], which is expressed with greater poignancy in 'O Crist! Þi lawe is hid ȝit; whan wilt Þou sende Þin aungel to remove þe stone, and shewe Þi treuþe to Þi folk?' [O Christ! Thy law is still hidden; when wilt Thou send Thine angel to remove the stone, and show Thy truth to Thy people? ibid., I. 78–79, 129] Many other problems of social and devotional practice are aired in the 800 printed pages of the sermons—pre-destination, useless prayers for the soul after death, the need for making a will, princes as guardians of the church, Christian avoid-ance of secular law-courts, and (in the closing sentences) teaching the people on Sundays; but enough has been cited to prove the extraordinary range of Wyclif's huge and heartfelt thesis. *Vae Octuplex* is a tract on a biblical text which Arnold rightly prints with his second volume of the sermons; in it the friars and others preach on fables and anecdotes, dock Scripture, make up long prayers, entice children to join their orders, and bother about the colour of their habits; at the end there is a blast against Papal infallibility and, with a gentler cadence, a plea for faithful belief without speculation: 'And þus ech man shulde trowe þat God is beter þan ony oþer þing, and in generalte bileve alle þe treuþis þat God wole, and muse not in specialte aboute treuþis þat God wole hide, as God wole have hid fro þee wheþer þou shalt be saved or dampned, but He wole þat þou trowe, if þou beleve in Him to þe deeþ, þanne þou shalt be wiþ Him in blisse of hevene wiþouten ende. And þus God wole have hid fro þee þe our of tyme whan þou shalt die, and þe daie of þe laste doom, for God wole þat þou be ever wakinge. And þus God wole þat þou leve to muse on doutis þat He wole hide, as of Oure Ladi, and Seint Joon, and oþer seintis þat foolis glaveren, and bringiþ þis ynne as bileve, for þei hopen to wynne herbi. And þus, siþ God made al þing in mesure, we shulden holde us in His hondis, and trowe treuþis þat he haþ ordeyned, and tauȝt Cristene men to trowe, and putte us not in straunge perilis þat we han no nede to treete.' [And thus every man should be sure that God is better than any other creature, and wholly believe all the truths that God wishes, and not muse particularly about truths that God wants to hide, as God wants to keep hidden from you whether you will be saved or damned, but wishes you to be sure that, if you believe in Him to the death, then you will be with Him in the joy of heaven without end. And thus God wants to keep from you the hour of time when you must die, and the day of the last judgment, because God wants you to be always watchful. And thus God wants you to cease musing on doubts that He wants to hide, for instance about Our Lady and St John and other saints that fools tattle of, introducing it as an article of belief because they hope to gain by it. And thus, since God made all things adequately, we should hold ourselves in His hands, and believe the truths that He has ordained, and taught Christian men to believe, and not expose ourselves to strange perils that we have no need to deal with.]

Lastly, the weighty treatise *Of Feyned Contemplatif Lif* (F. D. Matthew, op. cit., pp. 187–96, and K. Sisam, *Fourteenth Century Verse and Prose*, Oxford, 1921 &c., pp. 119–28), now generally accepted as Wyclif's, is full of information on the contemporary church and its outward practices. The objects of its criticism are more than the first four words which the editors use for its title, and include current vogues in singing, the fashionable Ordinal of Salisbury and the spread of this 'Sarum Use', and the concern of priests with worldly affairs. Their claim that the contemplative life is superior to preaching Christ's Gospel is, says Wyclif, blind hypocrisy and heresy, dodging the plain mandate of Christ, forgetting that a priest is a prophet and must show the people their sins, and forgetting that Christ and the Baptist left the desert to preach. So 'hou dore we fonnyd heretikys seie þat it is betre to be stille, and preie oure owen fonnyd ordynaunce, þan to preche Cristis Gospel?' [how dare we foolish—as in *fondly imagine*—heretics say that it is better to be quiet, and pray our own foolish choice of prayers, than to preach Christ's Gospel?] When they adduce the Gospel, saying that Mary had chosen the better part by meditating at Christ's feet, they forget that she was a woman, unauthorized in God's law to teach and preach; when they say that Christ and St Paul tell us to keep on praying, they do not realize that the prayer is the holy life, not just 'babelynge of lippis' [babbling of lips]. They get their revenues, estates and appropriated parish churches by simony and lies, 'stynkynge gronyngys and abite of holynesse' [disgusting lamentations and show of piety]. As for the new type of singing, it is so complicated that it occupies priests' limited minds to the exclusion of studying and preaching; it inspires pride and levity, whereas true song in church is for meekness and contrition.

Þan were matynys, and masse, and euensong, *placebo* and *dirige*, and comendacion, and matynes of Oure Lady, ordeyned of synful men to be songen wiþ heiȝe criynge, to lette men fro þe sentence and vnderstondynge of þat þat was þus songen, and to maken men wery, and vndisposid to studie Goddis lawe for akyng of hedis. And of schort tyme þanne weren more veyn iapis founden: deschaunt, countre note, and orgon, and smale brekynge, þat stiriþ veyn men to daunsynge more þan to mornynge; and herefore ben many proude lorelis founden and dowid wiþ temperal and worldy lordischipis and gret cost. But þes foolis schulden drede þe scharpe wordis of Austyn, þat seiþ: 'As oft as þe song likiþ me more þan doþ þe sentence þat is songen, so oft I confesse þat I synne greuously.'

[Then matins, and mass, and evensong, vespers and matins of the dead, commendation of souls, and matins of Our Lady, were ordained by sinful men to be sung with loud shouting, so as to hinder men from the sense and understanding of what was sung in that way, and to make men weary and indisposed to study God's law because of headache. And within a short time further empty tricks were devised: descant, counterpoint, diaphony, and broken notes, which stir idle men to dancing rather than to sorrowing; and for this reason many proud louts are provided and endowed with temporal and secular estates and large means. But these fools ought to dread the sharp words of Augustine, who says: 'As often as the song pleases me more than does the sense of what is being sung, so often I confess that I am sinning grievously'.]

They excuse all this singing by reference to song in the Old Testament, and even to the angels' song in heaven; but angels 'ben in ful victorie of here enemys, and we ben in perilous bataile, and in þe valeye of wepynge and mornynge' [are in full victory over their enemies, and we are in perilous battle, and in the valley of weeping and sorrowing.] This new 'knackynge and taterynge' [trilling and fragmentation] is eagerly subsidized with 'many markis and poundis' [many marks—they were 13s 4d each—and pounds] that should go for alms and good causes; 'whanne þer ben fourty or fyfty in a queer, þre or foure proude lorellis schullen knacke þe most deuout seruyce þat no man schal here þe sentence, and alle oþere schullen be doumbe, and loken on hem as foolis. And þanne strumpatis and þeuys preisen Sire Iacke, or Hob, and William þe proude clerk, hou smale þei knacken here notis; and seyn þat þei seruen wel God and Holy Chirche, whanne þei dispisen God in His face, ande letten oþre

Cristene men of here deuocion and compunccion, and stiren hem to worldly vanyte.' [When there are forty or fifty in a choir, three or four proud louts will trill the most devout service so that no man will hear the meaning, and all the others will be dumb, and stare at them like fools. And then harlots and thieves praise the Reverend Jack, or Bob, and William the proud cleric, for trilling their notes so tinily; and say that they serve God and Holy Church well, when they despise God to His face and hinder other Christian men in their devotion and repentance, and stir them to worldly vanity.] Sarum Use is being given more status than the Gospel, and a priest's failure in it is accounted more reprehensible than his breaking the commandments of God; the old function of the priest is being scandalously revised and depraved. Then Wyclif skilfully introduces a favourite subject: 'A Lord! ʒif alle þe studie and traueile þat men han now abowte Salisbury vss, wiþ multitude of newe costy portos, antifeners, graielis, and alle oþere bokis, weren turned into makynge of Biblis, and in studiynge and techynge þerof, hou moche schulde Goddis lawe be forþered and knowen and kept, and now in so moche it is hyndrid, vnstudied, and vnkept.' [Ah, Lord! if all the study and hard work that men are now devoting to Sarum Use, with its pile of new costly breviaries, antiphonaries, graduals, and all the other books, were applied to the making of Bibles, and the study and teaching of them, how much God's law would be furthered and understood and kept, and now to the same extent it is hindered, unstudied, and unkept.] He has a lot more to say about the office of the priest, ending with a prayer to God that He will stir them to their true calling of preaching the Gospel in word and in their lives. The control, the variety, the probing, of this great treatise show how Wyclif was the first of his countrymen to examine, with restless curiosity and a new illumination, the whole grounds of medieval being; his early questioning of Papal interference in English affairs, whether by levies or by the intrusion of foreign clergy into our benefices, had been only the beginning of a process by which he zealously overturned all the religious, political, and social assumptions of his day, in defiance of entrenched authority and all its weapons.

Secular Heterodoxy: Clanvowe

Even as the body of English writings by clerical followers of Wyclif is comparatively small, and often monotonous and ineffective, so vernacular utterances by his lay converts are now hardly to be found; such laymen's witness may have perished through proscription and burning, but the silence can be more reasonably attributed to the simplicity and poverty of those members of the laity who were chiefly touched by Lollardy, though some were of the upper classes. In the next century, with the accession of Henry IV and the act *De Haeretico Comburendo*, a few aristocrats and gentry such as Sir John Oldcastle, styled Lord Cobham after his marriage, asserted with incredible courage or foolhardiness the faith that was earning the fire, and the Lollard Knights continued a force and a menace until their extirpation by those most Catholic kings Henry IV and Henry V; but they were not vocal in English, or at any rate nothing from their pens has come down to us. Before 1400 the silence is broken only by one remarkable man—soldier, diplomat, courtier, poet, crusader, and, in one extant treatise, writer of English religious prose: Sir John Clanvowe. (His career is examined by V. J. Scattergood in 'The Two Ways: an Unpublished Religious Treatise by Sir John Clanvowe', English Philological Studies, Vol. X, 1967, pp. 33–56, and in 'The Authorship of "The Boke of Cupide" ', *Anglia* 82, 1964, pp. 137–49). The mere catalogue of his rôles suggests that he was not an epitome of Lollardy, and only the mildest feeling of heresy breathes in his treatise, but he is associated in judicial and state documents with notorious heretics, and by the orthodox John Capgrave (*Chronicle of England*, ed. F. C. Hingeston, Rolls Series, 1858, pp. 244–45) with an especially obnoxious group—Sir William Neville, Sir Lewis Clifford, Sir Richard Stury, Sir Thomas Latimer, and ('werst of alle') Sir John Montagu, third Earl of Salisbury—who would not doff their hoods in the presence of the Sacrament. Montagu went further, and physically insulted the Sacrament in a way that even the doughtiest Protestant would hardly defend, but the secular arm (if this be not too flattering a term for the mob that lynched him at Cirencester) finally removed him in 1400. Neville was Clanvowe's bosom friend, and died of grief hard on

Clanvowe's strange death in a village near Constantinople; Clifford was a close friend of Chaucer; Stury is documented along with Sir Philip Vache, to whom Chaucer addressed his grave balade *Truth*, and who married Clifford's daughter; Clanvowe's *Boke of Cupide* seemed so Chaucerian that it even wormed its way into the Chaucerian canon; and the 1385 will of Joan, the Fair Maid of Kent, who had rescued Wyclif, mentions among her executors Neville, Clifford, Clanvowe, Stury, the unfortunate Simon Burley, and others clearly forming 'the court party' and a highly Lollard party at that.

Clanvowe's treatise is not strikingly heretical in doctrine; rather, it is grave and puritanical, a big man's response to the clean new teaching of Wyclif. Writing as he makes his last voyage to his death in a far land, and now about fifty years of age and elderly by medieval standards, he compiles no Chaucerian 'Retraction' but faces fairly the two ways of life open to men. Stylistically, he has learnt much from Wyclif, especially a great ease in translating from the Bible which makes the professional Hereford's version look all the sillier; there is nothing slavish or Latinized in 'Brethren, beþ soobre and waketh, for ʒoure aduersaire the deuel, rooryng as a lyon, aboute goth seechyng whom he may swolewen and distroyen; to whom withstoonde ʒe, stroonge in feith.' [Brethren, be sober and keep watch, because your adversary the devil, roaring like a lion, goes around seeking whom he can swallow and destroy; strong in faith, withstand him. ll. 231–35 of V. J. Scattergood's edition of *The Two Ways*. I have throughout these excerpts supplied my own punctuation and capitals.] From the very outset there is grace, clarity, and conciseness:

The gospel telleþ þat in a tyme whanne Oure Lord Ihesu Crist was heere vpon eerthe a mon com to Hym and askede Hym ʒef þat fewe men shulden be saaued, and Crist answerede and seyde, 'The gaate is wyde, and þe way is brood þat leedeth to los, and manye goon in þat wey, and how streit is þe gate, and þe way nargh, þat leedeth to þe lyf, and few fynden þat way.' By thise woordis of Crist we mown vndirstoonde þat þe way þat leedeþ to þe peyne of helle is a brood wey, and þat þe wey þat leedeþ to the blisse of heuene is a nargh wey. For Crist cleepeþ the peyne of helle los, and þe blisse of heuene lyf, and þerfore it weer ful good þat we shoopen vs for to eschewe þat broode way and for to goo in þat nargh wey, for we been euery day goyng ful faste towardis anoþer place and we wyten neuere how soone we shuln out of þis world.

[The gospel tells that once when Our Lord Jesus Christ was here upon earth a man came to Him and asked Him if few men were going to be saved, and Christ answered and said, 'The gate is wide, and the way is broad, that leads to loss, and many go by that way, and how strait is the gate, and narrow the way, that leads to life, and few find that way.' By these words of Christ we can understand that the way that leads to the pain of hell is a broad way, and that the way that leads to the joy of heaven is a narrow way. For Christ calls the pain of hell loss, and the joy of heaven life, and therefore it would be very good for us to contrive to eschew that broad way and go by that narrow way, because every day we are going very fast towards another place and never know how soon we must leave this world. ll. 4–19]

The vocabulary throughout the treatise is markedly Anglo-Saxon, in Wyclif's simpler manner; in the foregoing passage only five words (saaued, streit, peyne, eschewe, place) are of French origin, and of these all save 'eschewe' are very simple and familiar early borrowings.

Among the more obvious stylistic features here, in the tradition of Wyclif and older native writers, is alliteration. It is rarely obtrusive, and in fact is hardly given its usual functions of emphasis or antithesis or onomatopoeia or (with certain consonants) tenderness, but a few phrases give pleasure in the hearing: 'God . . . ʒeue vs grace to goo in at the streite gaate'; 'And sikerly we aughte weel to dreeden Him soore for we haue no beyng ne lyf ne weele ne wyt but only of Hym and by Hym'; 'þe worlde . . . is ful besy aboute to bryngen vs into the broode wey'; and (becoming monotonous now) 'þanne shuln we with Goddis grace goon in at þe streite gaate . . . God of His greete goodnesse haþ ʒeuen vs grace.' [May God give us grace to go in at the strait gate./And surely we ought to be very afraid of Him, because we have no being or life or wealth or understanding save only from Him and through Him./The world is very anxious to bring us into the broad way./Then we shall with God's grace go in at the strait gate . . . God of His great goodness has given us grace. ll. 119–20, 128–30, 363–65, 584–88] In one place alliteration is subtly combined with assonance, the half-rhyme of closed and open long *e*: 'For whan þat we haan moost neede it may stonde vs in noo stede.' [For when we have the greatest need it may stand us in no stead. ll. 425–26] There is little of the crudity—found at its worst in the early fourteenth-century mystic Rolle—of rhyming jingles in strings of present participles or verbal nouns, though 'bacbitynges, chidynges' [backbitings, upbraidings] in l. 704 gives a hint of it. At its best, the prose moves in fine Wyclifite cadences that rise to period sentences, in which the clause structure never goes astray, and can deliberately fall to the 'muk' of the closing lines:

> For þat þat is cleped richesse it is greet trauaill to geten it, and it is greet dreede to keepen it, and to departe þerfro it is greet heuynesse, so that fro the first getynge to the laste forgoyng it is alle sorewe. And þei þat haan þe greet rychesses of þis world þei been as ofte sithes ateened, as ofte adrad, as ofte seeke, and as soone deede, as þei þat haan noon swiche richesses, and whan thei been deede it letteth hem to comen to heuene moore than it helpeth hem. For Crist seide þat it was harde for a riche man to entre into the kyngdom of heuene. And þerfore þat muk of þis world þat is cleped richesse it shuld bee cleped sorewe and noo richesse.

> [Because what is called riches is great labour to get, and great dread to keep, and great misery to part from, so that from the first getting to the last relinquishing it is all sorrow. And those who have the great riches of this world are as often annoyed, as often afraid, as often sick, and as soon dead, as those who have no such riches, and when they are dead it hinders them from coming to heaven more than it helps them. Because Christ said that it was hard for a rich

man to enter into the kingdom of heaven. And therefore that
dung of this world that is called riches should be called sorrow
and not riches at all. ll. 413–25]

The simplicity, and the logical flow of the argument, are likewise Wyclifite. Easy little catalogues are given—'euele, vneesie,
vnsikere, and not lastynge' [evil, uneasy, unsure, and not lasting]
in ll. 384–85; and some of the summings-up are noble despite
their pithiness—'for to leeuen yuel for dreede of God and for to
doo goode for þe loue of God'. [to leave evil for the fear of God
and to do good for the love of God. ll. 299–300] The real progress
of the argument is pointed, as in Wyclif, by the frequent recapitula-
ting or anticipating particles 'So . . . And þus . . . And þerfore . . .
For . . . And also . . . And eeke', whereby the planned thesis sweeps
convincingly on; the principal interruption—and a welcome one—
is by imagery taken from various walks of life. Thus the merchant's
wise investment is used as a symbol of our putting away evil
desires to gain the joy of heaven: 'For þei ȝat been holden wyse
merchantz in þis world, þouȝ thei louen money neuer so wel,
what tyme that any of hem seeþ that he may with puttyng out of
twenty pounde wynne an hundrede pounde he is faynere to putte
forþ þoo twenty pound þanne he wolde bee to drawe to hym forty
or fifty pound.' [Because those who are considered wise merchants
in this world, however well they love money, whenever one of
them sees that by an outlay of twenty pounds he can gain a hundred
pounds he is keener to lay out those twenty pounds than he would
be to gain for himself forty or fifty pounds. ll. 141–146] God's
gifts to us in moderation are illustrated by 'a good leche, that
kepte not that the seeke man tooke moore þanne shulde turne
hym to goode, al þouȝ þe seeke man desire ofte tymes to taake
and vse out of measure aȝens his lyf and his heele also'. [a good
doctor, who did not care for the sick man's taking more than
would do him good, although the sick man often desired to take
and use it beyond moderation, to the danger of his life and his
health, too. ll. 336–39] And the devil uses evil companions as
his decoy, even 'as a foulere þat taaketh first a brid and maake
þerof a wacchebrid and setteþ it bisyde his net for to synge; and

þanne whanne þat oother briddes seen it and heeren it synge þei fallen alle doun to it'. [as a fowler that first catches a bird and makes it into a decoy and sets it near his net to sing; and when other birds see it and hear it singing they all fall down to it. ll. 522–26]

The subject is not, of course, such as to bring out the polemic that Wyclif taught so well, but there is violence, combined in the following instance with sharp fricative alliteration, when an abuse earns it: 'And therfore, for þe loue of God, sette we not oure hertes so muche vpon the foule stynkyng muk of þis false faillynge world.' [And therefore, for the love of God, let us not set our hearts so much on the filthy stinking dung of this false failing world. ll. 377–79] A proper Wyclifite sneer is reserved for those who cannot leave their piffling sins: 'For a babel is an instrument þat is maad of þing þat is litel worth, and with þat a fool beeteþ ooþere men and ofte tymes oothere men beeten hym þerwith aȝen, so þat he smyteth and is smyten aȝen þerwith, and it serveth of not elles, and þat a fool wol alwey haaue neiȝ hym, and he wol leeue it for noo thyng.' [For a bauble is an instrument made of materials of little value, and with it a fool beats other men and often men beat him back with it, so that he hits and is hit back with it, and it serves for nothing else, and a fool will always have it near him, and he will not give it up for anything. ll. 61–7]

Amid so much that is orthodox and even hackneyed—such as our 'ful hard werre' [very hard war, l. 173] against our three foes, the world, the flesh, and the devil—a little of the Lollard campaign emerges. First, despite Clanvowe's military prowess, there is pacifism: 'þe world holt hem worsshipful þat been greet werryours and fiȝteres, and þat distroyen and wynnen manye londis, and waasten and ȝeuen muche good to hem that haan ynouȝ, and þat dispenden oultrageously in mete, in drynke, in clooþing, in buyldyng, and in lyuyng in eese, slouþe, and many ooþere synnes.' [the world considers them honourable who are great warriors and fighters and destroy and conquer many lands, and waste and give much property to them that have plenty, and spend outrageously on food, drink, clothing, building, and living in ease, sloth, and many other sins. ll. 459–64] The attack here is almost on rank, and Clanvowe is disgusted that it is of these proud and vengeful people that 'men maken bookes and soonges, and reeden and syngen of hem for to hoolde þe mynde of here deedes the lengere here vpon erth'. [men make books and songs, and recite and sing of them so as to keep the memory of their deeds the longer here on earth. ll. 467–70] Then, with significant elaboration in a great period sentence extending to fourteen lines, he gives oblique praise to the Lollards:

> And also swiche folke þat wolden fayne lyuen meekeliche in þis world and ben out offe swich forseid riot, noise, and stryf, and lyuen symplely, and vsen to eten and drynken in mesure and to clooþen hem meekely, and suffren paciently wroonges that ooþere folke doon and seyn to hem, and hoolden hem apayed with lytel good of þis world, and desiren noo greet naame of þis world ne no pris therof, swhiche folke þe world scoorneth and hooldeþ hem lolleris and loselis, foolis and shameful wrecches . . .

> [And moreover such people as would like to live meekly in this world and be away from such aforesaid revelry, noise, and strife, and live simply, and be accustomed to eat and drink in moderation and to clothe themselves demurely, and patiently suffer wrongs that other people do and say to them, and keep themselves satisfied with few of this world's goods, and desire no great reputation in this world and none of its praise, such people the world scorns, and considers them Lollards and scamps, fools and shameful wretches. ll. 476–85]

The puritan sternness here is extended to those whom the world calls 'goode felawes', but who in reality are the devil's decoys, seeking to 'waaste þe goodis þat God hath sent hem in pruyde of the world and in lustes of her flessh, and goon to þe tauerne and to þe bordel, and pleyen at þe dees, waaken loonge anyȝtes, and sweren faste, and drynken, and ianglen to muche, scoornen, bakbiten, iapen, gloosen, boosten, lyen, fiȝten, and been bandes for here felawes, and lyuen al in synne and in vanitee—þei been hoolde goode felawes. And (moore harme is) þere is now in þis world muche swich curside felashipe.' [waste the goods that God has sent them in the pride of the world and in the desires of their flesh, and go to the tavern and the brothel, and play at dice, stay up late at night, and swear hard, and drink, and quarrel too much, deride, backbite, jest, flatter, boast, lie, fight, and are minions for their fellows, and live entirely in sin and in emptiness—they are considered good fellows. And (the more's the pity) there is now in this world plenty of such cursed company. ll. 548–57]. The cumulative force of this is worthy of Wyclif, and there is even a touch of authoritarianism in Clanvowe's treatment of the Ten Commandments, where he makes it clear that the mother whom we must honour signifies our 'gostly moodir Holy Chirche' [spiritual mother, Holy Church, l. 628] and that all slayers in word or deed break the fifth commandment save those having authority to put men to death if they deserve it by God's law.

But, fortunately, it is the best of Wyclif that inspires the great climax of the treatise—his unwavering faith and his real tenderness. Clanvowe's disciplined plainness keeps him rigidly to the word of scripture when a statement of doctrine is called for: 'Thou shalt loue þi Lord God of all þin herte, of alle þin soule, of alle þi mynde, and of alle þi strengthes; this is þe firste and the gretteste comaundement. The seconde is lyke to þis; þou shalt loue þi neiȝebor as þi self, and in þise two comaundementz hangeþ alle þe lawe and þe prophetes.' [Thou shalt love thy Lord God with all thy heart, with all thy soul, with all thy mind, and with all thy strength; this is the first and greatest commandment. The second is like it; thou shalt love thy neighbour as thyself, and on these two commandments hangs all the law and the prophets. ll. 664–69] When to this plainness was added a strong and experienced man's compassion, the picture of Our Lord's birth is touching indeed: 'And þe tyme of His blesside berthe was in þe cooldeste of þe wynter and in a poore logge and a colde. And whanne þat He was born His blesside moodir wrappide Hym in a fewe poore clooþis and leyde Hym in a maungeor bitwene an oxe and an asse for to warmen Hym, and þere was no grettere aray.' [And the time of His blessed birth was in the coldest of the winter and in a poor, cold lodging. And when He was born His blessed mother wrapped Him in a few poor clothes and laid Him in a manger between an ox and an ass, so as to warm Him, and there was no greater splendour. ll. 688–93] So on to a quite majestic version of the Crucifixion story, its harsh alliterative phrases blended with long supple sentences and the staccato words of innocence and pity:

And afterwarde þei tooken Hym and bounden Hym as a þeef and ladden Hym to here bisshop, and þere þei acusiden Hym with fals witnesse and buffeteden Hym and blyndefelden Hym and scoorneden Hym and spitteden on His blisside face as þei wolden haue don on a dogge. And after þat He was ylad bifore Pilat of Ponce, and þere He was falsly accused and enprisouned, and afterward ystript naaked and bounden to a pilar and beeten with scharpe scoorges til that al His blesside boody ran on bloode, that neuere dede synne. And after þei setten on His blisside heed a coroune of greete scharpe þornes, and clooþiden Hym as a fool, and scorneden Hym, and after þat þei deemeden Hym falsly to þe deeth, and maaden Hym go bitwene two þeeues, as weery and al forbled as He was, and maden Hym to bere Hys heuy cros, þat He shulde dyen on, vpon His owene bak þoruȝ the citee in siȝte of His blissede moodir, His kyn, and His oothere freendis. And whanne þat He coom in to þe place of comun iustyse thei naylleden His blessed feet and Hise hoondis with greete boistouse naylles to the cros, and al todrowen His hooly lymes vpon þe cros. And ȝet in alle Hise greete peynes þis innocent preyede for His enemys and seide, 'Fadir, forȝeue hem þis gilt, for þei witen not what þei doon'. And þoo þei heengen oo þeef on His riȝt half and anooþer on His lyft half, and Hym for dispit þei heengen bytwene hem two, and þanne He þurstede soore for þe greete peynes þat He had suffred, and þe bleedyng þat He hadde bled, and þoo þei ȝeeuen Hym eysel and galle for to drynke, and whanne He had assayed what it was He wolde not drynke it, but boowide His blessede heed adoun and ȝelde vp þe goost. And þanne þere coom a knyght ycleped Longens and smoot Hym þoruȝ þe herte with a spere, and þere coom out waatir and bloode, and alle þis He suffrede for vs. And after þis His blesside body was taaken doon of the cros and buried. And þanne He wente doun in to helle, and þere He fette out þilke þat He louede.

[And afterwards they took Him and bound Him like a thief and led Him to their bishop, and there they accused Him with false evidence and buffeted Him and blindfolded Him and reviled Him and spat on His blessed face as they would have done on a dog. And after that He was led before Pilate of Pontus, and there He was falsely accused and imprisoned, and afterwards stripped naked and bound to a pillar and beaten with sharp scourges until all His blessed body, which had never done sin, was running with blood. And afterwards they set on His blessed head a crown of big sharp thorns, and clothed Him like a fool, and reviled Him, and after that they falsely condemned Him to death and made Him go, as weary and all weakened by loss of blood as He was, between two thieves, and made Him carry His heavy cross, that He was to die on, on His own back through the city in sight of His blessed mother, His family, and His other friends. And when He came into the place of common punishment they nailed His blessed feet and His hands with big clumsy nails to the cross, and dragged His holy limbs quite apart on the cross. And yet in all His great pains this innocent prayed for His enemies and said, 'Father, forgive them this sin, because they do not know what they are doing'. And then they hung one thief on His right side and another on His left side, and they spitefully hung Him between the two of them, and then He thirsted sorely because of the great pains that He had suffered, and the blood that He had lost, and then they gave Him vinegar and gall to drink, and when He had tasted what it was He would not drink it, but bowed His blessed head down and yielded up the spirit. And then there came a knight called Longinus and struck Him through the heart with a spear, and there came out water and blood, and all this He suffered for us. And after this His blessed body was taken down from the cross and buried. And then He went down into hell, and there He fetched out those that He loved. ll. 707–43]

6: Chaucer's Religious Views

Now did Chaucer share the dangerous beliefs of this circle, his proven friends? Did the strictly orthodox Gower exclude him from the revised epilogue of the *Confessio Amantis* from alarm at his heterodoxy? How far were Princess Joan and her daughter-in-law, Richard II's loved Queen Anne of Bohemia, touched with Lollardy when Chaucer read *Troilus and Criseyde* to them in that still-smiling garden of Corpus Christi College, Cambridge, MS 61? It might be easy for a commentator of the 'Catholic' or the 'Protestant' school to make out a case for Chaucer as one of his persuasion, and some of the facts seem equivocal. From the beginning of his poetical life, Chaucer could spin into his fabric a lot of conventional Christian remarks, as if in easy acceptance; the 'C' version of *The Romaunt of the Rose*, which is probably not his, is typical of this unquestioning use of doctrine, and the very early *A.B.C.*, derived and contrived and flat, is an elaborate restatement of the non-scriptural dogma of the Blessed Virgin as sole mediatrix:

> Soth is, that God ne graunteth no pitee
>   Withoute thee; for God, of His goodnesse,
> Foryiveth noon but it lyke unto thee.
>   He hath thee maked vicaire and maistresse
>   Of al the world, and eek governeresse
>   Of hevene. . . .

[The truth is that God grants no mercy without you; because God, in His goodness, forgives no one unless you are willing. He has made you vicar and mistress of all the world, and also governess of heaven. *A.B.C.*, ll. 137–42]

Though the hostile word 'mariolatry' could be ascribed to Chaucer, and certainly to his age, there is a warmth and strength in the cult; even Wyclif accorded Mary an exalted position, and so it strikes us as curious when so devout a writer as Langland hardly makes mention of her. The *Gawain* poet is quietly confident of her efficacy: the hero has his trust in her five joys, and can always draw courage in battle from her image painted on the inside of his shield (ll. 644–50); he naturally prays to her in the wilderness for a shelter where he can attend his Christmas mass (ll. 754–55); and he has all the time been making his plea to her (l. 737); he and the seductive lady of the castle swap the Virgin's name—he carefully, with 'May Mary repay you', she casually, with a mere 'By Mary' that means no more than the 'Marry' of post-Reformation speech (ll. 1263 and 1268); her husband uses the same oath in its briefer form (l. 1942), and Gawain even stoops to do so when he is in the throes of his ordeal at the Green Chapel (l. 2140); only Mary saves Gawain from the sin of adultery by keeping him in mind (l. 1769). The tender strength of faith in this poet comes out best in such simple lines as that describing the Christ child as

> þat syre, þat on þat self nyȝt
> Of a burde watz borne oure baret to quelle.
> [That lord, who on that same night was born of a virgin to end our troubles. ll. 751–52]

Instances of the more perfunctory kind could be multiplied in Chaucer; since the oath of her name is used or quoted by the sailor, the host, the merchant, and the canon's yeoman, in *The Canterbury Tales*, she is not honoured by their different kinds of unworthiness; even the eagle in *The House of Fame* says it twice in succession (II. 573). But Chaucer can speak of her more gently—and more intensely; in the Prologue of his *Astrolabie* she is God's 'mother the maid', and the second nun's long, paradoxical invocation to her before her tale (spoilt rather by her calling herself an 'unworthy son of Eve') is certainly capped by the brilliant hymn in which the prioress, her superior, turns from praise of Christ to that of His mother:

> O moder mayde! O mayde moder free!
>   O bush unbrent, brenninge in Moyses sighte,
> That ravisedest doun fro the Deitee,
>   Thurgh thyn humblesse, the Goost That in th' alighte,
>   Of Whos vertu, when He thyn herte lighte,
>   Conceived was the Fadres sapience,
>   Help me to telle it in thy reverence!

[O mother virgin! O noble virgin mother! O bush unburnt, burning in the sight of Moses, who plucked down from the Deity, through your humility, the Spirit that alighted in you, by Whose efficacy, when He had illuminated your heart, the Father's wisdom was conceived, help me to tell this story in honour of you! *Prioress's Tale*, 1657–1663]

However much this may owe to the liturgy, it is able music on the mystery of the Incarnation, and since its first line alone contains the figures alliteration, apostrophe, paradox, and chiasmus, it cannot be said to be other than carefully wrought; the stanza is one great period sentence of classical skill, but in it throbs the passionate devotion of a nun who was not totally concerned with table-manners, lap-dogs, and discreet finery.

Certainly, the unthinking oaths are distasteful enough, and the saints come in for a fair measure of misuse. To take the extreme case of a foul-mouthed speaker, the miller's tale uses 'St Thomas of Kent' once and 'St Thomas' twice (ll. 3291, 3425, 3461), but each time for the sake of a rhyme: the first asseverates an adulterous assignation; the other two rhyme conveniently with the 'hero' Nicholas. Because his tale is of Oxford, the oath by St Frideswide (l. 3449) is apt—but it also rhymes; St 'Note' (apparently Neot), used in mid-line (l. 3771), is harder to explain. The reeve's tale lets one of the two Northern students swear (in the rhyme, l. 4127) by the favourite Northern saint Cuthbert, ill-spelt as 'Cutberd'; the other, in the obscenest context, wastes a whole line merely boasting 'by that lord that is called St James', again for the sake of a rhyme. The sailor scatters saints' names freely in *his* lewd story: Martin, Denis of France, Peter, Ive (who, like Neot, had a church in Hunts), Augustine, James (ll. 1338,

1341, 1404, 1417, 1449, 1545)—all, save Peter, for rhymes, and Ive with the same wasteful formula that the reeve had used for James. The woman from Bath rhymes in her Prologue on St Thomas (l. 666)—after all, he was the object of their pilgrimage—, and the canon's yeoman on St Giles (l. 1185). The friar uses an anecdote of St Dunstan, an apt carter's oath by St Loy his patron, and reckless mentions of the Blessed Virgin and 'sweet St Anne' (ll. 1502, 1564, 1604, 1613). The host, not surprisingly, seems not to care what saint he invokes: apart from his many blasphemies, he has a local oath 'by St Paul's bell' (nun's priest's head-link, l. 3970), the mysterious 'precious corpus Madrian' (monk's head-link, l. 3082), and—with different spellings, stresses, rhymes, and syllable-counts—St Ronyan/Ronyon in the physician's end-link (ll. 310, 320); a London cult of the Scots saint Ninian/Ringan/ Ronyan seems unlikely, and the name may be jestingly made up from the abusive noun *runnion*. The only other Chaucerian charac-ter to exploit the saints like these second-rate people is the eagle in *The House of Fame*, who stirs in with his little asides to the Godhead the names of James, Julian (with due relevance to the saint's gift of granting shelter for the night), Peter twice, Clare (but only to rhyme), Thomas of Kent, and Giles (II. 885, 1022, 1034, 1066; III. 1131, 1183, 2000); the bird is a worthy character, but otherwise there is little doubt that Chaucer, in limiting this careless swearing to the most callous of his pilgrims, is showing his distaste for it—a distaste which was part of Lollard practice.

How differently the saints are invoked in *Sir Gawain and the Green Knight*! Only four are used, and each one with utter appropriateness to the speaker: Gawain thanks St Julian the Hospitaller for helping him to a lodging (l. 774) and swears by St John to the lady, little knowing that he will nearly, like the Baptist, have his head cut off through the wiles of a woman (l. 1788); the jolly Bertilak swears by St Giles, the patron of his favourite hunting pursuits (l. 1644), and even the porter's 'Peter!' suits the keeper of the castle keys (l. 813). It is the same with every reference to God, a known yet intangible friend, the only One that Gawain had to talk to on his toilsome quest (l. 696), the One Who can easily manage to save His servants (ll. 2138–39), the

Lord Who for our destiny was born to die (1. 996). These vibrant words shame the easy blasphemies of the miller, who 'swore by arms and blood and bones' at his first speaking, went on to God's soul (a theological concept surely beyond him), and used 'pardee' as a mere line-filler; once his tale gets under way, he is glib with his 'Jesus, King of Heaven', Christ's 'holy blood', 'Him that harrowed Hell', 'by Jesu' and 'For Jesus's love'—both in grossly unsuitable contexts—, and 'Christ's sweet tree'. The snappy reeve is temperate by comparison, and his use of the 'holy cross of Broomholm' (1. 4286), a Norfolk relic introduced there in 1223, could be taken as a pious reference to his native county. The host, with his 'Goddes dignitee' in the head-link to *Melibeus* (1. 2109), is a bad influence on Chaucer himself, who replies with 'Goddes swete pyne' (God's sweet torment); but the host is always liable to lapse into oaths, some of them in ungrammatical Latin—'by nails and by blood' and 'By corpus bones' in the pardoner's head-link, 'by corpus dominus' and 'By St Augustine' in the prioress's head-link. The pardoner, having attacked swearing at the start of his tale, is on his best behaviour and merely calls on 'the cross that St Helen found' (1. 951); the woman from Bath, at the end of her tale, prays lewdly to Christ, but the merchant speaks with seeming reverence of 'God that sits in Trinity' (1. 2290), and the franklin gravely invokes the Trinity when trying to talk genteelly to the squire (1. 682). The really good characters abstain from this discourteous familiarity; but here, again, *The House of Fame* is exceptional: its theology is coarsened by the inclusion of a few members of the pantheon, but the first two lines invoke God and swear 'by the rood'. Even after a devout mention of the god of sleep, Chaucer goes on to Him 'Who is mover of all' and to a very vengeful prayer to 'Jesus God' (I. 81, 97), then a reference to 'the shrine of St Leonard' (I. 117), three too-quick prayers to 'Christ, that art in bliss', 'God, that madest Nature', and 'God that made Adam' (I. 492, II. 584, 970), and 'Swelp me God so wise' (II. 700). In giving himself this uncharacteristic manner of speech, he appears to be painting in *The House of Fame* a special self-portrait unlike the other autobiographical details in his poems.

For there is little doubt that he detested swearing, and was most a Lollard in this. Our authority is not the pardoner (whom we are not to credit) in the eloquent and climactic opening of his tale, but the little-noticed sailor's head-link or sergeant-at-law's epilogue, where the parson (whom we *are* to credit) is the central figure in a remarkable exchange of views. The pardoner admittedly pleads in words that would draw tears from any audience that did not know him; he mentions, as particularly reprehensible in his roistering youngsters, that

> Hir othes been so grete and so dampnable
> That it is grisly for to here hem swere.
> Our blissed Lordes body they totere;
> Hem thoughte Jewes rente him noght ynough.

[Their oaths are so extreme and so damnable that it is horrible to hear them swear. They tear Our blessed Lord's body to pieces; it seemed to them that Jews had not rent him enough. *Pardoner's Tale*, ll. 472–75]

But since he goes on to upbraid drinking and gambling, sins of which he sounds fully capable, the force of his plea is lost; he returns to it, and with the support of St Matthew, St Jerome, and the Ten Commandments, which put swearing before murder in their list. In fact, he illustrates two of his characters' vices in a quoted speech of hideous authenticity:

> 'By Goddes precious herte, and by His nayles,
> And by the blode of Crist that is in Hayles,
> Seven is my chaunce, and thyn is cink and treye.
> By Goddes armes, if thou falsly pleye,
> This dagger shal thurghout thyn herte go.'

['By God's precious heart, and by His nails, and by the blood of Christ that is in Hailes, seven is my special number, and yours is five and three. By God's arms, if you cheat, this dagger will go right through your heart.' ibid., ll. 651–55]

The sailor's head-link is unfortunately suspect in its order, its chief speaker, and even its authenticity, but it is a fine dramatic interlude and strongly suggestive of Chaucer's serious views on swearing:

> Our hoste upon his stiropes stood anon,
> And seyde, 'Good men, herkneth everich on.
> This was a thrifty tale for the nones!
> Sir parish prest,' quod he, 'for Goddes bones,
> Tel us a tale, as was thy forward yore.
> I see wel that ye lerned men in lore
> Can muche good, by Goddes dignitee!'
> The persone him answerde, '*Ben'cite!*
> What eyleth the man, so sinfully to swere?'
> Our hoste answerde, 'O Jankin, be ye there?
> I smelle a Loller in the wind,' quod he.
> 'How! good men,' quod our hoste, 'herkneth me;
> Abydeth, for Goddes digne passioun,
> For we shal han a predicacioun:
> This Loller heer wil prechen us somwhat.'
> 'Nay, by my fader soule! that shal he nat,'
> Seyde the shipman; 'heer he shal nat preche.
> He shal no gospel glosen heer ne teche.
> We leve alle in the grete God,' quod he.
> 'He wolde sowen som difficultee,
> Or springen cokkel in our clene corn. . . .'

[Our host stood up in his stirrups at once, and said, 'Good men, listen every one of you. That really was a useful tale! Sir parish priest,' he went on, 'by God's bones, tell us a tale, as was your agreement earlier. It's obvious to me that you men of learning know what's what, by God's dignity!' The parson answered him, 'Bless us! What's wrong with the man, to swear so sinfully?' Our host answered, 'Oh, Johnny, are you there? I can smell a Lollard in the wind. Hey! good men, listen to me; wait, by God's noble passion, because we're going to have a sermon: this Lollard here is going to preach to us a bit.' 'No, by my father's soul, he shan't,' said the sailor; 'he's not going to preach here. He's not going to interpret or teach any gospel here. We all believe in the great God.

He would plant some seeds of difficulty, or make cockle grow
in our clean grain. . . .' *Shipman's Head-link*, ll. 1163–83]

The parson stands out here as a lonely justified figure; while
coarser men curse round him, he isolates himself from them by
merely speaking of them in the third person, and the orthodox
(conventional and unthinking, rather) host at once suspects, or
pretends to suspect, him of being a Lollard; so rudeness is not out
of place, and he cuts the frequent generic name for a priest, John,
down to its mocking diminutive. With another oath to vex his
victim, he is just accusing him of the heretical activity of Lollard
preaching, when an odd champion of orthodoxy—the heartless,
thieving, piratical sailor—pushes forward and claims the tale for
himself. It is disappointing that some Chaucer MSS give this last
speech to the squire, and that the sailor goes on to refer to his
'jolly body' in a way that suggests that the women of Bath's tale
will follow; but, despite the mysteries in it, the little scene is
powerful evidence for Chaucer's Lollard sympathies.

There could be Lollard scorn, obviously, in the cool destruction
of the summoner and pardoner in the Prologue to the *Tales*,
especially when they are seen balanced against the parson and
that blameless layman, his brother; but this does not mean
that the parson stands for Wyclif or for a Wyclifite 'poor priest',
in whom the distinguishing marks included the repudiation of
the Papacy, of auricular confession, and even of the Real Presence
at the Eucharist, rejections which are not even hinted at in the
picture of the parson. But the cult of St Thomas Becket, almost
rapturously depicted at the beginning, is wholly orthodox, and it
cannot be too often emphasized that the grave criticism of the
monk, the waggish smiles at the expense of the prioress, the heavy
hand raised against the friar, and the frontal attack on the scum
that summoned and that sold pardons, is not intrinsically a blue-
print for the abolition of the Church and its hierarchy; it might
even be a wistful dream of reform, in the mind of one who loved
the Church and its services deeply, yet it must be conceded that the
churchgoers depicted are basely motivated. The woman from
Bath had to head the queue at the offertory, and was furious with

any woman who usurped her place; church gave her an excuse for dressing up, and it sounds as if her pilgrimage (as daring as Mrs Kempe's) gave her a welcome opportunity for male company. The miller assures us that Alison, the carpenter's wife, went to her parish church 'so as to do Christ's own works' (*Miller's Tale*, l. 3308), but her only stated gain was meeting that flippant member of its staff, the parish clerk. The reeve, when he came to retaliate, made his miller's wife the parson's daughter; because of this irregularity, her father, who sounds a deplorable and grasping priest, had paid handsomely to get her married off, but at least she was convent-educated, and this and her spouse's natural arrogance made their parading on holy-days an odious and contentious thing (*Reeve's Tale*, ll. 3943 ff.). There are a few examples, too, of the ignorance and superstition of the laity; the miller's cuckolded old carpenter is waiting for 'Nowel's' flood, and his 'night-spell', whatever its antecedents and analogues, is a farrago of St 'Benedight', the white paternoster, and St Peter's sister; the last forty-five lines of the manciple's tale are a string of intolerable platitudes trotted out by his old mother in support of keeping your mouth shut, and he is very prim and apologetic over having used the word 'lemman' [sweetheart, l. 204], as if he had said something unrepeatable.

The earnest, educated or skilful pilgrims who choose religious tales handle them very capably. After all, the pardoner's sermon—grave, yet thrilling, and beautifully dovetailed—is admirable and salutary, however much it has been vitiated by his previous exposé of himself and his methods. The monk, after half-promising a life of St Edward, uses the Bible for a few of his 'tragedies'—those of Lucifer, Adam, Samson, Nebuchadnezzar, and Belshazzar, but doesn't include the persecution of Christians in his story of Nero. The 'sweet' and 'goodly' nun's priest, quite apart from telling an absorbing and varied story, phrases and illustrates it as becomes his vocation; the old widow lived on what God sent her (l. 4018), and in and out of the story dart St Kenelm the boy martyr, Daniel and Joseph the readers of dreams, Adam and his experience of woman's counsel, *Physiologus* and its bestiary lore, *Ecclesiasticus* on flattery, Iscariot and St Paul, and the date of Creation in

March. This is good homiletic method, but perhaps it goes deeper: in ll. 4424–25 Chaucer says sedately that 'what God foreknows must needs be, in the opinion of certain scholars'—he has launched himself perilously on to the sea of altercation over freewill and predestination; in Book IV of *Troilus and Criseyde* he had let Troilus come to a gloomy fatalistic conclusion on the matter, but here his mind is freer and he dares to leave the matter open. The choice between simple necessity and conditional necessity (he of course knows and quotes the terms) had so long been debated that he ascribes the literature of the subject to 'a hundred thousand men' (1. 4429); but he chooses for mention St Augustine of Hippo, who had initiated it, Boethius, who had developed it, and Archbishop Bradwardyne of Canterbury, who had brought it up to date. Could Chaucer have taken it further?—he is probably admitting his limitations when he escapes with the words

> I wol not han to do of swich matere;
> My tale is of a cok, as ye may here.

[I'll not have anything to do with such a subject. My tale is of a cock, as you can hear. *Nun's Priest's Tale*, ll. 4441–42]

To be a poet, and to be a philosopher, are each full-time occupations, and it would be wrong to expect depth in Chaucer's contributions to these topics; names like Bradwardyne's are very prettily dropped, but the whole technique of this particular tale is teasing and tangential, and here as elsewhere Chaucer is not profoundly philosophical or philosophical for long. But even if he made no lasting contribution to theology and none of any kind to mystical record, his dependence on the Bible as the source of his reasoning and conclusions is vast; no mere tally of his quotations from Scripture is possible here, but W. Meredith Thompson, in an important essay in *English and Medieval Studies Presented to J. R. R. Tolkien* (London, 1962; pp. 183–99), exhibits him as a lifelong and effective translator of the Bible, even in contexts where we have little cause to expect such quotations, as in the tales of the merchant and the summoner. The five hundred or so texts that he uses are Englished in an admirable style, and do not suggest anything but original versions made for their occasion; no dependence on an early Wyclifite Bible seems possible, and in any case Chaucer discreetly amplifies or fuses the texts that illustrate his points. Biblical echoes and, more obviously, Biblical names are everywhere, though this may be counted as no more than the medieval technique of producing *exempla*: the woman from Bath, her mind on marriage, starts off with that at Cana, but is soon learnedly (perhaps too learnedly for verisimilitude) trotting out Jerome *versus* Jovinian and other items from her husband's obnoxious book, in which the dangerous Eve and Dalilah figured along with classical ladies as bad as Xanthippe or Clytemnestra. The *Melibeus*, second only to the parson's tale in its lacing of Biblical texts, uses not just Solomon and Isaac, Judith and Abigail, but portions of the Apocrypha and such commentators and apologists as Jerome, Augustine, and Petrus Alphonsus. The merchant, in a story not polite though highly polished, cites Jacob, Judith, Abigail, Esther, Solomon, Sarah, Rebecca, Joab (the same kind of characters that had appeared in the Prologue to *The Legend of Good Women*); Lollards hated the kind of preaching that used the Troy story, and other romances, as illustrations, and it is likely that they would have hated even more this perverted quotation of Scripture to shed light on lewdness. Meredith Thompson thinks Chaucer's versions of texts so good that he wishes Chaucer had translated the Bible entire, rather than leaving it to the Wyclifites and rather than wasting his time over his *Boethius*, his *Melibeus*, and his parson's tale; but it is the use to which Chaucer puts these bits which is so often objectionable in its professional secularity.

When he ventures out alone as a theologian there are hardly any serious lapses; for an educated writer at the time, the situation was made tricky by humanist studies of pagan classics, and his *Former Age* goes back to a Golden Age which has some archaeologically sound points but ignores Eden and our first parents. The beginning of the bitter *Envoy to Bukton* has a tasteless reference to Our Lord before Pilate, and then proceeds to make fun of marriage and suggest how nice it is to be a widower; but such remarks as that he has heard of heaven and hell, but that no one has ever been there, at the beginning of *The Legend of Good Women*, would cause no clerical offence—even the wholly orthoddox and wholly mendacious Mandeville, who had been everywhere in the known and unknown world, admitted that he couldn't speak plainly of Paradise because he had never been there. And we should be quite wrong in seeing the vicious anti-Semitic yarn told by the prioress as an attack on her principles, or as a gloss on her sentimental regard for mice and lap-dogs to the exclusion of humans; the Jews are drawn by wild horses because it was felt that this was the right way to treat them, and Chaucer stands condemned by his own intolerance. The second nun's piffling etymology of the name *Cecilia* is no worse than many wild medieval guesses.

At the end of his parson's tale, and probably at the very end of his life poetical and earthly, he notoriously 'retracted' most of what he had written: the implicit 'sin' of *The House of Fame*, *Troilus*, *The Legend of Good Women*, and the young poems, with 'many a lecherous lay'; but he was pardonably thankful for *Boethius* and for works relating to 'legends of saints, homilies, morality and devotion'. These last must include the lost translations of Pope Innocent III's *De Contemptu Mundi* and of Origen's *De Maria Magdalena*, mentioned as his in the Prologue of *The Legend of Good Women*, A. 414–18. But if he wanted to make a lasting contribution to Christian literature, why did he not translate St Thomas Aquinas, since Boethius was not overtly Christian in the writing of his famous treatise, and the *Melibeus* is a shallow work without challenge to thought? The answer may be a lack of theological depth on his part; but it may equally be that those who could wrestle with Aquinas's thought had no need of an English version, and that those without sufficient equipment (including Latin) were the very audience that he was trying to reach in such things as his *Boethius* and the dull composite 'tale' of the parson. Much more dismaying to many than the Retraction is Chaucer's dismissal of *Troilus and Criseyde* at the end of the fifth book; thousands of lines have built up a convincing picture of Troilus's ennobling love, his chivalry, his pre-Christian devotion—then suddenly death in battle engulfs him. In swift stanzas he is raised to the neatly-constructed heaven of current belief, looks down to 'this little spot of earth', and laughs at those who are making so much fuss over his death; he even gives way to a moral judgment on the kind of desires that have motivated him, and abruptly and permanently turns from it all and accompanies Mercury to his new quarters. That is the end of Troilus, Chaucer immediately says, and 'for love'; other things in him had end, too—even his worthiness and his royal status, and beyond his personality 'the brittleness of this false world'. Then comes a lovely, lilting, yet austere and wintry, stanza:

> O yonge fresshe folkes, he or she,
>   In which that love up groweth with your age,
> Repeyreth hoom from worldly vanitee,
>   And of your herte up-casteth the visage
>   To thilke God That after His image
>   Yow made, and thinketh al nis but a fayre
>   This world, that passeth sone as floures fayre.

[O young, fresh people, youths or girls, in whom love grows up as you grow in age, return home from worldly idleness, and lift up the visage of your heart to that same God Who made you according to His own image, and reflect that this world, which passes as quickly as pretty flowers, is nothing but a fair. *Troilus and Criseyde*, V. 1835–41]

Only Christ is to be loved, for His sacrifice and His faithfulness; why look for 'feigned loves'? Another seven lines fling the whole story aside as the 'cursed old rites of pagans', the 'wretched appetites of the world', the reward you get for following a gang of gods, the principles of old poets; then a plea to Gower—'moral Gower'—and the anti-Wyclifite philosopher Strode to go through the poem for heterodoxy ('to correct where there is need'), and finally a dignified hymn as the safe waters are entered. Much has been written of this startling repudiation, and it is not my purpose to add more by way of excusing it; but it is eminently sensible and Christian for him to point out that any love other than that of the

Divine is at best second-rate and, in comparison with eternity, as doomed as the daffodil.

His informal remarks on religion are sometimes delightful, as if of a studied simplicity. In *The Book of the Duchess*, he says that he had never heard of *gods* who could make men sleep, 'Because I never knew of any God but One' (1. 237), and wistfully admits—as many a medieval man must have thought when authentic miracles grew short—'Such marvels used to happen then' (1. 288). The sergeant-at-law is made to shed some light on the epilogue of *Troilus* when he recounts in his tale the reunion of Alla and Custance; they felt such joy as has never before been known, and never shall be known, while the world lasts, 'save for the joy that lasts for evermore' (1. 1076). This tale, in fact, is a more interesting theological medley than any of the others; pious and exceedingly superstitious, wildly anti-Moslem in its picture of the sultan's mother and her henchmen, absurd and repetitious in Custance's ordeals by banquet and water, it yet has some noble stanzas of rhetorical questions in which God the Redeemer is seen miraculously preserving her:

> Men mighten asken why she was not slayn.
>> Eek at the feste who mighte hir body save?
> And I answere to that demaunde agayn,
>> Who saved Daniel in the horrible cave,
>> Ther every wight save he, maister and knave,
>>> Was with the leoun frete er he asterte?
>>> No wight but God, that he bar in his herte . . .

> Wher mighte this womman mete and drinke have?
>> Three year and more how lasteth hir vitaille?
> Who fedde the Egipcien Marie in the cave
>> Or in desert? No wight but Crist, sans faille.
>> Fyve thousand folk it was as gret mervaille
>>> With loves fyve and fisshes two to fede.
>>> God sente his foison at hir grete nede.

[People might ask why she was not killed. Who could have saved her body even at the banquet? And in return I reply to that question, who saved Daniel in the horrible den, where every person, master and servant, except for him was eaten by the lion before he could escape? No one but God, Whom he kept in his heart. . . . Where could this woman get food and drink? How did her victuals last for three years and more? Who fed Mary the Egyptian in the cave or the desert? No one but Christ, and without fail. It was as great a miracle to feed five thousand people with five loaves and two fish. God sent his abundance at her great need. ibid., ll. 470–476 and 498–504]

The same tale has a nice sense of the history of religion: how the Christians had fled from the pagan invaders of Britain and taken refuge in Wales, though a few remained and continued in secret worship, and there was even 'A Briton book, written with Evangels' (1. 666) available for swearing on (and a very effective one, too; a perjuror's eyes popped out when he used it). The same interesting kind of comment occurs in the Prologue of the *Melibeus*, when Chaucer himself discourses to the pilgrims on how far the Gospels are synoptic; learned Gospel harmonies were in use, but the grounds for their existence are very winningly summed up:

> ye woot that every evangelist
> That telleth us the peyne of Jesu Crist
> Ne saith nat al thing as his felaw dooth,
> But natheles hir sentence is al sooth,
> And alle acorden as in hir sentence,
> Al be ther in hir telling difference.
> For somme of hem seyn more, and somme lesse,
> When they His pitous passioun expresse;
> I mene of Mark and Mathew, Luk and John.
> But doutelees hir sentence is al oon.

[You know that every evangelist who narrates to us the suffering of Jesus Christ does not say everything in the same way that his fellow does, but nevertheless their meaning is entirely true, and they all agree as far as their meaning is concerned, although there may be some difference in their narrative. For some of them say more, and some less, when they describe His pitiful passion. I refer to Mark, Matthew, Luke and John; but certainly their meanings are all the same. Prologue to *Melibeus*, ll. 2133-2142]

Similarly, the conversion of Valerian in the second nun's tale is made the occasion for a pithy statement of faith,

> Oo Lord, oo feith, oo God withouten mo,
> Oo Cristendom and fader of alle also,
> Aboven alle and over al everywhere,

[One Lord, one faith, One God without any more, One Christendom, and also Father of all, above all and over everything everywhere]

though within a tale of great exaggeration; St Cecilia is too good and enduring to be true, but her toughness is more convincing when she is faced with the bullying prefect Almachius. To set their dialogue out in dramatic form:

Almachius: What kind of woman are you?

Cecilia: I am a woman of gentle birth.

Almachius: I'm asking you, even if it annoys you, about your religion and your belief.

Cecilia: You have begun your questioning stupidly, by trying to include two answers in one question; you asked ignorantly.

Almachius: From where do you get such rude answering?

Cecilia: From where?—from conscience and from unfeigned good faith.

Almachius: Don't you take any notice of my power?

Cecilia: Your strength is very little to be feared; because every mortal man's power is only like a bladder, full of wind, indeed. And when it is blown up, all the boast of it can be laid very low with the point of a needle. . . .

This tale has a happy ending, in that the principals are martyred into eternal joys; the franklin's tale has one, too, but because all the characters behave so very decently, even the magician in his

S

alarming house at Orleans; the sergeant-at-law's is oddly realistic, in that Custance's long sufferings are rewarded with only one year of wedded bliss before her husband Alla dies ('Now let us pray God to bless his soul!'), but her father and her promising son are depicted as providing consolation enough.

I have left until late the story of the patient Griselda told by the respectable and industrious, though rather bookish and un-practical, Oxford student, since it has been considered either an extreme and absurd demonstration of wifely devotion and of a ruthless husband's determination to be sure of it, or a magnificent religious allegory of God (Walter), omniscient and omnipotent, testing the human soul (Griselda) until He is convinced that nothing can shake her love for Him, whereafter they have transcen-dental joy together. In its folk-lore origins the story certainly did not have anything like the latter meaning; and even if it is assumed the double story sometimes creaks badly at its joints: if an omni-scient lord knows that nothing will unseat his wife's obedience to him, will he really pretend that he has killed their children and that she must prepare the bridal chamber for her successor—and just to find out whether she *will* give way? But this is allegory, where the parallels often have little external resemblance, or something much less than allegory, by which the student at the end suggests that Griselda's patience is just a homely reminder to us that we ought 'much more', and on a totally different plane, to receive what God sends. Distasteful as it may all seem to readers, and especially female readers, nowadays, it was a familiar parable: generations earlier, the writer of *Ancrene Wisse* had a more reasonable story in which the wife had *some* trivial faults, but the husband pretended not to notice them; rather, he did all he could to make her love him, but when he was confident of her deep love he began to rebuke her openly for what she did amiss, turned stern, and even bared 'the grim tooth'—all to find out if he could shake her devotion to him. When he realized that she loved him no less for all this, but even more, he showed her how utterly he loved her, too, and did all he could to please her; and that is how God tries and tests recluses in the early, though not the earliest, days of their solitary life. 'Finally, after the test, that is when the great joy is.' (*Ancrene Wisse*, in Corpus Christi College, Cambridge, MS 402, fol. 59r) Fortunately, Griselda's story in the hands of the gentle student has glories that enhance its pious but confusing status; when she must deliver her first baby to an officer, apparently to be killed, she shuts out from her prayer any self-pity and speaks with the most marvellous tenderness:

> And thus she seyde in hir benigne voys,
>   'Far weel, my child; I shal thee never see.
> But, sith I thee have marked with the croys,
>   Of thilke fader blessed mote thou be
>   That for us deyde upon a croys of tree.
>   Thy soule, litel child, I him bitake,
>   For this night shaltow dyen for my sake.'

[And she said as follows in her gentle voice, 'Farewell, my child; I must never see you again. But, since I have marked you with the cross, may you be blessed by that same Father Who died for us on a cross of wood. Little child, I commend your soul to Him, because this night you must die for my sake.' *Clerk's Tale*, ll. 554–60]

Likewise, no self-pity, but only self-realization, touches her leave-taking when she must seemingly relinquish the palace to her supplanter; she renders again the rich clothes which Walter has given her, and even her jewels, and then continues in her bland, unquestioning way, unconsciously filling in by biblical reference some of the details of the religious experiment of which she is the victim:

> 'The remenant of your jewels redy be
>   Inwith your chambre, dar I saufly sayn.
> Naked out of my fadres hous,' quod she,
>   'I cam, and naked moot I turne agayn.
>   Al your plesaunce wol I folwen fayn;
>   But yet I hope it be nat your entente
>   That I smoklees out of your paleys wente.'

['The rest of your jewels are ready inside your chamber, I

am quite sure. I came naked out of my father's house,' she said, 'and naked I must return. I will gladly act according to all your pleasure; but yet I hope it is not your intention for me to go out of your palace without a smock.' ibid., ll. 869–75]

The parson, of course, tells no real tale at all, but simply gives a stern sermon largely devoted to sin; in his Prologue he warns the host that they will get no 'fable' from him, but 'a pleasant prose story to knit up all this entertainment and round it off'. And, as he speaks (in verse for the moment), the idea of pilgrimage emerges, as if the whole purpose of this travel to Canterbury had been only to reflect that pilgrimage through life which is every man's lot. It is strange how the greatest writers of their age were obsessed with this thought: Langland with his endless, interrupted, snakes-and-ladders quest, the dream of the missed bus, yet shot through by sudden visionary gleams of truth and eternity; the *Gawain* poet starting with a mention of Aeneas, as if his poem is to be another of those moralized Virgils that the Middle Ages knew, and his hero the human soul on its voyage through sins and virtues; and Chaucer ending his 'comedy' with a grave peep at

> thilke parfit glorious pilgrimage
> That highte Jerusalem celestial.

[that same perfect, glorious pilgrimage which is called celestial Jerusalem.]

7: On Being Alive in the Late Fourteenth Century

It has become customary to suppose that Chaucer gives us in *The Canterbury Tales* all that we need to know, or need as clues, about the social life of his time, and phrases such as 'cross-section of society' have occurred; this forgets that easily his poorest fellow-pilgrim was the tenant farmer styled 'plowman', with his opportunity for honest competence by very hard work, and with an honoured parson for a brother, and we have seen already that even the poor widow in one of the tales had a cosy little tally of advantages. To know the extent of the fulness of his social scene, there is no proper guide save a diligent reading of his *Tales*, and it would be far too long a study to consider here the closeness of his translations from verifiable fact; in any case, it would be repetitive of famous old books, often well illustrated and normally well documented, such as J. J. Jusserand, *Wayfaring Life in the Middle Ages*; L. F. Salzman, *English Life in the Middle Ages;* H. W. C. Davies, *Medieval England;* E. Power, *Medieval People*; and the weighty works of the convinced anti-papist G. G. Coulton. But consideration of many non-modern concepts must be held firmly in mind as we read the *Tales*; we must find out, from Robinson's sumptuous notes or any other source, what if any is the symbolism of the colour of the pilgrims' clothes, what weight Chaucer attaches (or is it but a pretence of attaching?) to the 'humours' that go to form their physical and psychological make-up, what possible redemption there is for the unstomachable summoner and pardoner, whether the woman from Bath really *is* 'good' and 'worthy' in any sense at all, whether the highly-trained and quite learned physician is just on the make, why so many proper names (never to be taken up again) are scattered around—even to calling the reeve's horse Scot, whether the cook's ulcerated leg is to be in some way horribly linked with his blancmanges and the prioress's *Amor* brooch with human *amour*, and many other mysteries left scrupulously recorded by Chaucer but not now always within our reach. To see the cavalcade as one shapely and colourful frieze, as William Blake and Thomas Stothard depicted it for us, is an over-simplification only if we believe that their tales are part of their characters; and since Chaucer was writing a long-planned comedy that he had prayed for at the end of his *Troilus*, and not a *Thoughts on the Cause of the Present Discontents*, it is pardonable to savour this assembled slice of life as a slab of rather rich fruit cake with not all the cherries at one end.

But some modern commentators have become impatient with Chaucer's self-imposed limitations, as if suspecting that the insulated courtier in him rejected Lazarus and found Dives fascinating; and they have of course called on Langland to fill in the gaps. Again, it would need the fullest quotation from the whole of *Piers Plowman* to test the accuracy of this view, and since the poem starts with a Field Full of People it certainly is a promising study for the sociologist, but Chaucer is not so exclusive as a mere catalogue of his pilgrims suggests; the stuff of poetry was for him extremely wide, and there is omnivorous tolerance in his remark on the encountered canon that 'it was joy to see him sweat! His forehead was dripping like a still'. Sweating can apparently be good and interesting *of its kind* (Hesiod had 2,000 years before said that the deathless gods put it before virtue), and interesting pardoners and pirates and husband-hunters, good of their kind, give us an impression of Christian charity as worthy as the desperate pity and admiration for the way that

> Souters and shepherdes, suche lewed iottes,
> Percen with a paternoster the paleys of heuene.

[Cobblers and shepherds, and ignorant peasants like that, penetrate with the Lord's Prayer the palace of heaven. *Piers Plowman*, B.X.460–461]

I have never felt so near to Chaucer and his holiday party as on first reading the reeve's sly dig at Chaucer himself in the Prologue to his tale, 'Lo, Grenewich, ther many a shrewe is inne' ['Look, Greenwich, where so many bounders live', 1. 3907], and remembering the charabanc guide of my childhood with his grinned apology, 'This is the slum district of Bournemouth, where the driver lives'. Langland's indignation, when imitated by a lesser mind (as in *Mum and the Sothsegger*), raves; Chaucer knew faithfully that under Christ every mortal is imperfect, but his hand was rarely on the first stone.

These two great contemporaries at first sight appear to bestride all society; yet still the picture is not complete. The unknown poet of *Sir Gawain and the Green Knight* chose to write an Arthurian novel (some say, with religious overtones or a religious motive or even odder intentions), and this has rather disqualified him from figuring richly in this book; but he gives an enthusiastic and convincing picture of a society—well-off provincial society, with its classes happily dovetailed and bestowing service and patronage. The poem must be read with the utmost care; for a composition so attentive, and words so poised and neighbourly, any other kind of 'reading' would be merely flippant, and Norman Davis's 1968 revision of J. R. R. Tolkien and E. V. Gordon's Oxford edition leaves nothing to chance in its glossary and other apparatus. To many tastes, including my own, it is the greatest poem in all Middle English; it is certainly the happiest. Its writer is at home, as an equal, in a noble court of great luxury and taste, where splendid meals were put on at the chief festivals and hospitality was dispensed, where Christmas parties included dancing and games and sometimes too much wine, where due order of rank was observed but nobody groused, and where fine men were experts in hunting, composing song-dances, talking with glittering eloquence, and balancing their religious duties with the claims of their delightful world. We know enough of the menus and recipes of the day to be confident that the feasts are not one whit exaggerated, and of the importance of a knight's ritual arming to feel the same confidence in the elaborate preparations of Gawain and in the eager crowd of courtiers who feel honoured to be 'despoiling' him of his armour when he arrives for Christmas. Heraldry may now seem to many a curiosity; it engaged the poet's attention—

and, we believe, his audience's—for nearly fifty lines on one device. Further, the courtesy is not just mentioned, but reported verbatim, and it is not just the courtesy of refined and privileged equals: the porter is polite to Gawain and is thanked for his services; the grooms are thanked for stabling Gawain's horse so well; the monstrously rude visitant at Arthur's court is addressed as if he were an invited guest; Gawain and his host cannot agree on which of them is more honouring the other over the holiday, and he and his temptress make similar remarks of self-depreciation and do not go back on them even when the seduction fails. Most striking to the observant ear, and strange for our century, is the subtle balance of 'þou' [thou] and 'ȝe' [you]; we have lost the old distinction between these by the simple expedient of shedding *thou, thee, thy* and *thine* altogether, though a Bristolian saying 'thee bist' sounds over-familiar to the purist, and this leads us to the old rule: *thou/thee* (apart from its application to the Triune God) was for use by superiors to inferiors (including kings to almost everybody) and by familiar equals to one another, and *ye/you* (apart from its obvious plural meaning) was for more gingerly equals and for inferiors addressing superiors (including almost everybody addressing kings). What is so interesting here in *Gawain* is the occasional infringement, with a quite violent enhancement of the sense.

The first character to use a second person pronoun is Arthur, to the already truculent and insolent Green Knight; by every right, he keeps to *þe* and *þy*. But the Knight, although he has now learned the King's identity, shows no manners at all when he replies with *þe* and *þy* and twice *þou* (a ȝe is stirred into the middle of his speech, but this is probably a lapse on the poet's part rather than a sudden onset of decency on the Knight's). To the end of his unwelcome stay, he continues in this style, but the courteous Gawain, as soon as he opens his mouth, is found addressing Arthur with *ȝe, yow, your, yourseluen*; then, when it is clear that he and the Knight are going to converse, we wonder whether Gawain's courtesy will stretch to ignoring any implied insult, but to the Knight's *þe* and *þou* he answers bluntly with three similar forms, and their colloquy shows no variation from this despite the formal 'sir' equivalents which they insert from time to time. Before the scene ends, we hear Arthur bestowing a *yow* even on his beloved Queen.

The next exchanges are brief and normal; arriving at the mysterious castle, Gawain calls the porter *þou* and gets ʒe/*yow* back, and the unnamed lord later gives him the compliment of ʒe/*yow*/*yowre* and is of course repaid with the same. Such speech as they have together continues thus until l. 1068, when the lord astonishingly starts a friendly speech with *þe*, reverts to *yow* twice and ʒe, back to *þyn* in the very same line, and *yow* twice more. Norman Davis calls this inconsistency 'remarkable', and no certain interpretation can be put on it; Gawain, at all events, takes no hint from it, and the rest of a longish talk is on the formal level. A more piquant opportunity for handling the idiom arises when the lord's wife comes to Gawain's room to tempt him; for the most part she uses the distant plural (nineteen times on her first visit), so that the two occasions when she uses *þe* (ll. 1252 and 1272) may have had the effect of a sly 'darling' suddenly breathed, a flicker of the eyelids, or a caress. Even when saying 'ʒe are welcum to my cors' [You are welcome to my body, l. 1237] she is grammatically formal; but it is no longer credible that this remark means anything blunter than 'I like having you here', so that the even reticence of Gawain's immediate reply is to be seen as a matter of courtesy, and not as a rebuke for importunity. He shows no signs of *thou*-ing her, and the interview safely ends; even the return of the lord, in a back-slapping mood after his day's hunting, finds jovial expression in the stiffer idiom, as do his two other home-comings and all the mild horseplay when he and Gawain are together, save that the arrangements for the fateful third day of bargaining are made by him as if he were the master and mentor, with *þou*, *þy*, *þow*, *þy*, *þyn*, *þe*, *þe*, *þe*, and not a single plural in the ten lines. The lady's second visit finds her using two dozen plurals, and one exploratory *þou* at the beginning of her plea; Gawain does not descend from the heights. Her third visit is strikingly different: it begins with her irritating entry into his bedroom, when she throws open the window (and it *is* late December) and gaily chides him for sluggishness: 'Oh, man, how canst *thou* sleep when the morning is so bright?' Then, after a formal exchange and what seems like a last parting kiss, she puts into action her plan for persuading him to the deed that will damage him—no adultery now, but the acceptance of a supposedly magical life-protector unworthy of a Christian knight; and her opening gambit uses only *þy, þi, þe*. Significantly, he picks up this mood, and for the first and only time uses *þy* in 1. 1802; but his vigilance is now relaxed, and although he at once reverts to the plural (and she likewise) the process set on foot is soon fulfilled by his taking of the girdle.

Another simple and enjoyable demonstration of the rules of politeness is seen when Gawain is given a squire to guide him to his fearful tryst with the Green Knight; this young man, part of the elaborate plot against the hero, must clearly put on an act of admiration, of delight at being of service, of gratitude for Gawain's stay in the castle, and so forth, and when the last stage of the journey is reached he addresses Gawain in a thirty-five-line speech, at first fulsome and then of earnest plea and warning, in which his awareness of their respective ranks is conveyed by the score of plural forms, among which the stray 'I say thee' of 1. 2110 must be as impersonal as a later *prithee*. His endeavour is to make Gawain shun the encounter and flee like a coward, and he promises not to tell anyone, distastefully backing this 'by God and all His good saints, swelp me God and relics and plenty of oaths'; he gets the reply he deserves—grudging thanks and the resolve not to comply. At once, his mission a failure, he drops his mask of courtesy and turns to a discouraging insolence:

> 'Mary!' quoþ þat oþer mon, 'now þou so much spellez
> Þat þou wylt þyn awen nye nyme to þyseluen.
> And þe lyst lese þy lyf, þe lette I ne kepe.
> Haf here þi helme on þy hede, þi spere in þi honde . . .'

['Marry!' said the other man, 'now thou art talking so much that thou wilt bring on thyself thine own hurt. If it pleases thee to lose thy life, I don't care to hinder thee. Here, take thy helmet on thy head, and thy spear in thy hand. . . .' ll. 2140–43]

And so on, with four more singular forms throughout his directions as to the way; this infringement of rules is thus the means of making an insignificant character abound.

Finally, Gawain meets the Green Knight, the blithe host in his enchanted guise, and as expected finds himself back in the idiom with which the tale started. *Thou* is swapped coolly and inimically, and sees them through the Knight's first feinted blow and the mental torture of the second; Gawain's protest at this is in the same convention, and when he has had his tiny token wound he defies the Knight with a *þy* and a *þow*—though a colloquial 'þerto ʒe tryst' [be sure of that] slips in, too. Is it meant as a warning of the impending change in their relationship?—whereby the Knight will be mentor again, and even priest and confessor if we accept the wholly religious interpretation of the story. The Knight, from the moment that his explanation makes everything become clear and right, is the arbiter of the situation, and he speaks as a superior for thirty lines; then suddenly he seems to promote Gawain to equality and dignity again—after all, the wound has cleansed him and gone a long way towards full recompense for his fault:

> 'Bot here yow lakked a lyttel, sir, and lewte yow wonted.
> Bot þat watz for no wylyde werke, ne wowyng nauþer,
> Bot for ʒe lufed your lyf; þe lasse I yow blame.'

['But here you were slightly at fault, sir, and fell short of fidelity. But that was not because of any brilliantly-made needle-work, or any love-making either, but because you loved your life; I blame you all the less.' ll. 2366–68]

Gawain, in great wrath with himself, which he at once transfers to the cowardice and covetousness that had toppled him, refers to 'þy knokke' [thy blow], but soon recovers his poise and in great humility twice uses the plural as he begs to regain the Knight's goodwill. Again the Knight uses both forms: the singular when he is speaking of confession and punishment, both ʒe and þou when he suggests that Gawain should all his life wear the girdle as a salutary reminder, and the plural thrice when he invites Gawain back to relaxation and reconciliation at the castle.

Gawain's dignified reply (a little tarnished by his reference to Biblical temptresses as an excuse for his lapse) is entirely in the plural form, but the Knight in his friendly and inviting last speech keeps his privilege of talking down to Gawain, and uses the singular.

Nothing is known of the identity of this remarkable writer, not even whether his status was clerical or lay; whatever he was, he must have been writing for a prepared audience that shared his knowledge, his views, and his taste for a hard and demanding poetic idiom. Chaucer, in contrast, is informative by stages, often spoonfeeding his readers with fare in a simple colloquial idiom; it is not unfair to remind ourselves that he was a literary civil servant, and that his leisure was occupied in making poetry out of the circumstances that were real to him. So the English countryside does not appear in his lines; it was not a poetical terrain in the Middle Ages, but often trackless, muddy, densely wooded, infested with outlaws and dangerous beasts, and not even a novelty—the heart of London was only about a mile from meadows and farms. The dream-wood in *The Book of the Duchess* is a moment never returned to; the whelp that comes to be tickled and lays its ears back, and the squirrels chewing high up in the trees, are succeeded by the catalogues of trees and birds in *The Parliament of Birds* and by Criseyde's garden with its railed and sanded walks, its blossomy boughs, and its new benches. But the *Gawain* poet in addition to the exhilarating journey through the seasons from which we have already quoted, makes powerful poetry out of a landscape far tougher and, in its colouring, more drab and monotonous than anything that Chaucer would have encountered near London. The harsh winter of the quest is conveyed in jagged consonants:

> claterande fro þe crest þe colde borne rennez,
> And henged heȝe ouer his hede in hard isse-ikkles.

[the cold brook runs crashing from the crest, and hung high over his head in hard icicles. ll. 731–32]

But its implications are noticed, too; with great tenderness, its baneful effect on the helpless is brought out in the wan chirpings of the line (747) about birds

> Þat pitosly þer piped for pyne of þe colde.
> [that were piping there pitifully for pain of the cold.]

This is a dead world; but after Gawain's apparently safe sojourn at the castle, with few hints of hardship save the 'warbling wind' that sings him such a ghastly aubade on his last morning, he is exposed again to a countryside alive with menace, its savagery thumped out in lines where every operative word alliterates:

> Þay boȝen bi bonkkez þer boȝez ar bare.
> Þay clomben bi clyffez þer clengez þe colde.
> Þe heuen watz vphalt, bot vgly þervnder.
> Mist muged on þe mor, malt on þe mountez.
> Vch hille hade a hatte, a myst-hakel huge.
> Brokez byled and breke bi bonkkez aboute,
> Schyre schaterande on schorez, þer þay doun schowued.
> Wela wylle watz þe way þer þay bi wod schulden,
> Til hit watz sone sesoun þat þe sunne ryses
>> Þat tyde.
>> Þay were on a hille ful hyȝe.
>> Þe quyte snaw lay bisyde.

[They moved along slopes where the boughs were bare. They climbed along cliffs where the cold was clinging. The clouds were high up, but it was threatening under them. Mist was drizzling on the moor and melting on the mountains. Each hill had a hat, a huge cloak of mist. Brooks were bubbling and foaming on their banks all around, dashing brightly against their shores, as they made their way down. They had to take a very confusing path through the wood, until suddenly it was the time when the sun rises at that season. They were on a very high hill. The white snow lay around them. ll. 2077–88]

The close of this passage is suddenly calmed by the *s* alliteration of the sunrise and by the Wordsworthian simplicity of the last two lines.

Further disappointments await us if we expect Chaucer to record at least the urban scene. His keen eye dwelt little on real buildings, but he interestingly observed one architectural detail, and that out of its context: Absolon, the dandyfied parish clerk in the miller's tale, had 'Paul's window carved on his shoes'. In footwear of this type, the leather of the upper was cut away in a tracery-pattern, and the bright hose showed through; the resemblance, in method and appearance, to a Gothic window caused such shoes to be called *calcei fenestrati*, and here Chaucer has noticed that Absolon's rosette is the same as a rosace in Old St Paul's Cathedral, either that at the east end or a simpler transeptal one. Someone else wanted to record the same building—the doodler, perhaps an itinerant mason, who scratched the graffito of Old St Paul's on the tower wall of Ashwell Church, Hertfordshire, some time after 1350; his attention was particularly taken by the high flying-buttresses of the tower, a rose-window, the detached campanile, and the tallest spire in England. But in general the great architectural experiments of the Middle Ages went unrecorded in the vernacular, and with all their sense of wonder no writers were stirred to make topographical records of any depth or understanding; a chronicler copied from an older chronicler rubbish about places that lay within easy reach, when a week-end's journey would have shown him how wrong he was and given him a first-hand account. Thus Trevisa, who earlier seemed to us pretty enlightened, is eminently slapdash in listing the supposed marvels of Britain (K. Sisam, *Fourteenth Century Verse and Prose*, Oxford, 1921 etc., pp. 146–48): Wimborne Minster is 'not far from Bath' (it must be over sixty miles); Loch Lomond (not named) has sixty habitable islands and tributary streams, and a hundred and twenty cliffs and eagles' nests; Stonehenge looks like 'gates set on other gates' (in fact, there is no sign of such building in two storeys); in charge of the springs at Bath is Minerva ('in *his* house the fire lasts always'), a jotting which Trevisa, only twenty miles away in Berkeley, translated from Higden, who had got it out of the twelfth-century Alfred of Beverley. Some of the information in this passage is merely credulous, especially the salt-wells that turn fresh every week-end, and it is disappointing that such stuff had currency when no one left, for us to share, his rapture at seeing Lincoln Cathedral with the three lost spires that must have made it almost the most exciting pile in Christendom.

Yet there was a sort of architectural criticism, even in a world where the beauty of Gothic art was after all a commonplace: in the north aisle vaulting of St Mary Redcliffe, Bristol, a roof-boss is a model of the high vault in the nearby north transept, and one of its fellows is a model of a very shapely, though somewhat monotonous, rose-window; with them, and on the same plane, is a spiritual model which exploits the natural roundness of a boss—a uni-cursal maze symbolizing our journey. These break a long silence during which many daring things had been achieved in our archi-tecture. We had glanced very briefly at a curvilinear Gothic of quirks and flickers, summed up its beauties and pitfalls in the east window of Carlisle Cathedral, passed on to formulate our own national 'Perpendicular' at Westminster and in the very cloister and chapter-house of the cathedral of the capital, and by 1370 had devised fan-vaulting in the exquisite cloisters at Gloucester. But the buildings that were rising were less an amenity than an essential, and taken for granted in the same way that we leave unsung our admirable drains and post offices; the immanence of the Church and its buildings, the bells never long out of earshot, the enviable colours and the beetle-killing incense and the con-trolled sounds, precluded a detached view or an aesthetic judgment —after all, the tall towers were in use as lighthouses, daymarks, guides over marshes, and houses for bells (and even for priests), and the pinnacles added weight to buttresses. Our first great architect, Henry Yevele (grown tangible from John Harvey's recent research), died in the same year as Chaucer and with a record of equal magnitude; whereas Chaucer wrote Duchess Blanche's memorial poem, Yevele wrought her tomb, but his art was 'mechanical', not 'liberal', and in the collective task of church-building a lonely genius had to sink his personality and fuse his work with the traditions of the years. The west front of Bever-ley Minster, rising by 1400, is its own lyric and inspired no surviving word; nor did the screen of sculptures at Exeter.

However, even in this field we can expect the *Gawain* poet to write with perception and enthusiasm; in the whole canon of his works there is evident a willingness to scrutinize objects closely. The architecture of the heavenly Jerusalem in *Pearl* may be pardoned for sounding rather extreme, and we are cheated of a great poet's description of a great church when we read that there was no church, chapel or temple inside, the Almighty being their goodly minster; for this, as for the glittering stones, the Apocalypse is his authority. The one technical term employed here is *bantel*, the horizontal coursing of masonry; *Cleanness* gives the poet more scope for architectural minutiae, since there is an account of the siege of Jerusalem, with its battlements and a big wooden breastwork, and of Belshazzar's palace, with its carved battlements, pinnacled towers, and strong bratticing; furthermore, the covered cups from the Temple remind him of castles, since their lids apparently come down on to what look like corbel-tables under a battlement, and their finials are like crocketed spirelets. Above all, through no mist of over-statement he allows us to see with Gawain's expert eye the latest thing in military architecture (*Sir Gawain and the Green Knight*, ll. 786–802): a deep double ditch right up to the wall; the wall 'wading' very deep in it and then rising to 'a very huge height', all of hard masoned stone up to the cornices; machicolations under the battlements 'in the best style'; and very pretty turrets at intervals, with admirable loopholes. He 'had never noticed a better barbican'. But this is only the outwork of the castle; his gaze now rises above the outer wall and takes in the high hall, the spaced-out towers bristling with spirelets, the tall pinnacles and their carved finials, the chalk-white chimneys rising from the roofs of the towers, and in fact so many painted pinnacles scattered everywhere—especially in the embrasures of the battlements—that it all absolutely seemed to be cut out of paper. This is a magnate's castle, built regardless of cost and in the latest fashion, but it is credible, and its details are verifiable from buildings of the period in both France and England; the *painted* pinnacles at first sound exaggerated, but the delicate paper-white beauty of the whole suggests that whitewash may have been used (as we know it was on the White Tower of London). Compared with this, Chaucer's dream-architecture in

The House of Fame and *The Book of the Duchess* is crude and contrived, the former breathless with gold and with windows as frequent as flakes 'in great snows'; in the latter poem, he dreams that he is in a bedchamber with stained glass in all the windows, depicting classical figures that include characters from the Troy story, and with wall-paintings that present the 'text and notes' of the *Roman de la Rose*!

But we must thank the friars, indirectly, for the greatest piece of architectural criticism in Middle English, the description of a Dominican friary in *Piers Plowman's Creed*. The poet is soon in conversation with a Franciscan, who praises his own order for various qualities, including its megalomaniac building-schemes; the words 'broad . . . large . . . aloft . . . wide . . . high' are the mood of three adjacent lines (118–20), and the poet is asked to help glaze the huge windows, in which his name will then be inscribed and in which he can be depicted kneeling before Christ in a golden surround, 'and St Francis himself will enfold you in his cope and present you to Trinity'. Wearying of this, he tries the Dominicans, but his description of their house (ll. 153 ff.) subordinates any real admiration for skill to horror at wicked waste: he had not seen such a building for a long time, with its painted and polished pillars, its cleverly-carved capitals, its windows tall and wide, and the long circuit of its wall, with 'private posterns, to get out when they wanted'. Around were orchards and gardens, and there was a brilliantly-carved cross with tabernacle-work on it—the price of a ploughland in round coins would have been too little to pay for it. As for the church, it was marvellously well built: there were arches on every side, with crockets and golden foliage capitals; the wide windows were inscribed with names of donors and studded with their shields and their merchants' marks (the power of money and rank shown more blatantly than on a herald's roll). High canopied tombs in recesses were rendered in alabaster and marble, with effigies of armed and surcoated knights and their lovely ladies in garments covered with gold leaf—all looking like saints sanctified on earth! A ten-year tax would not have paid for that church, and the cloister was equally stupendous: pillared, painted, lead-roofed, paved with painted tiles in a pattern, with

T

bright tin conduits and brass lavers beautifully fitted—the produce of the land in a great shire would not have covered the cost of it. The chapter-house was like a huge church in itself, and it was carved and vaulted and quaintly fretted; it had a lovely ceiling, and paintings all around like a parliament-house. The refectory was big enough to be a king's hall and to hold a household; the tables were wide, the benches spotless, the windows glazed like those of a church. It was the same with all the rest of the precinct: high halls, chambers with fireplaces, pretty chapels, kitchens big enough for a king's castles, the dormitory with strong doors, the infirmary and its own refectory, 'many more houses', the great boundary-wall turreted handsomely and with glazed windows, and buildings good enough to lodge the Queen. The source of all the necessary money is pointed out by Piers himself (ll. 501–02): 'they work hard at building tombs, to load their church floor, and and change it often.'

Of the public worship that went on in such buildings we are told very little in English, but John Myrc, Austin canon of Lilleshall in Shropshire, writing about 1400 of the duties of a parish priest, leaves us some incidental information on conditions (ed. E. Peacock, *John Myrc's Instructions for Parish Priests*, Early English Text Society No. 31, London, 1868): one must not stand in church, or lean against pillar or wall, but kneel on the floor; however uninviting the church, one must not spare to go 'for heat or cold'; a midwife may baptize in emergency, but she must then burn both water and vessel, or bring it to church and pour it into the font. Myrc writes carefully; he even tells us what to do if a spider falls in the chalice, and we can regret that he does not say more about the ordinary parish church that just begins to live under his pen.

It is, indeed, very hard to visualize precisely the people of the time as they dealt with their everyday lives; facets of their work and leisure have come down to us, but the reactions of ordinary people to ordinary events (since Margery Kempe was extraordinary by any standard) were not held to be the province of literature, and nothing approaching an imaginative novel was written, save the framework of *The Canterbury Tales*, to suggest the interplay of characters out of humdrum life. Where we might expect compassion and understanding we may read only snobbishness and callous denunciation, as when Langland declares (in the afterthought of the C-text, VI. 65 ff.) that

> Bondmen and bastardes and beggers children,
> Thuse bylongeth to labour, and lordes kyn to seruen
> Bothe God and good men, as here degree asketh.

[Serfs and bastards and beggars' children belong to labour, and lords' families should serve God and good men, as their degree requires.]

But now,

> bondemenne barnes han be mad bisshopes,
> And barnes bastardes han ben archidekenes,
> And sopers and here sones for seluer han be knyghtes,
> And lordene sones here laborers, and leid here rentes to wedde
> For the ryght of this reame ryden aȝens oure enemys.

[serfs' children have been made bishops, and bastard children have become archdeacons, and soap-boilers and their sons have been made knights for money, and lords' sons have become their labourers and mortgaged their land to ride out against our enemies in defence of this realm.]

These words, misleadingly convincing in their emphasis and with no subsequent denial of them, are only on the lips of the fallible dreamer in his cheeky mood, when he can tell Reason 'I live in London and *on* London, too'; but the taste of them lasts.

This chapter, by keeping to English record, has made no deep contribution to social history or sociology; indeed, no -ology emerges interestingly from the vernacular writings of the time, and it would be sheer humbug to speak of an Age of Aquinas or an Age of Dante in relation to English expression. Even Wyclif's English, *flos Oxoniae* as he was, limps behind the Latin of Ockham and Bradwardine, and is sometimes derived from nothing more intellectual than the Spiritual Franciscans or the Franciscans' great enemy Fitzralph. It is laughable to read the ideas on cosmology embedded in a poem on the 'leaps' that Christ took, in Corpus Christi College, Cambridge, MS 294: Rabbi Moses tells us that there are seven heavens and seven planets, with 500-year journeys between them; which leads on through fumbling calculations in wretched doggerel to the idea that Christ leapt 7,000 miles when He ascended into heaven. Since this kind of thing was *fact*, it is not surprising that the most emancipated prose style of the half-century, perhaps the most influential in shaping an all-purposes prose for later years, was that in which the English translator of 'Sir John Mandeville' couched the outrageous fiction of his world travels, always with a protestation of truth but basking in the freedom to invent and to open up to his readers an absorbing new world of one-footed men, lamb-bearing pods, male and female diamonds that have children, griffins, men with heads on their chests, and hippopotamuses that 'eat men, when they can catch them' (which statement of the obvious blinds us to the lie in the main clause).

But one big field of social comment was, naturally enough, the relationship between the sexes; marriage itself, once it had occurred, ceased to be interesting to writers, who could make nothing special out of its ordinariness and its pleasant monotony, but unhappy marriages (with the wife normally as the dominant and unreasonable partner) were occasionally recorded or imagined, and young love was celebrated so often and with such sameness that a cynic might be excused for thinking it to be all nothing but fiction written to a formula. It might be hoped that the love of lad for lass in fourteenth-century England would be expressed in fresh and unsophisticated terms with the dew of the early world still on them; on the contrary, love was celebrated to a set of rules, whereby the lady was pinnacled and unattainable, her beauty peerless, her rank superior, her disdain not haughty but justified, her status often that of married woman; her glance emboldened you for days, her discreet smile kept you going for lonely weeks, and the possession of her handkerchief must have seemed the heights of requital. Much has been written recently on this strange and dignified love, and on its origins in lonely grass-widows of crusaders, in young victims of parentally fixed marriages with old magnates, in the cult of the Blessed Virgin as the epitome of all that is best in womanhood, and in the languors of Ovid and *The Song of Songs*; a now famous summing-up of the tradition and its literature is C. S. Lewis's *The Allegory of Love* (Oxford, 1936 etc.), which necessarily gives plenty of emphasis to such continental analogues as the *Roman de la Rose*, but in our literature we can find one or two careful treatments of the theme and many informal sketches of it. Chaucer's *Troilus and Criseyde* is a real handbook of the procedure, right down to the realization that this love is only second-rate, anyway, compared with the love of Christ; but it will be more interesting for our purpose to trace the picture of an up-to-date lover—the poet himself—that John Gower weaves through the many stories of his *Confessio Amantis*.

Gower was Chaucer's friend and contemporary, a participator in his borrowing of French words though not in his metrical experiments, and a more pessimistic beholder of affairs; in his French and Latin works (for he was competent in the three tongues) he was a reformer such as Chaucer never chose to be, and we were disappointed that his huge English poem is rather silent, after the Prologue, on political and social matters. But the lover lives, as the most convincing picture in depth of one of these self-sacrificing and decent young men quite hopelessly in love; towards the end of the eight books the picture fades, and Gower even shows himself enfeebled by sickness and age, but while it lasts it is sympathetic and credible. This is achieved because the lover lets us share his reaction to the lady's charms, and does not just paint her flatly (as Chaucer tends to, in his young *Book of the Duchess*, with the dead Blanche); nor does he let his symptoms overstay their welcome, but gives us a story or two by way of punctuation. From the beginning, circumstances are noted that any lover will recognize.

Within a few lines of some pretty exaggeration (his heart has turned to stone, and his lady has engraved a print of love on it) he says that when he hears her speak his wits lose their bearing (I. 553 ff., 559 ff.). He has never been a hypocrite and feigned love (I. 712 ff.), and he has been disobedient to her only in staying loyal to her at a time when she commands him to close his mouth on the subject of love (I. 1274 ff.); on these occasions she tells him to give her up and choose a new lover, adding that if he knew how hopeless his suit was he would 'love in another place' (I. 1310 ff.). He murmurs and grouses, but inwardly, not daring to speak a word to displease her (I. 1382 ff.). In a sudden outburst to his Confessor, he cries

> Bot wolde God that grace sende
> That toward me my lady wende
> As I towardes hire wene!

[But would that God might send me grace that my lady felt towards me as I feel towards her! I. 2373–75]

He has written love-poems to her; they sound of the artificial type—rondeau, balade, and virelai—, but they and his lighter songs and song-dances move her not at all, and she will not listen to them (I. 2726 ff.). The second book shows how his infatuation affects his dealings with other men: he is jealous of them when they approach her, and consumed with misery when she gives them her ear (II. 39 ff.); he has committed the sin of joy at another's grief, when he hears that they are rebuffed, and when Fortune's wheel turns down for them

> Thanne am I fedd of that thei faste,
> And lawhe of that I se hem loure;
> And thus of that thei brewe soure
> I drinke swete, and am wel esed
> Of that I wot thei ben desesed.

[Then I am fed on what they can't eat, and laugh at what I see them frown at; and thus I drink sweetly from what they brew sourly, and am made comfortable by what I know has upset them. II. 244 ff.]

Worse, he maligns them to her (II. 456 ff.), and gains their confidence only to betray it; if he suspects that one of the lady's admirers is making headway with her he 'throws water on the fire' and overturns 'his cart in the middle of the mire' (II. 1962 ff.). Nor is this the only adverse way that he affects others: he is so melancholy and distempered that his servants are afraid of him and think that he is going mad with rage (III. 41 ff.); and ultimately he has wished a thousand times a day to die (III. 1503 ff.).

The fourth book shows a slight recovery from this mood, and something of a rationalization of his behaviour. He can observe how often he puts off speaking to her, or decides to write a letter instead, and though he expresses this as Procrastination's evil advice to him, it is plain that he can see his worse self failing in these little points (IV. 28 ff.). When he reaches her presence, he forgets the lines that he has so carefully composed, and stands deaf and dumb so that 'all's not worth an ivy leaf' (IV. 557 ff.); yet when he is alone again afterwards, he rebukes himself for his timidity, reminding himself that she is as harmless as a three-year-old child (IV. 594 ff.). His obedience to her is absolute, and he loves to do her any office; he bows and offers her his services in private room or hall, tries to escort her to the chapel for mass and back again, and is delighted to give her his arm, but his devotions ignore his book and centre on her in hopes of a miraculous change of heart (IV. 1122 ff., V. 7110 ff.). He does what she bids him do, goes where she orders, comes when she calls, follows her with his eyes, kneels near when she sits, stands when she stands, watches admiringly when she weaves or embroiders, and finds himself thinking or talking or singing or sighing; but if she does not care to stay, and busies herself in other matters, he hangs around to consume the long day somehow, not wishing to leave, and in his humility plays with her little dog on the bed or the floor, or with her cage-birds, or talks affably to the little page or the simple chambermaid. If she wants to ride out on pilgrimage or to any other place, he comes unbidden and lifts her gently into the saddle, and then leads her out by the bridle; if he finds that she wants to ride in her carriage, he mounts and rides by the side of it, sometimes talking and sometimes singing a love-song out of Ovid (IV. 1161 ff.). His time with her is delightful; if she wants to stay up for songs and dances, he eagerly accompanies her, clasping her hands and dancing and skipping like 'the roe that runs on the moor'; if she wants to play dice for fortune-telling, or to have the story of Troilus read, he consents at once, sometimes stirring in a bit of his own pleading—but that is when she tells him to go, remarking that it is far into the night. He prolongs his leave-taking until he sees that it is inevitable,

> And thanne I bidde Godd hire se,
> And so doun knelande on mi kne
> I take leve, and if I schal,
> I kisse hire, and go forth withal.
> And otherwhile, if that I dore,
> Er I come fulli to the dore,
> I torne ayein and feigne a thing,
> As thogh I hadde lost a ring
> Or somwhat elles, for I wolde
> Kisse hire eftsones, if I scholde,
> Bot selden is that I so spede.

[And then I pray God to guard her, and so kneeling down on my knee I take my leave, and if I must, I kiss her and just go away. And at other times, if I dare, before I have quite reached the door I turn back and pretend to have lost a ring or something else, because I should like to get another kiss after, if I could, but I am not often as lucky as that. IV. 2777 ff.]

His only avarice is his desire to possess her:

> Fy on the bagges in the kiste!
> I hadde ynogh, if I hire kiste;

[Fie on the moneybags in the chest! I would have plenty, if I could kiss her. V. 83–84]

> I axe nouther park ne plowh.
> If I hire hadde, it were ynowh.

[I ask for neither parkland nor ploughland. If I had her, it would be plenty. V. 2849–50]

But, equally, no gift will win her; she will take nothing from him (V. 4758), and she gives him nothing—not a kind word, not a single 'thank you' (V. 4503, 4518). Yet one glance from her eyes wins his whole heart, and on long, cold nights he rises from bed and stands at his window watching across the rooftops the chamber where she lies asleep (V. 4493–94, 6659 ff.).

Of a franker, more ingenuous, love there is some trace in the surviving lyrics. One lover (in R. H. Robbins, *Secular Lyrics of the XIVth and XVth Centuries*, No. 9) is particularly choked and incoherent; and no wonder—he is drunk and deserted:

> Wer þer ouþer in þis toun
> Ale or wyn,
> Isch hit wolde bugge
> To lemmon myn.
> Welle wo was so hardy
> Forte make my lef al blody;
> Þaut he were þe kynges sone
> Of Normaundy,
> ȝet icholde awreke boe
> For lemman myn.
> Welle wo was me tho—
> Wo was me tho;
> Þe man that leset þat he louit
> Hym is also.
> Ne erle ne lerde
> Ne—no more in can!
> But Crist ich hire biteche
> Þat was my lemman.

[If there were in this town either ale or wine, I would buy it to my sweetheart. It would be very hard on anyone who was so rash as to make my darling all bloody; even if he were the King of Normandy's son, I would still be avenged for my sweetheart. It was very hard on me then—hard on me then; that's just how it is for a man who has lost what he loves. No earl or lord or—nothing left in the pot! But I commend to Christ the girl who used to be my sweetheart.]

This MS (Bodley Rawlinson D.913) has other little trifles where the beauty of the beloved is compared with the peerlessness of the hawthorn in flower (Robbins, op. cit., No. 16) and where a baser poet riddlingly sees his night's companion as a rose now de-flowered (ibid., No. 17); the attitude of the latter poem is seen in coarsened form in poems of the next century where a callous joke is made out of the betrayed servant-girl or simple country wench, but for the time being this blunted humour was either non-existent or not given to costly parchment. In the same MS hides the haunting and mysterious incremental song 'Maiden in the mor lay' [Maiden stayed in the wilds, ibid., No. 18], where the tuneful but uneconomical repetition builds up a picture either of a fairy girl living in the open (for eight days, anyway) on a diet of primroses and violets, with cold spring-water, and no shelter save the red rose and the lily, or—in view of the normal associa-tion of these two last flowers with the Incarnation—of the blessed Virgin in the unredeemed wilderness of the world.

One love poem (ibid., No. 160) was so popular—and deservedly so—that even the cock and the head of his harem, in the nun's priest's contribution to *The Canterbury Tales*, sang it in harmony when the sun shone:

> My lefe ys faren in a lond.
>   Allas, why ys she so?
> And I am so sore bound
>   I may nat com her to.
>   She hath my hert in hold
>   Where euer she ryde or go,
>   With trew love a thousand fold!

[My darling has gone away. Alas, why has she done so? And I am so grievously constrained that I cannot get to her. She has my heart in her keeping wherever she may ride or walk, with faithful love a thousandfold.]

But this brings us back, however gossamer the discipline, to the rules of stately loving. Even the uncomplicated pleasure of the *reverdie*, the song of delight at the return of spring, may be meant to stem from more tender feelings; when the poet of a brisk little quatrain (ibid., No. 141) lists the nice qualities of May as the bright blossoms on the trees, the around-the-clock bird-song, the

fun and music on every greensward, and no more, his gusto must
be attributable only to love.

So the loves of poor folk are little recorded; and it is the same
with their simple fare, save that there are a few wistful catalogues
of what they would like to eat if they could afford it. The attempt
to satisfy Hunger in *Piers Plowman* B.VI.282 ff. lets Piers list some
of these luxuries, none of them exotic: pullets, geese, piglets, salt
bacon, and meat and egg 'coloppes'; all he can manage to serve at
present are two green cheeses, a bit of curds and cream, an oatcake,
two loaves of beans and bran, parsley, leeks, and plenty of cab-
bages, to which the frightened poor add pea-pods, beans, baked
apples, spring onions, chervils, and ripe cherries. But that they
wasted such sustenance in better times, and especially in the cities,
is seen in the disgusting performance of Glutton in B.V. 304 ff.,
who is tempted from his church-going by the promise of good ale,
the hot spices of pepper and peony, garlic, and fennel-seed, and
after drinking more than a gallon spews it all up in the lap of
Clement the cobbler; he admits in his confession that he often
vomits whole suppers and mid-day meals in this way, when the
food could have been devoted to the hungry. The whole scene of
his drinking is vividly vulgar and grubby, but the low life depicted
seems by no means short of money. The attempt to transmit
drunkenness succeeds again in another scrap in the Rawlinson
D.913 MS (ibid., No. 117), which begins with repeated mention
of the word 'drunken' and goes on to plead with everyone to stand
still while the drinker totters into a more relaxed state:

> Hay, suster, Walter, Peter!
> 3e dronke al depe,
> And ichulle eke.
> Stondet alle stille—
> Stille, stille, stille—
> Stille as any ston;
> Trippe a lutel wit þi fot,
> Ant let þi body go!

[Hey, sister, Walter, Peter! You've drunk very deep, and so

shall I, too. All stand still—still, still, still—still as any stone;
trip a little with your foot, and let your body go!]

Chaucer must have the last word. But a trenchant opinion on
another side of low life—the misery of living near an all-night
workshop—lives on in the brilliant and famous *Blacksmiths* (ibid.,
No. 118), where the resources of a pounding alliteration are
exploited to the full. The victim, whom we can imagine nowadays
writing indignant letters about Heathrow, has as his neighbours
a set of insensitive smiths who add to the intrinsic noise of their
work by shouting and spitting and telling yarns and lumbering
around:

> Swarte smekyd smeþes, smateryd wyth smoke,
> Dryue me to deth wyth den of here dyntes.
> Swech noys on nyghtes ne herd men neuer.
> What knauene cry, & clateryng of knockes!
> Þe cammede kongons cryen after 'Col, col!'
> & blowen here bellewys þat al here brayn brestes.
> 'Huf, puf!' seyth þat on, 'Haf, paf!' þat oþer.
> Þei spyttyn & spraulyn & spellyn many spelles,
> Þei gnauen & gnacchen, þei gronys togydere,
> And holdyn hem hote wyth here hard hamers.
> Of a bole hyde ben here barm-fellys,
> Here schankes ben schakeled for þe fere-flunderys;
> Heuy hamerys þei han þat hard ben handled,
> Stark strokes þei stryken on a stelyd stokke.
> 'Lus, bus! Las, das!' rowtyn be rowe.
> Sweche dolful a dreme þe deuyl it todryue!
> Þe mayster longith a lityl & lascheth a lesse,
> Twyneth hem tweyn, and towchith a treble.
> 'Tik, tak! Hic, hac! Tiket, taket! Tyk, tak!
> Lus, bus, Lus, das!'—swych lyf þei ledyn!
> Alle cloþemerys Cryst hem gyue sorwe;
> May no man for brenwaterys on nyght han hys rest!

[Swarthy, sooty smiths smutted with smoke are driving me to
death with the din of their strokes. No one has ever heard such

noise night after night. What shouting of assistants, and clatter-
ing of bangs! The snub-nosed changelings shriek out for
'Coal, coal!' and blow their bellows till all their brains burst.
'Huff, puff!' goes one; 'Haff, paff!' goes the other. They spit
and lope around and tell a lot of yarns, chew and gnash their
teeth, groan in concert, and keep themselves hot with their
hard hammers. Their aprons are made of bull-hide, and their
legs are gaitered against the sparks; they have heavy hammers
that get toughly wielded, and they strike rough blows on a steel
anvil. 'Luss, buss! Lass, dass!' they roar in turn. May the
devil make off with such a grim noise! The boss lengthens a
little piece, belabours an even smaller one, twists them
together, and strikes a treble note. 'Tick, tack! Hick, hack!
Ticket, tacket! Tick, tack! Luss, buss! Luss, dass!'—that's
how they carry on! May Christ give sorrow to all horse-
clothers; no one can get his rest at night because of water-
sizzlers!]

There is no sympathy here for the hard-driven staff of a filthy
factory; instead, the poet's indignation works on two features of
the language now lost to us—not only is this the most extreme
passage of alliteration surviving from Middle English, but it
shows remarkable inventiveness in compounding nouns: 'lap-
skins', 'fire-flinders', 'clothe-mares' and 'burn-waters' are either
not instanced elsewhere or very rare. The loss of this rich source
of new words is particularly grievous. Old English compounded
nouns easily and picturesquely, as do all other Germanic tongues
(as we admit when we borrow *kindergarten* or *ombudsman*) and
Greek (now vitally in use in such medical terms as *appendicectomy*);
Latin (like Welsh) compounded little, and French inherited this
characteristic from its parent and alas! handed the tendency on
to English during the three hundred years of Norman French
ascendancy. In the process we lost a multitude of expressive and
economical words.

Money has never been, until recently, a fit topic of gentlemanly
conversation or of poetry. It is a melancholy fact, therefore, that
we must round off this century with a mention of Chaucer's

'complaint' to his purse, originally a *balade* of three seven-line stanzas and perhaps intended for Richard II: the poet's purse is empty, and he longs for it to be heavy again. But between Henry's reception as King by Parliament on 30 September 1399 and a royal grant to Chaucer doubling his pension to forty marks on 3 October, the poet added an *envoy* in a different rhyme-scheme, begging Henry, who could put everything right for the country, to take notice of his supplication. Had Chaucer sincerely changed camps?—he was old by medieval standards and a year off death; the mood that induced his 'Retraction' was perhaps upon him, and the religious views of many of his friends (such as Clifford) were discredited and risky; at Christmas he took a long lease of a house under the skirts of Westminster Abbey—hopefully, it would seem, since we know nothing for certain of offspring who could succeed him there; no bland tolerance such as his survived him, and the first martyred 'heretic' burned soon after. But the *envoy* remains regrettable; it cringes—the unhappy King who had granted him a yearly tun of wine just a year before is forgotten, and the usurper becomes

> O conquerour of Brutes Albioun,
> Which that by lyne and free eleccioun
> Ben verray king!

[O conqueror of Brutus's Albion, you who by lineage and free election are true king!]

Even forgetting the displaced and doomed Richard, this call on lineage is false; the nine-year-old Edmund Mortimer, fifth Earl of March, had the prior claim and was lucky to survive the usurpation. It is kindest to Chaucer, and only fair to Henry, to suppose that those closest to Richard had noticed in 1397 and thereafter his mounting madness, and had turned from him, perhaps with terrible pity, as the age closed.

Bibliography

This is a bibliography of primary sources, the texts themselves of writers from 1350 to 1400; almost all are annotated and glossed by their editors in such a way as to make them accessible to modern readers who are willing to take the trouble to use the apparatus provided. No other commentaries, and no histories or critical essays, are suggested here, since the endeavour of this book is to let the period give its testimony in its own language.

ed. W. W. Skeat, *The Works of Geoffrey Chaucer*, 7 volumes (Oxford University Press, 1894–97).

ed. W. W. Skeat, *The Complete Works of Geoffrey Chaucer* (Oxford University Press, 1895 etc.); from which the line-numbering in this book is taken.

ed. F. N. Robinson, *The Works of Geoffrey Chaucer*, 2nd edition (Boston: Houghton Mifflin, 1957).

ed. D. J. Price and R. M. Wilson, *The Equatorie of the Planetis: a Manuscript Treatise ascribed to Chaucer* (Cambridge University Press, 1955).

ed. W. W. Skeat, *The Vision of William concerning Piers the Plowman . . . together with Richard the Redeless, by William Langland*, 2 volumes (Oxford University Press, 1886 etc.).

ed. J. R. R. Tolkien and E. V. Gordon, revised by Norman Davis, *Sir Gawain and the Green Knight*, 2nd edition (Oxford: Clarendon Press, 1968).

ed. G. C. Macaulay, *The English Works of John Gower*, 2 volumes, Early English Text Society Extra Series Nos. 81 and 82 (Oxford University Press, 1900 and 1901 etc.).

ed. J. A. W. Bennett, *Selections from John Gower* (Oxford: Clarendon Press, 1968).

ed. Carleton Brown, revised by G. V. Smithers, *Religious Lyrics of the XIVth Century*, 2nd edition (Oxford: Clarendon Press, 1957).

ed. R. H. Robbins, *Secular Lyrics of the XIVth and XVth Centuries* (Oxford: Clarendon Press, 1952).

ed. R. H. Robbins, *Historical Poems of the XIVth and XVth Centuries* (New York: Columbia University Press, 1959).

ed. R. T. Davies, *Medieval English Lyrics* (Evanston: Northwestern University Press, 1964).

ed. R. L. Greene, *A Selection of English Carols* (Oxford: Clarendon Press, 1962).

ed. H. A. Person, *Cambridge Middle English Lyrics* (Seattle: University of Washington Press, 1953).

ed. Sir I. Gollancz, *Winner and Waster* (Oxford University Press, 1930).

ed. F. W. D. Brie, *The Brut, or the Chronicles of England*, 2 volumes, Early English Text Society Nos. 131 and 136 (Oxford University Press, 1906 and 1908). The final composition and polish of much of this is later than our period; but its basis, and much of its wording, must be contemporary.

ed. J. Hall, *The Poems of Laurence Minot* (Oxford: Clarendon Press, 1914).

ed. E. Brock, *Morte Arthure*, Early English Text Society No. 8 (London: Kegan Paul, 1865 etc.).

ed. W. W. Skeat, *Pierce the Ploughman's Crede*, Early English Text Society No. 30 (London: Kegan Paul, 1867).

ed. E. V. Gordon, *Pearl* (Oxford: Clarendon Press, 1953 etc.).

ed. Phyllis Hodgson, *The Cloud of Unknowing . . .*, Early English Text Society No. 218 (Oxford University Press, 1944 etc.). See page lxxxix of Dr Hodgson's book also for bibliography of Walter Hilton, to which can be now added Fumio Kuriyagawa, *Walter Hilton's Eight Chapters on Perfection* (Tokyo: Keio University, 1967). Dame Julian's writings have been subjected to editorial tampering and 'modernization'.

ed. S. M. Brown and Hope Emily Allen, *The Book of Margery Kempe*, Early English Text Society No. 212 (Oxford University Press, 1940).

ed. T. Arnold, *Select English Works of John Wyclif*, 3 volumes (Oxford University Press, 1869–71).

ed. F. D. Matthew, *The English Works of Wyclif Hitherto Un-*

printed, Early English Text Society No. 74 (London: Kegan Paul, 1880).

ed. H. E. Winn, *Wyclif: Select English Writings* (Oxford: Clarendon Press, 1929).

ed. C. Lindberg, *MS Bodley 959*, 4 volumes continuing (Stockholm: Almqvist and Wiksell, 1959 etc.).

ed. V. J. Scattergood, '*The Two Ways* . . . by Sir John Clanvowe', *English Philological Studies*, Vol. X (1967), pp. 33–56.

Many good things to our purpose will be found in the following anthologies:

ed. K. Sisam, *Fourteenth Century Verse and Prose* (Oxford: Clarendon Press, 1921 etc.).

ed. O. F. Emerson, *A Middle English Reader* (London: Macmillan, 1905 etc.).

R. M. Wilson, *The Lost Literature of Medieval England* (London: Methuen, 1952).

Index